Ancient Civilizations

Previous page: A cow and calf from the Nimrud Ivories. These were trade goods made by the Phoenicians, and found in the palace of an Assyrian king. This page: An Assyrian relief showing how timber from the forests of Lebanon, after being dragged through the mountains, was transported downriver to the site of a new palace. The cedars and firs of Lebanon were immensely valuable, since few large trees grow in the Mediterranean lands. The winged bulls represent protective spirits.

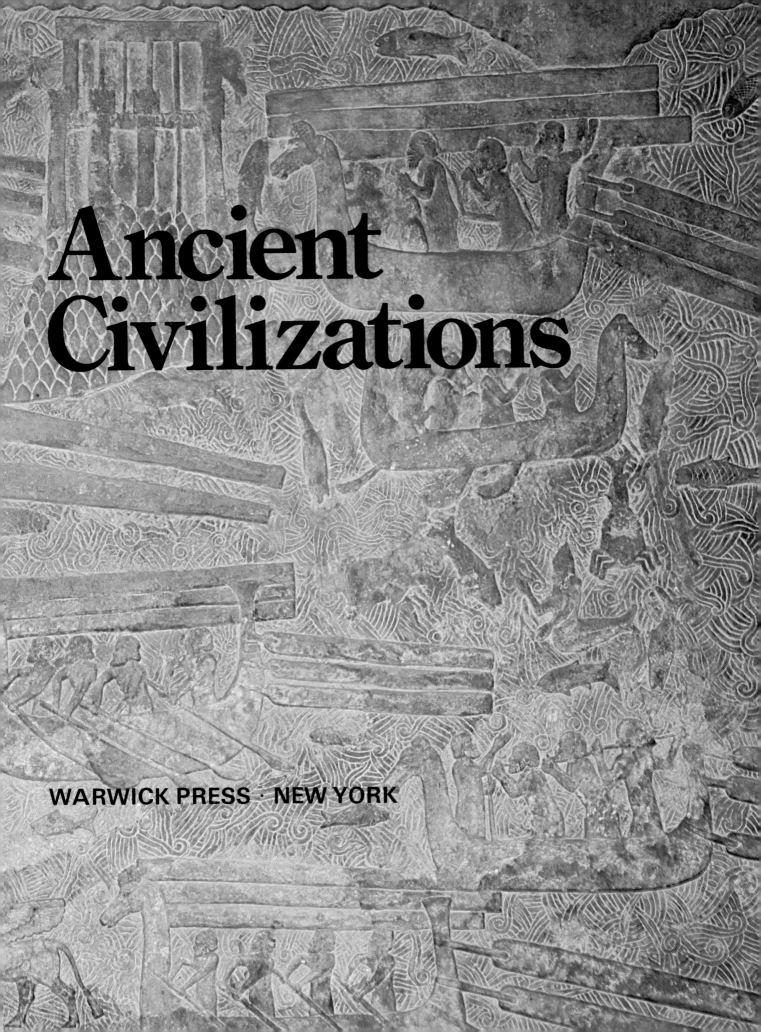

Ancient Civilizations

WARWICK PRESS · NEW YORK

Consultant Editor

Amélie Kuhrt B.A.

Editor

Frances M. Clapham

Assistant Editor

Abigail Frost M.A.

Contributors

Christopher Fagg B.A.
J. R. Knox M.A.
Anne Millard B.A., Dip.Ed., Ph.D.
Amélie Kuhrt B.A.

Martin O'Connell M.A.
Robin Place M.A.
Anton Powell B.A., Ph.D.
Patricia Vanags B.A.

Illustrators

Nigel Chamberlain
Brian Dear
Constance Dear

Richard Hook
Angus McBride
John Sibbick

Published 1978 by Warwick Press, 730 Fifth Avenue, New York, New York 10019

First published in Great Britain by Sampson Low, 1978

Copyright © 1978 by Grisewood & Dempsey Ltd

Printed in Hong Kong by Mandarin Publishers Ltd

6 5 4 3 2 1

Library of Congress Catalog No. 78–50676

ISBN 0–531–09091–4
ISBN 0–531–09073–6 lib. bdg.

Contents

Opposite, top left: A seal ring, found in a shaft grave at Mycenae, showing a stag hunt. Below left: Alexander the Great; detail from a mosaic, perhaps a portrait from the life. Opposite right: Bronze figure of a cat from Egypt, made about 600 BC. Below: Roman baths at the Greek city of Ephesus. Right: Part of the staircase relief from the palace of Darius at Persepolis. Below right: A bronze yu (wine-jar) made in China during the Shang Dynasty. Page 8: A scene from the gold shrine found in the tomb of the Egyptian pharaoh Tutankhamun, whose tomb is one of the most famous archaeological finds of this century.

Ruins of vast monuments stand today where the ancient empires once reigned. North Africa is rich in such reminders of its days as a Roman province, when it was more prosperous than ever since. This arch, built in AD 216, stands in Djemila, Algeria, commemorating the Emperor Caracalla; the once-flourishing town has been half-buried by desert sand.

Setting the Scene

When agriculture developed in the Near East some 8000 years ago, it became possible for men to change from a nomadic way of life and settle in permanent communities. Most lived in villages, but some gathered together in towns with populations of several thousands. Such towns, which probably grew up as trading centres, might have their own distinctive cultures – characteristic patterns of behaviour and artefacts. But we do not class them as civilizations. Archaeologically and historically, the term civilization is applied to a culture which is maintained by a large population, over a long period of time, which includes an established political organization centred on cities, palaces, or temples; the use of writing; and the development of specialized occupations. L. civitas, city

The first great civilizations which emerged some 2500 years later grew up not around the early farming towns, but in arid or semi-arid areas centred on the great river systems in north China, north India, Mesopotamia, and Egypt. We will never know what determined people to settle in such areas. Possibly the more easily cultivated regions were even then becoming over-populated; perhaps they migrated from declining hunting and grazing grounds. Climatic changes around 4000 BC may have made once-fertile homelands barren. In the areas where they now settled, it was possible to produce plenty of food – but only by building complex irrigation systems.

The irrigation of valleys calls for the co-operation of large numbers of people over a wide area. So too does flood control, another necessity in these regions. These two factors must have played an important part in the development of social organizations. Successful water-control schemes must have some overall direction, and as a result political structures grew up which were powerful enough to compel everyone to act together in the community's interests.

Irrigation schemes would inevitably lead to disputes among the water users; these demanded an arbitrator. And the irrigation structures were a community's most important assets, which needed to be defended – with force if necessary – against any outside threat. The combination of these factors resulted in the emergence of a ruler who was an organizer and lawgiver, a protector and a war leader. In some areas such as Egypt and China the ruler was regarded as divine; because of his ultimate control over all aspects of agriculture, he came to be thought of as the originator of all fertility.

In all four areas the complex organization and political structure led to the emergence of massive bureaucracies, to carry out the administration. And in these four areas, too, writing systems – essential for the keeping of adminstrative records – developed independently. Complex and surprisingly accurate calendars were worked out in order to keep precise records of floods and seasons. To do this careful observations were made of the movements of the stars, and the mass of information recorded led to the development of astronomy.

This 'hydraulic' theory of the development of civilization applies to the first four major civilizations; but there are others which it does not fit. The island of Crete developed all the features of a

26

A fragment of a glazed faience vase from Ashur showing a grazing goat standing on a stylized mountain. The goat was one of the first animals to be domesticated. It could survive where there was only sparse grazing, and provided skins, hair, and meat as well as milk.

Two Assyrian scribes of the 7th century BC list the booty from a conquered Babylonian city. The invention of writing was a response to the need to record the property of the state, and is a criterion for civilization.

Scene from a Sumerian commemorative stele (about 2500 BC). The patron god of the city of Lagash, Ningirsu, grasps the enemies of Lagash in his net.

The frieze on the staircase of Darius's palace at Persepolis shows peoples from all over the Persian empire bringing tribute to the King. The growth of empires spread civilization among some of the subject peoples.

Part of the Lion Gate at Hattusa, the ancient Hittite capital. The mighty Hittite empire dominated Anatolia between about 1650 and 1200 BC, but little is known of its history.

civilized society, including a complex palace-centred economy and an independent writing system; yet it had no great riverine system. In Elam (about whose social and economic organization we know very little) a civilization with writing developed; in this case, perhaps, it was related to the needs of trade.

The emergence of specialists

As societies became increasingly complex in structure, specialists developed in various fields. The community had to be able to grow food enough to support them; but whether an existing food surplus allowed the development of such specialists, or whether the emergence of specialists stimulated extra food production, is a problem on which scholars have not reached agreement. There were temple and government administrators, who used the services of scribes. Specialist metal-workers supplied weapons and luxury objects of gold and silver. The increasing demand for luxuries led local industries to develop and refine their products by training specialist workers – weavers, stone-cutters, and so on. It led too to an increase in trade and the emergence of merchants.

The increase of trade throughout the ancient world also brought conflicts of interest, such as competition for the domination of trade-routes and of commodity supplies. Such conflicting interests led to attempts by one state to dominate others, by depriving them of independence and thus establishing undisputed claims to their wealth. This factor may well have played a part in the establishment of one of the earliest empires known – the Akkadian empire of Sargon, who conquered the Sumerian city states and vast areas to the north and west, and so gained control of trade throughout the area. The growth of an empire resulted in the spread of its civilization through the area, and its adaptation to local conditions. Some regions went on to develop their own civilizations; and some of these first became powerful independent states and then built up their own empires, as in the case of the Hittites.

Another factor in the emergence of an imperialist structure is the struggle against encroaching neighbours or invaders. This applies to some extent to the Assyrian empire, which developed to counter the Aramaean invasions. And Athens, in struggling to maintain independence against the threat of Persia, became leader of a defensive league which effectively became a tributary empire.

Outside the empires

As these empires spread, many local groups lost their identities and were absorbed into the dominant civilizations. But there were a number of peoples who retained their individuality within the empires, as did the Israelites; while others (such as the Scythians) were never included in them, despite frequent trading contacts. In many cases we know little about these peoples and what we do know may be inaccurate, since our only written source of information is the records of the civilized societies with whom they came into contact. Frequently groups of nomadic or semi-nomadic peoples lived in peaceful co-existence with the settled populations, often acting as caravaneers and traders for the larger civilizations. Among these were the Amorites in Mesopotamia during the Third Dynasty of Ur, and the Mongols in China. But sometimes, for no clear reason, such peoples came to be regarded as a threat – to such an extent that walls were built to keep them out.

An important and recurring phenomenon of the whole period

covered in this book is the disruption wrought by movements of peoples. Some of these were definitely marauding mass-movements of peoples whose identity is not clear, as in the case of the 'Sea Peoples' around 1200 BC (see page 43). In other cases, the names and even something of the cultures of these peoples is known – among them, for example, the Celts and the Huns – but the reason for their movement is not. In the wake of such migrations established political groupings almost totally disappeared. Invaders from the north destroyed the Mycenaean civilization and plunged Greece into the Dark Ages; other migrants swept away the Hittite empire; and shifting masses of barbarians broke up the western half of the Roman empire. Other migrations took the form of gradual infiltration, the evidence for which is difficult to trace and to interpret. The time-span and extent of the 'Aryan' invasion of India, for instance, is hotly disputed by scholars.

Some sort of cataclysm overtook the first great Indian civilization – that of the Indus valley. The new Indian civilization that grew up, like that of China, developed continuously without any major check. But in the 5th century AD the barbarian invasions of Europe, culminating in the fall of Rome in 476, reshaped the Rome-dominated Mediterranean world. The eastern Roman Empire, which sucessfully resisted the barbarians, continued with only slight changes the old pattern of large scale empire. But while its links to the east remained unaltered those with the west decreased – a reorientation emphasized by the spread of Islam through much of the area. The western part of the empire changed radically. Although the Roman patterns of life were not swept away without trace by the barbarians, their lack of any strong central political organization led to the growth of the feudal system and small-scale national states, linked together by their common Christianity. The concept of the East and West of today had been born.

Around the lid of a bronze vessel found in southern Italy gallop Scythian horsemen. The Scythians were a nomadic people who wandered about north-eastern Europe, remaining independent despite frequent contact with civilized peoples. p. 80

In November 1977 Greek archaeologists discovered the tomb of King Philip of Macedon near Vergina in northern Greece, in the area where they had long believed the ancient Macedonian capital of Aeges to have been sited. Near the massive golden coffin containing the King's bones were armour, a shield, a sceptre, and a diadem. There was also a set of five miniature ivory portraits of Philip, his parents, his wife, and his son Alexander the Great. Our knowledge is constantly being expanded by fresh discoveries – few as spectacular as this, but all helping to build up a detailed picture of the past.

NEW-WORLD CIVILIZATIONS
The civilizations of the Near and Far East and of Europe are all to some extent connected with one another, if only through trading contacts. But in the Americas civilizations arose which have no proven connection with those of the Old World. On the whole these were a later development. In South America really large settlements appeared only after 1800 BC, while the first recognizable civilization in central America was that of the Olmecs in the forest regions of the Gulf Coast of Mexico, who flourished between 1300 and 400 BC. But it was only after the period covered by this book that the great American civilizations, those of the Incas of Peru and the Aztecs of Mexico, grew up. They had no contact with the Old World until the arrival of the Spanish at the very end of the 15th century when with appalling cruelty and speed their complex and sophisticated civilization was utterly destroyed.

Above: Excavations in progress on the Greek island of Kithira. Archaeology began in the Mediterranean area, but much work still remains to be done there.

Below: A cache of jars and a skull on Kithira, photographed with a measuring stick to give scale. Such photographs form an important part of the archaeologist's final record of his work; the position of objects may in itself reveal valuable information.

Archaeologists at Work

Archaeology is the study of Man through his material remains. By recording and interpreting objects from an excavated site the archaeologist tries to reconstruct the life of people long ago. Archaeology's status as a scientific discipline is only comparatively recent. Before the end of the 19th century most excavations were little more than treasure hunts, and much important information was either overlooked or destroyed in the search for exciting or spectacular finds. As early as the Renaissance, sites in the Mediterranean were ransacked for statues and other works of art. Curiosity about the past and interest in travel led antiquarians as far afield as Persia and Africa in the 17th and 18th centuries, and a large number of the objects they unearthed now form the basis of European museum collections.

A president of the United States, Thomas Jefferson, carried out the first scientific excavation. Jefferson's intelligent interpretation of an Indian burial mound in Virginia in 1784, based on careful observation and recording, was unequalled for almost 70 years.

Victorian amateurs hack their way through the local Bronze Age barrow – archaeology as a rather serious picnic. Early excavations, conducted as a search for curios rather than for scientific information, have damaged many important sites.

GEOPHYSICAL SURVEYING

Archaeologists today often use geophysical surveying to find a site. The most common methods are resistivity surveying and magnetic surveying. Resistivity surveying, like the interpretation of crop marks, relies on changes in the soil's ability to hold water when an archaeological feature is present. An electric current is sent into the ground and the soil's resistance to it is measured. The resistance will be lower than what is normal for that particular soil where there is a filled-in pit or ditch. This is because the soil filling the feature will be wetter than the surrounding soil, and water is a good conductor of electricity. Conversely, where a stone building or metalled path is buried the resistance will be greater. Magnetic surveying uses the fact that a buried object or structure may well have a stronger magnetic field than the soil around. Metal objects are a good example of this, but other things can be found this way. Firing and burning tend to increase magnetism. Kilns, hearths, and other fired clay structures can be especially well detected by magnetic surveying as their magnetism is permanent.

In both types of survey readings are generally taken at measured intervals on the site. The problem is then to turn a series of numbers or readings into an easily understood picture. In large surveys the dot density method is used. Here, each reading is converted by a computer into a number of dots. So a series of high readings, representing a resistivity survey of a stone wall, will show as a cluster of dots. It is often possible to pick out individual buildings and streets in this way.

How underground features can be detected with resistivity surveying.

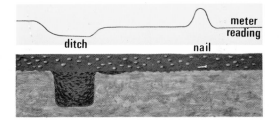

It was then that Meadows Taylor, a British officer and administrator in India, excavated several megalithic tombs there with a remarkable degree of care and technical ability. But unfortunately most 19th century excavations were still undisciplined, destructive scrambles for ancient relics. Heinrich Schliemann undoubtedly made a significant contribution to our understanding of the early civilization of Greece by his discovery of Troy and later Mycenae and Tiryns from the 1870s (see page 51). But his excavation techniques were a travesty of correct archaeological procedure.

A British general, Augustus Lane-Fox Pitt-Rivers, can be regarded as the founder of modern archaeological science. After inheriting the Rivers estate in the south-west of England in 1880 he devoted himself to meticulous excavation and recording of the local archaeological sites. Pitt-Rivers showed how important it was to understand the different deposits that make up a site, and to appreciate the value of ordinary objects such as potsherds and domestic utensils, in our interpretation of the technological development of ancient Man.

The 20th century has seen significant advances in archaeology. Archaeologists like Mortimer Wheeler and Kathleen Kenyon have pioneered a systematic method of excavation aimed at retrieving the greatest possible amount of information from a site. Ill-directed and disorganized excavations, still common in the 1930s, are now the exception. Science has an increasing part to play; modern dating methods have made our dating of past events and stages in the development of Man far more precise.

'Rescue archaeology' is a field that has become important today. The size and scale of modern redevelopment schemes, such as office building and road construction, has meant that more and more archaeological sites are threatened with destruction. The foundations of a tower block can be up to 30 metres (100 feet) deep – penetrating well below any archaeological layer. In Britain professional teams of excavators have been formed to examine at least a few sites before they are destroyed. The time available to excavate before construction takes place is often limited, and some information is inevitably lost. Unless archaeologists and building contractors co-operate a wealth of archaeological data beneath many towns and fields may be swept away unrecorded.

Detecting sites

Finding an archaeological site can be difficult. Not every ancient site leaves identifiable surface features, and often only a scatter of pottery or tiles in a field indicates the presence of an old settlement. A study of maps and documents is often a great help. The existence of a long-buried building or town may be preserved in the local name for a particular area; although Pompeii had been completely sealed beneath several metres of volcanic ash and pumice and the land was used by farmers, the area was still known as *Cività* (*civitas* or *city*) as late as the 18th century.

Fieldwork – the detection and interpretation of unusual surface features in fields and open areas – is important in the discovery of archaeological sites. It can also provide information about the development of agriculture in the ancient world. Unusual features can be geological in origin but may well have been caused by Man, through farming, settlement, or industry. Continual ploughing of small areas has produced a variety of field shapes. The need to mark the limits of one's land has resulted in field boundaries consisting

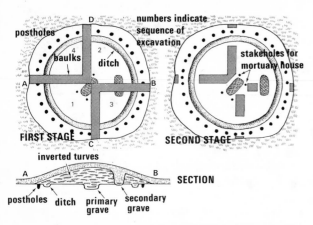

postholes
numbers indicate sequence of excavation
baulks
ditch
stakeholes for mortuary house
FIRST STAGE
SECOND STAGE

inverted turves

SECTION
postholes   ditch   primary   secondary
grave   grave

Diagram of a burial mound, excavated by the quadrant method.

Archaeologists often find that to reach one site, they must dig through another. The features that first attracted settlers to a place (such as a river or an easily defensible position) may well have been as attractive to many later peoples. In this excavation on Crete a Roman villa overlies a Minoan site; the villa must be as carefully excavated and recorded as the earlier buildings. This modern approach contrasts with that of some 19th-century excavators, who would dig straight through any later material in which they did not happen to be interested. Here, workers clean the surface ready for photography and drawing; an ordinary household brush is a delicate and efficient tool for the job.

of ditches or lines of stones. Such land divisions or field systems, often dating from prehistoric times, can still be seen in parts of Europe. Some fine examples of the Roman system of land divisions, where fields were laid out in a series of squares, are discernable in parts of northern Italy and southern France.

Archaeologists have been quick to adapt new inventions for their own use. More archaeological sites have probably been discovered by means of aerial photography than by any other method. The possible usefulness of aerial photography for archaeology was first appreciated at the beginning of this century, when people realized that a complex system of earthworks is easier to understand from above, while many features which are invisible to men on the ground will show up clearly from the air.

Geophysical surveying – measuring the electrical or magnetic properties of the ground to find buried archaeological features – is another example. There are two main types available to the archaeologist. *Resistivity surveying* uses electrical currents to find filled-in ditches or buried buildings. *Magnetic surveying* measures variations in the magnetic field of the ground; it is obviously useful in finding metal objects but will also identify other features.

Stratigraphy

If a site is continuously occupied its level will gradually rise, as deposits or layers accumulate. This happens in a number of ways. A new settlement is often built on top of earlier occupation sites. Successive rebuilding over many years has resulted in the huge mounds or *tells* in the Near East, where several cities have been built on top of one another. An inhabited area deserted because of floods will be covered by a layer of silt, while soil and vegetation will soon encroach on an abandoned settlement. As a general rule the lower layer is earlier than the higher. An archaeologist tries to find out the history of a site by making a vertical cut or section through it, and then distinguishing the different layers. In the same way every feature (such as a pit or ditch) must also be sectioned, in order to understand how it filled up or what it was used for. It is very unusual for all the layers to be clearly separated. More usually layers are disturbed or confused by later interference like the digging of wells and rubbish pits, or burrowing animals. Often layers can be distinguished only by slight differences in colour or feel; a great deal of experience is needed before a section can be properly understood.

Methods of excavation

The excavation of a site consists of removing each layer in turn. Every find from a particular layer must be recorded and kept separately. The method of excavation depends on the type of site and area, and the time and money available. Three important methods are trenching, the quadrant method, and open-area excavation.

When it seems likely that an area contains archaeological material but detection methods such as aerial photography or geophysical surveying have proved inconclusive, a series of trenches may be excavated. This will show whether there is a site and, if so, establish its extent and nature. Trenching may be only the first stage in investigating a much larger area if it produces evidence of a settlement. Trenching by itself has serious deficiencies as a great deal of important information will be lost unless a more complete examination is undertaken.

Defensive earthworks or boundary ditches are often excavated by cutting a trench at right angles to their alignment. The section on each side of the trench will show how the bank or ditch was constructed, when it went out of use, and how the ditch filled up. If a defensive system is connected with a settlement site, it will then be necessary to excavate a larger part of the ditch and the area it enclosed in order to see how the two are related.

The quadrant method is often used to examine individual features like burial mounds. The mound is divided into four sections or quadrants. These are removed one by one until the original land surface on which the mound was built is reached. Walls of earth (*baulks*) are left so that the sections they preserve can be recorded. The baulks are finally removed so that the whole feature can be examined. The principal burial that often lies at the centre of the mound can be recorded and extracted in one operation. Secondary burials are sometimes discovered in the process of excavation and are dealt with first.

The best way of understanding the history and development of a settlement is to open up large areas. This shows each phase of the habitation site in one operation. Each successive layer and feature is completely examined, recorded, and then removed. No permanent baulks or sections are left which might obscure the overall picture of the site. At one time a large area was excavated by laying out a grid and then excavating a series of square trenches separated by baulks. But this method did not allow the excavator to examine buildings or structures as a whole at certain stages in their development, while the baulks themselves, if left, occupied too much of the area investigated.

Open-area excavation requires great care and discipline. Before a large area is opened up a grid is laid out, made up of pegs spaced at regular intervals. This makes it easier to record each find and feature. As in the old method, it is necessary to record vertical sections. This can be done by leaving temporary baulks along fixed lines across the site; these are removed once they have been recorded or if they interfere with a particular structure or feature. If a large site is to be excavated it is usually divided into several areas, each of which is supervised by a skilled and experienced excavator. The director oversees the whole operation.

Plants and animals

Excavations teach us not only about the physical appearance of past structures and settlements, but also about the environment of ancient Man. We can find out about the climate, flora, and fauna of different periods by analysing the pollen and cereal grains, insect remains, and bones which, under certain conditions, are preserved in the soil. Animal bones on the site can tell us about the wild animals Man hunted or domestic animals he kept at different stages of his history. Sometimes an ancient land surface may be sealed under a burial mound or building and pollen grains may be preserved. As some vegetation will only grow under certain conditions these will provide information about the climate of the period. Cereal grains from rubbish pits or middens can tell us about the agriculture and diet of ancient Man. If large numbers of human bones are available for study from a cemetery, an osteologist can work out the rate of adult or infant mortality or the range of diseases people suffered from at a particular period. Even the remains of cremated bones can yield valuable information.

CROP MARKS

When the Sun is low on the horizon any features on the Earth's surface will cast long shadows. As a result a whole series of mounds and interconnected ditches may be revealed. Even if such features have been completely levelled by ploughing they can still be detected by their effect on crops. Because crop growth depends on the soil, the existence of a buried pit or ditch (which has a greater depth of soil, holds more moisture, and has a larger organic content) will give rise to a stronger though slower-growing crop compared with the rest of the field. Such features can then show up from the air as dark lines or circles. Buried stone walls or metalled roads will be largely impenetrable by roots and will retain less moisture: so a faster-growing but stunted crop will be produced. Outlines of buildings and streets may then appear as white lines in an aerial photograph.

Variations in crop growth depend on the nature of the soil, the type of crop, and the climate. Crop marks are particularly clear on well drained soils like gravel and sand. Clay will tend to be disappointing because it retains moisture even after a long dry spell. Cereal crops are very revealing but sugar beet may show nothing because of the large size of the individual plants. A drought will emphasize differences in crop growth but after a wet spring growth will be more even.

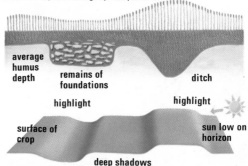

How the Sun's rays on a field can reveal archaeological features by showing up cropmarks.

Open area excavation of a Roman fort at Nijmegen, in the Netherlands. The square pattern of baulks does not follow the shape of the fort; the baulks are left according to a fixed grid to allow the recording of sections. A new area is being cleared in the distance.

An archaeological site may appear to be a chaotic mass of people and tools but in fact order and method are never forgotten. In this photograph workers carefully scrape away soil with mason's trowels so that no 'find' or slight variation in the soil is missed. The key to the whole site is the grid of string. This allows each section of the site to be given a number, used later in identifying finds and in mapping the site at different stages. Finds are placed in the labelled boxes which can be seen dotted about the site. Spoil — the earth turned up by the trowel — is put into buckets and taken away in wheelbarrows to a spoil tip (again marked to follow the grid) where it will be sieved in case any small find has been missed. At intervals, the whole site is cleared and photographs and accurate drawings made to record each layer before it is destroyed by the next stage of the excavation.

Organic materials such as leather, cloth, and wood are sometimes preserved, particularly in stagnant water. Here oxygen is absent and the normal process of decay stops. Deposits like peat are particularly valuable to the archaeologist. In 1950 in a peat bog in Denmark over 150 bodies were found in an almost perfect state of preservation. They were people who had died nearly 2000 years earlier, as part of some ritual.

A famous and dramatic example of preservation can be seen in southern Italy. The towns of Pompeii and Herculaneum were buried beneath volcanic ash, pumice, and mud in AD 79. This preserved every aspect of the two ancient cities: buildings, streets, domestic objects, wall-paintings, and even electoral posters. Where the ash had suffocated and buried unfortunate people who were unable to escape in time, it hardened round the corpses. When the bodies disintegrated the ash formed a perfect mould. By filling such moulds with plaster the archaeologist Fiorelli was able to produce casts of the bodies. This process was also applied to objects such as wooden doors, furniture, and food.

Dating methods

For an excavation to be valuable, a date must be given to the site. Pottery is the most common artefact found in most excavations and is often the only method of dating a phase of a site or a particular layer. Vessels for cooking and serving food have a relatively short existence as they are easily broken. If they can be dated, therefore, they can give an approximate date for the layer in which they are found. But not all pottery types are closely datable and rubbish survivals from an earlier period can confuse the picture. Coins can be dated quite accurately – often to the year of manufacture – but they usually remain in circulation for a number of years; some Roman coins stayed in use for more than a century. So when an archaeologist finds a coin in a layer the only assumption he can make is that the deposit was not laid down before the date the coin was minted.

Only through scientific methods can one assign an absolute date to an event or an object. Two of the best-known methods are carbon-14 and dendrochronology. Carbon-14 is a radioactive form of carbon. All living matter absorbs radioactive carbon-14. When that matter dies it ceases to absorb carbon-14 and the radioactive element decays at a fixed and measurable rate. Half the element will have disappeared after about 5570 years. Knowing this, it is possible to date a piece of organic matter such as wood or bone by the amount of radioactivity present. Dendrochronology uses the fact that every tree forms a growth ring each year. This varies in thickness according to climatic conditions. A dry year will cause a narrower ring than a wet year. By matching up tree ring sequences from trees of different dates it is possible to construct a time scale for a particular region which can be used to date timbers from ancient structures there.

Experimental archaeology

When a large part of a building or an object is found in an excavation it is often possible to produce a reconstruction. A study of similar objects shown on sculptured reliefs or pottery can assist in this process. For instance, the discovery of well-preserved waggons or chariots buried with the dead in the second millennium BC in eastern Europe, and in other areas of Europe in the first millennium, have enabled the archaeologist to reconstruct and appreciate the development and workings of wheeled vehicles in prehistoric times. Thor Heyerdal's seagoing version of an Egyptian reed boat, modelled on representations of such boats from tomb paintings and on similar boats still in use in the Near East, has shown what the archaeologist can learn from experimental archaeology. Heyerdal used his boat to prove that long sea voyages were possible in such flimsy craft, and found out that some apparently useless parts of their structure played a vital part.

Working models of ancient kilns and furnaces based on excavated examples, and experiments in minting coins and casting weapons using ancient methods, are increasing our appreciation of early Man's technical ability. At Butser Hill in south-east England a complete Iron Age farmstead has been recreated. The farm buildings have been modelled on excavated remains; emmer, the type of wheat grown in the Iron Age, is cultivated in the fields; cattle of a similar breed to prehistoric stock are reared and experiments in the firing of pottery are being made. This experiment has not only helped us to understand the workings of an ancient farm; many questions have been answered and others raised. The building of huts has caused shallow features of a type found before on archaeological sites, but never previously explained. Experiments in crop growing and storage have changed our idea about the efficiency of prehistoric farmers. It is now obvious that they did not simply produce enough for subsistence alone; farmers could have produced a surplus which may have been traded. Experiments at Butser Hill have also highlighted the way some early structures (such as storage barns, fences, and pottery kilns) often leave scanty or confusing evidence for their existence. To discover the full range of activities on an ancient settlement, future excavators must use even more skill and care.

Experimental archaeology in action, at Lunt in the English Midlands. Top: Modern soldiers perform one of the tasks of Roman legionaries – raising timbers to form part of a 'Roman' fort. Reconstructions like this help archaeologists to understand how such buildings were constructed; the evidence of paintings or other visual sources is often too confusing to explain clearly the features of a site. Seeing the work being done can often solve a mystery at once. Bottom: The completed fort. As well as acting as a kind of museum exhibit, the reconstruction will give valuable information about such things as the effect of weather on its timbers.

Time Chart of the Ancient World

BC	MESOPOTAMIA	REST OF NEAR EAST	EGYPT AND AFRICA	GREECE
3000	c 3100 First pictographic tablets c 2600-2400 Royal Graves of Ur. 2372-2255 Akkadian empire, founded by Sargon. 2113-2006 Third Dynasty of Ur. 1792-1750 Hammurabi rules Babylonia. 1590 Hittites raid Babylon. 1509-1245 Kassite Dynasty established in Babylon. 1124-1103 Nebuchadrezzar I rules Babylon.	3000s Elamite civilization in south-west Iran. 2200 Burials at Alaca Hüyük, Anatolia. 1460-1180 Hittite empire at its height. 1300 Iranians move into Iran. c 1200 Raids of Sea Peoples. 1050 Greeks colonize coast of Asia Minor. 1000-926 Israel's United Monarchy.	c 3118 Unification of Egypt c 3000 Sahara begins to dry up. 2686-2181 Old Kingdom. 2500 Land becomes more arid south of the Sahara. 2133-1633 Middle Kingdom. 1674-1567 Egypt ruled by the Hyksos invaders. 1567-1085 New Kingdom; Egypt's period of greatest power. 1197-1165 Ramesses III; defeats the Sea Peoples. 1140 First Phoenician colony in North Africa. 814 Phoenician city of Carthage founded.	2000-1900 Greek-speaking tribes arrive in Greece. 1650-1450 Minoan civilization in Crete; Mycenaeans on mainland. 1450 Cretan civilization destroyed. 1150 Dorians invade Greece; destruction of Mycenaean civilization.
1000				
	745-630 Assyria at its height. 612 Nineveh sacked by Medes and Chaldaeans. 605-562 Nebuchadrezzar II, king of Babylon. 539 Cyrus II of Persia conquers Babylonia.	549 Persians under Cyrus II defeat Medes. 424 Assassination of Artaxerxes I of Persia. 360s Weakening of Persian empire; revolts in many satrapies.	525-404 Egypt ruled by Persians. c 500 People of Nok – skilled iron-workers – living in northern Nigeria. 407 Carthaginian Hanno sails down coast to Senegal. 343-332 Egypt's second period of Persian rule.	900-750 Rise of city-states. 700-500 Sparta dominates Peloponnese. 700-600 Athenians expel their kings. 507 Athenian democracy begins. 490-479 Persian Wars. 477-405 Athens dominates Aegean. 431-404 Peloponnesian War 356-338 Philip of Macedon makes himself master of Greece.
500				
	332 Alexander the Great conquers Mesopotamia. 304-64 Seleucids rule Mesopotamia.	334 Alexander the Great invades Persian empire. 304-64 Seleucids 247-227 Parthian kingdom established.	332 Alexander the Great invades Egypt. 304-30 Ptolemaic period. 218-201 Second Punic War; Hannibal crosses Europe with elephants. 183 Suicide of Hannibal.	336 Assassination of Philip. His son Alexander becomes king. 323 Death of Alexander. 280-197 Former city states try to throw off Macedonian rule. 171-168 Macedonia tries to re-establish rule over Greece; defeated by Rome, it becomes a Roman province. 145 Romans destroy Corinth.
200				
		133 King of Pergamum bequeaths his lands to Rome. 64 Pompey gains Seleucid empire for Rome. 55 Partition of Roman provinces. 53 Crassus defeated by Syrians. 5 Probable date of birth of Jesus.	149-146 Third Punic War; destruction of Carthage. 111-105 Romans at war with Numidia. 32 Octavian declares war on Antony and Cleopatra.	
AD				
100	117 Roman conquest under Trajan.	115-117 Trajan extends Roman empire. 162-165 War between Romans and Parthians. 267-273 Revolt of Zenobia, Queen of Palmyra.	130 Hadrian visits Egypt. 193-211 Septimius Severus (African-born), Emperor of Rome.	
300		330 Constantinople becomes 'second Rome'. 325 Nicean Council. 441-453 Attila the Hun advances into eastern Roman empire.	300 Great citadel of Zimbabwe built. 326 Ethiopia converted to Christianity. 429 Vandal kingdom of North Africa established.	286 Goths sack Athens, Corinth, and Sparta.
476				

22

ROME AND ITALY	REST OF EUROPE	CHINA	INDIAN SUB-CONTINENT	BC
				3000
	c 2000 Spread of Indo-European peoples.	2500 Lung-shan neolithic culture in Taiwan.		
	c 1500 Building of Stonehenge and other megalithic monuments.	1500-1027 Shang Dynasty. A feudal empire, centred on Anyang.		
		1027 Defeat of Shang; foundation of Chou Dynasty.		1000
900s Rise of Etruscans	1100s Phoenician colonization in Spain?	700-500 Weakening of Chou as vassal states grow in power.	900-700 Iron Age.	
735 Traditional date of founding of Rome.	600 Greeks found Massilia (Marseilles).	660 Nomads devastate north Honan.	c 600 Early cities in Ganges valley.	
		551 Birth of Confucius.	c 563 Birth of the Buddha. 533 Achaemenid invasion of India.	
509 Etruscan kings expelled from Rome; founding of Republic.				500
493 Aristocracy forced to recognize plebians' tribunes.	450 Rise of Celtic La Tène culture.	481-221 Warring States period. 400 Iron-casting practised.	430-364 Shishunaga dynasty rules.	
			364-324 Nanda dynasty rules.	
343-275 Rome establishes its domination of central Italy.			326 Alexander the Great in India. 324-187 Mauryans; drive out Greeks, unify empire.	
264-241 First Punic War.		256-221 Ch'in defeat Chou and unify empire for the first time.	232 Death of Ashoka.	
218-201 Second Punic War; Rome defeats Carthage and gains its first provinces.	201 Rome defeats Carthage and gains its territory in Spain, Sardinia, and Corsica.	206 Collapse of Ch'in Dynasty. 206 BC-AD 220 Han Dynasty.	187-75 Shunga dynasty.	200
133-91 Power-stuggles between aristocratic and popular parties.	113-101 Northern tribes defeat Romans; leads to reform of Roman army.			
82-80 Dictatorship of Sulla. 83-62 Rise of Pompey. 46-44 Dictatorship of Caesar.	58-51 Julius Caesar's conquest of Gaul.	50 BC- AD 50 Buddhism introduced.		
44 Assassination of Caesar. 40 Power-struggle between Mark Antony and Octavian.				
27 Octavian takes the title Augustus. He has become the first Roman Emperor.	15 Roman empire extended to upper Danube.			
14 Death of Augustus.	43 Claudius's conquest of Britain begins.	25 Han move capital after short usurpation.	15-300s Kushan invaders rule.	AD
98 Trajan becomes Emperor – the first to be born outside Italy.	101-107 Trajan's conquest of Dacia.			100
	122 Hadrian's Wall built. 257 Goths occupy Dacia.	166 Roman emperor Marcus Aurelius sends embassy to China.		
200s Financial crisis 212 Edict of Caracalla	274 Gauls set up brief rebel empire.	220-587 Six Dynasties period; China in turmoil.		
286 Diocletian divides empire. 312 Constantine defeats Maxentius at Milvian Bridge.	300s Increasing barbarian threats to empire.		320-600s Gupta empire extended.	300
313 First toleration of Christianity.	376 Visigoths admitted into empire.			
410 Goths under Alaric sack Rome.	406 Vandals overrun Gaul. 407 Last Roman troops withdraw from Britain.			
476 Last Western Roman emperor deposed.				476

23

Mesopotamia

One of the earliest definable urban civilizations grew up in a region which at first sight seems to be inhospitable and poor in resources – a swampy area in southern Iraq where the Tigris and Euphrates flow close together before reaching the Persian Gulf. Stone, timber, and metals are not available locally; the two rivers flood in spring just as crops are ready for harvesting, and the flood not only threatens the harvest but also deposits large amounts of silt. This can choke irrigation canals, cause sudden changes in the courses of the rivers, and sometimes make the soil excessively salty, and so unproductive.

Why and how did cities develop in this area, under such conditions, as they did toward the end of the fourth millennium BC? In the period between 7000 and 5000 BC communities which relied fully on agriculture developed in the hilly rainfall-zone of Western Asia, and for a while it was thought that this agricultural pattern was only gradually transferred to the swampy, relatively rainless area of southern Iraq. After a number of archaeological finds in southern Iraq it is now more generally accepted that, although this area was not a pioneer in developing agricultural techniques, it did adopt them swiftly. By about 4000 BC it had begun to outstrip the more northerly areas. Some archaeologists have thought that one reason for this rapid growth might have been the need for irrigation, flood diversion, and continuous cleaning out of canals – effective organization of all this would require a central authority. But recently it has become clear that irrigation can be practised quite effectively by small villages, without resulting in complex urban development; moreover, some archaeologists now maintain that the larger political structures of cities in southern Iraq predated the introduction of full-scale irrigation there.

Perhaps a more likely reason for the rapid development of this area is the existence of varied and reliable extra food supplies such as fish, wildfowl, and above all the date-palm. This has a high

Mosaic decoration from the temple of Inanna at Uruk. The mosaics were built up of a number of clay cones, the flat ends of which were coloured red, white, or black. Clay-cone mosaics were commonly used in the large, elaborate temples built at Uruk toward the end of the fourth millennium. Their zig-zag and lozenge patterns are similar to those of woven reed-mats.

tolerance of brackish water, and its fruit is harvested in the autumn, just at the time when the grain (harvested in spring) would be running low. These extra sources of food brought first a greater security in food supplies (leading to an increase in population) and second, the need for some degree of specialization of work, particularly in the production of dates. Such specialization and dependence on varied sources of food seems to have led to the emergence of large-scale institutions, usually temples, which could store produce and distribute it for food, processing, or cultivation. Interestingly, the oldest structure using solid building materials so far known from this area is a small shrine at Eridu dating from the fifth millennium BC.

A drawing of an alabaster vase found in the temple precinct at Uruk. It is decorated with a relief arranged in registers: at the bottom a wavy line indicates water, the source of all life; above it, ears of grain and herds of sheep represent the produce of the fields. The middle register shows a line of naked figures, probably temple attendants, bringing the fruits of the harvest to the temple. In the top register, the fruits are presented to a female figure – a priestess, or an image of the goddess Inanna herself. Behind her, two reed-bundles (the symbol of Inanna) guard the entrance to the store-house, which contains a pair of vases identical in shape to this one.

With the evolution of temples (and perhaps other comparable organizations such as manors) and the complex society that their existence implies, not only did writing (see page 36) develop, but *regular* irrigation seems to have been adopted. One of the main results of this may well have been the establishment of small permanent fields owned by families. Inevitably some would have had more, others less, productive fields, resulting in the growth of poorer and richer groups of landowners. The widening gap between these groups, with the poor eventually sinking to a state of serfdom, is illustrated by sale-documents from the middle of the third millennium, which show that small, impoverished landowners were forced by crop-failures to sell their plots to large landowners who incorporated them into their own estates, with the original owners remaining as share-cropping tenants.

Temple and king

The major sites excavated in southern Iraq are temples and their precincts. The reason for this lies in the fact that the people built and rebuilt sanctuaries on the same spot, so that large mounds (tells) were formed as walls and foundations accumulated on top of each other. These are easily identifiable as promising archaeological sites in the flat plain of south Iraq. But as a result, modern knowledge of the rest of the cities in which the temples stood is severely limited and frequently biased, and this led in the past to faulty interpretations of material. For example, for a long time it was thought, as the result of the work of the Sumerian scholar Deimel, that all the land of Sumerian cities was owned by the city-god and so by the temple, and that the political organization of the cities was a kind of 'theocratic communism'. It is now more usual, and probably more correct, to regard the temples as massive self-sufficient organizations (perhaps comparable in some ways to a mediaeval priory), existing within the Sumerian city-state, and wielding an enormous amount of political and economic power by reason of their wealth as much as their religious function.

Nevertheless on the evidence we have at present it does seem that temples provided at least one of the focal points

in the process of urbanization which reached its zenith in the brilliant civilization of the Sumerian city-states of the third millennium BC. Probably one of the most important factors in their development and political prominence had to do with the needs of animal-husbandry and the interdependence of this and agriculture. This is illustrated by a Sumerian legend which centres to some extent on the 'Cain and Abel' motif; it concerns the rivalry between a shepherd and a farmer (both gods in this legend). They compete for the hand of Inanna, a type of fertility goddess, and their conflict is resolved at

A white limestone cylinder seal from the Uruk period. The design here shows a figure in a net skirt – perhaps the en of Uruk – accompanied by an attendant holding grain.
Below: detail of an oblong alabaster trough with a rounded base, generally thought to come from Uruk. A ewe approaches a reed hut decorated with reed bundles from which a lamb is emerging. The stylistic similarity of the decoration to that of the Uruk vase opposite suggests that both were used in the Inanna temple at about the same time.

the end with the two agreeing to be friends and help each other:

> *Farmer God: Against you, O shepherd, why should I strive?*
> *Let your sheep eat the grass of the riverbank*
> *In my meadow let your sheep wander*
> *In the bright fields of Uruk let them eat grain*
> *Let your kids and lambs drink the water of my canal.*
> *Shepherd God: As for me who am a shepherd, at my marriage*
> *O farmer, may you be counted as a friend.*

Sheep and goats could always be grazed on stubble in the fields after harvest, at the same time providing on-the-spot manure; they were hardy, cheap to feed, and provided the basis for one of the most important industries in this area at all times – the manufacture of textiles. To produce and market these on a large enough scale to pay for the imports of essential raw materials such as metals and stone meant capital expenditure on a scale which could only be afforded by a large organization such as a temple.

The maintenance of large cattle provides an even better example of the central role of the temple in the development of complex social structure. The ox- (or donkey-) drawn plough was first used by the Sumerians, and these animals need more food than they can get by grazing. This resulted in their concentration in large herds within the temple which, since it also collected and distributed a major part of agricultural produce, could afford to maintain them. Once in control of the herds the temple also organized the ploughing – so that for their most funda-

This inscribed stele commemorates the final victory of Lagash, under its ruler Ennatum (about 2500 BC) at the end of a long border dispute with its neighbour Umma. This side shows two scenes from the battle. Above: Ennatum, wearing a royal helmet decorated with a bun of hair (compare the bronze head of an Akkadian ruler, page 28), and holding a throwing-stick, leads a closely formed phalanx of helmeted soldiers into battle. Below, Ennatum in his war chariot aims his lance, flanked by spear-carrying soldiers.

mental subsistence all smaller farmers were dependent on the temple.

It is against this background that we must seek for the origins of kingship. This is a very disputed question. One answer suggests that with the establishment of permanent fields and organized irrigation-works, boundary-disputes became more common – to the extent that a war-leader had to be appointed. This function eventually developed into a permanent kingship. In some cities (for example Uruk) this leader emerged from within the temple-structure itself, since his title *en* would seem to have 'temple-administrator' as its original meaning. But in other cities, such as Ur, the royal title is *lugal* which means 'great man'.

The cities grow

One effect of the almost continuous warfare that went on between the Sumerian city-states was a concentration of population within the larger urban centres; they began not only to build strong defensive walls around themselves but also to extend their protection to smaller outlying communities. As rich landowners moved into houses inside these protective walls, the population inside became much denser and their increased demands led to the creation and concentration of markets within these cities. The poorer

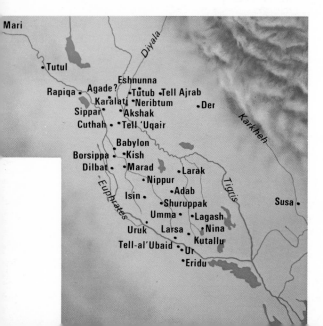

Gudea, ruler of Lagash in southern Babylonia about 2150 BC.

share-cropping peasants continued to live mainly outside these urban enclosures, in order to work the fields.

One of the hall-marks of this increasing social stratification was the demand for specialized craftsmanship. In the late fourth millennium this had been limited mainly to small-scale production of cult-objects of stone and shell-inlay within and for the temple; with the establishment of permanent kingship, technological progress was rapidly followed by an increased demand for such skills, but for quite different purposes and in totally different contexts. The main area of demand was of course military; craftsmen's skills went into the production of weapons and into four-wheeled, onager-drawn war-chariots. One glance at a representation of this complicated piece of war-machinery shows the high level of technological skill of which the Sumerian craftsmen were capable. Military demands were soon followed by royal and also private demands for luxuries. These are basically of two types – functional objects made in precious metals (a good example is a silver wine-skin found at Ur), and elaborately decorated ornamental objects. It is worth remembering that at the same time the people in the fields were probably still not using metals for their tools.

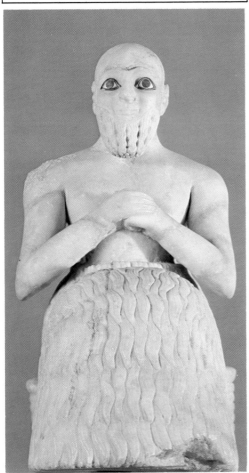

An alabaster statuette, inlaid with bitumen, shell, and lapis lazuli, of Ebih-il, an important functionary at the temple of Ishtar, in Mari. The inscription tells us that he himself dedicated the figure to the gods. He is dressed in a skirt of animal skins and sits on a reed stool.

THE SUMERIAN KING LISTS
A large clay prism, listing different local Sumerian dynasties successively, together with lengths of reigns and occasional remarks of a historical or legendary nature, is one of the very few sources for reconstructing Sumerian history. These lists were probably compiled during the Third Dynasty of Ur, but they must contain much older traditions. They try to reconcile the old ideal of independent city states with the newer ideas of empire. According to the lists, kingship was first 'lowered from heaven' in the city of Eridu, whence it passed in succession to other cities. The early kings are credited with reigns of thousands of years each, then 'the Flood swept thereover'. Archaeology has yet to provide conclusive evidence for this cataclysmic event, but the Sumerians were positive that there once had been a flood, more terrible than the usual spring floods. They told how the gods decided to destroy sinful mankind but warned one virtuous man, Ut-napishtim, of their intentions. He built a large boat and so he, his family, and 'the seed of all living creatures' were saved to repopulate the earth.

After the Flood, kingship was again lowered from heaven, this time to the city of Kish. Then came the dynasty of Uruk, the fifth king of which was the hero Gilgamesh. He was the subject of many legends; according to an Akkadian epic of much later date he and his onetime rival turned friend, the strange half-bull man Enkidu, enjoyed many adventures together till Enkidu died. Afraid of death for the first time, Gilgamesh set off to find Ut-napishtim and his wife, who were immortal, and could tell him the secret of eternal life. After more adventures Gilgamesh gained the secret, a plant from the bottom of the sea, only to lose it — on the way home he fell asleep and a snake ate the precious plant.

Fantastic though the time-span may appear, the king lists were not in any sense works of fiction. Some of the kings, such as Mes-annapadda of Ur and Me-barag-si of Kish, did actually live and rule in their cities for their names have been found on monuments and building inscriptions.

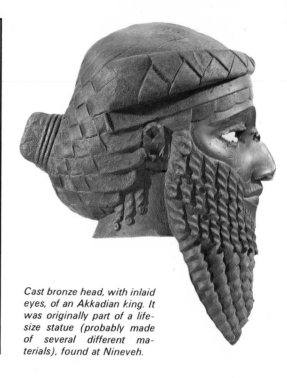

Cast bronze head, with inlaid eyes, of an Akkadian king. It was originally part of a life-size statue (probably made of several different materials), found at Nineveh.

Sandstone stele celebrating the victory of Naram-Sin over the Lullubi, a people living in the mountains to the east. The king's status is emphasized by his exaggerated size, and by his helmet decorated with the horns which symbolize his divinity. At the head of his troops, Naram-Sin advances up a wooded mountainside. Two dead Lullubi lie under his left foot, while others, dressed in animal skins, plead for mercy.

The rapid increase in the use of metallurgy brought about an extension of the administrative hierarchy in the temple and of the rapidly developing palace organization. On the one hand men had to be trained to do the necessary skilled work, while on the other the increased trade demands and the existence of groups of specialist professionals (metal-workers, goldsmiths, weavers, scribes) consumed ever more of the basic economic resources.

The fullest and best-illustrated period of this highly developed Sumerian city-life was from 2800 to 2400 BC; during this time kingship had become an integral part of the political organization, and wars against neighbouring states were undertaken in the name of – and with the blessing of – the city-god. But at the end of this period all the cities of Sumer were conquered by Sargon of Agade to the north, who incorporated them as a province in his extensive empire. Although the function and structure of the cities underwent a number of changes, they continued to exist as highly respected sacred cities. Several literary texts of slightly later periods illustrate the importance city-life held for the Sumerians: according to the texts cities had been founded by gods in 'pure' places for the specific purpose of functioning as cult-centres, and Man was only then created in order to serve the gods within them.

Sargon and after

Sargon was the descendent of the Semitic peoples who were settled in Mesopotamia before written records began. A legend tells how his mother, for reasons not disclosed, placed her baby in a pitch-covered basket and set him floating down the Euphrates. He was rescued by a shepherd who reared the child as his own, but on reaching maturity, Sargon became – it is not clear how – the cup-bearer of the king of Kish. He later overthrew his royal master and went on to conquer all of Mesopotamia, parts of north Syria, and Elam (across the Tigris in south-west Iran). At a site not yet discovered, he built a new capital called Agade for his state of Akkad. The cuneiform script of

This black stone weight in the shape of a duck bears the royal inscription of Shulgi (2095–2048 BC). Similar weights, in various sizes, were used from the time of the Third Dynasty of Ur to the late Assyrian period. The inscription guaranteed the weight and established a standard with which local units of weight had to conform, particularly for taxation purposes.

Sumer was adapted to fit the Semitic Akkadian speech of the new ruler.

Sargon's grandson, Naram-Sin, was also a warrior and ruler of genius, but the Akkadian empire was subject to great pressure from within and without, and eventually disintegrated – possibly as a result of pressure from a people called the Gutians of whom very little is known. The Sumerians eventually reasserted themselves, and for about a hundred years, enjoyed a renaissance of their culture and great prosperity under the leadership of the rulers of Ur. A great building programme was undertaken. The most impressive temple to be erected was the ziggurat (temple tower) of Ur, and other cities were not neglected.

But the old world of the city states was not restored. Thanks to Sargon, it had been replaced by the imperial ideal; and the Third Dynasty of Ur directed the affairs of a major part of Mesopotamia with an efficient and huge bureaucracy. From this period dates the earliest known law code, presumably drawn up to help judges (who represented the king) with the settlement of disputes throughout a large area. Measures and weights were standardized and a uniform calendar, in which each year received a name, was in use throughout the empire. The rulers of the Third Dynasty of Ur did not try to raise their own city-god (the Moon-god Nanna) to a position of pre-eminence; instead they emphasized the special status of the king in the structure of the empire by the ruler himself being regarded as a god – a practice introduced in the preceding period by Naram-Sin.

In spite of the obvious wealth and brilliance of the Sumerian empire, little (apart from some buildings) remains. One reason for this may be the dramatic and almost total destruction of Ur in about 2000 BC by the Elamites, who took the last ruler of Ur, Ibbi-Sin, into captivity at Susa. From now on Ur ceased to be politically important, but it remained a particularly sacred city. One of the most beautiful and moving Sumerian poetic compositions concerns its destruction and is called *Lamentation over the Destruction of Ur*; it was probably sung at a later time when the ziggurat and shrines of Ur were being rebuilt after the Elamite destruction. Some of the description

A god, possibly Marduk, in the act of slaying a one-eyed female creature. It has been suggested that this Old Babylonian terracotta plaque may illustrate an episode later incorporated into the Babylonian Epic of Creation.

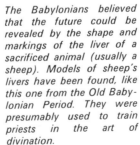

The Babylonians believed that the future could be revealed by the shape and markings of the liver of a sacrificed animal (usually a sheep). Models of sheep's livers have been found, like this one from the Old Babylonian Period. They were presumably used to train priests in the art of divination.

seems to echo an eye-witness account of the disaster:

> My city on its foundations verily was
>   destroyed;
> Ur where it lay verily perishes ...
> My house founded by the righteous,
>   like a garden hut, verily its side has
>   caved in.
> In Ur's lofty gates, where the people
>   were wont to walk,
>   dead bodies were lying about ...
>   in all its streets where they were wont
>   to walk,
>   the dead were lying.
> The mother left her daughter; the
>   people groan
> The father turned away from his son;
>   the people groan.

The beauty of this lamentation has at times been compared to the laments over the destruction of Jerusalem: and there is certainly a possibility that the Old Testament lament derived from this type of Sumerian lament.

Babylon

The Third Dynasty of Ur ended when Ur itself was sacked by raiding Elamites in about 2000 BC, but Ur had been under pressure for many years before that catastrophe. Provinces had broken away, and Western Semitic nomads had been infiltrating both the Mediterranean lands to the west, and Mesopotamia to the east. The newcomers were called *amurru* in Akkadian, and are usually identified with the Amorites of the Old Testament. They managed to take over large areas of land, and eventually Amorite dynasties established themselves in cities such as Mari and Ashur. About 1900 BC, one such family became the rulers of the small provincial city of Babylon. They spoke a dialect of Akkadian and, though naturally they were responsible for some innovations, on the whole they adopted the culture and way of life they found in their new home. The first five rulers of the dynasty were not particularly distinguished, but the sixth was the great Hammurabi.

Hammurabi inherited a small state, and during the first ten years of his reign such campaigns as he undertook were successful, though on a relatively modest scale. For the next 20 years he devoted himself to ruling his people, building temples, and erecting fortifications.

From the archaeological point of view, Babylon itself is a great disappointment. The city of this Old Babylonian period cannot be excavated, because it now lies below the water-table. But evidence from other sites supplies us with examples of Mesopotamian architecture from the years before and during the reign of Hammurabi. Splendid temples, some of great size with vast courtyards and numerous rooms, were still built as the houses of the god to whom they were dedicated, but the texts show that the king had increasing control over temple lands.

The scribes of the Old Babylonian period appear to have been particularly active, not only composing new texts but also copying out and editing Sumerian texts. Texts on mathematics and geometry are found for the first time; they show that the Babylonians had a good grasp of these subjects, and that they had a working knowledge of the theorem of Pythagoras, even though it was never abstractly formulated. Many texts deal with practical problems, such as the calculation of the area of disputed fields or the amount of earth required to build a rampart to scale a city wall of a given

THE LAW CODE OF HAMMURABI

The second year of the reign of Hammurabi bears the date formula 'The year he enacted the Law of the Land', which might seem to suggest that the great law code was promulgated in that year; some scholars have suggested, however, that this had nothing to do with the famous code, which in their opinion represents no more than a justification of Hammurabi's reign to the gods, and was not composed until his last years.

Hammurabi's code is not the earliest. Others are known from the Third Dynasty of Ur, but they have only survived in fragments on clay tablets, whereas the Hammurabi code has survived virtually intact on a stone stela, now in the Louvre.

At the top of the stela is a picture of the king before Shamash, the sun-god, who was also god of justice. In the introduction below the picture, Hammurabi says that it was his intention to cause justice to prevail in the land, to destroy the wicked and the evil, that the strong might not oppress the weak.

In the laws themselves, some elements are recognizable from earlier codes, but the principal of the *lex talionis* (an eye for an eye) is thought by some scholars to be an example of Amorite influence. The 282 laws listed cover such things as offences against people and property; disputes concerning trade, land, fees, professional services; and the family. Some of the punishments involving death or mutilation may be considered harsh by our standards; but on the whole the laws present a picture of a well-ordered society, which lived by certain recognized standards, and offered a measure of legal protection to all.

The stele inscribed with the law code of Hammurabi.

height. The texts, official and private, paint a picture of an efficiently run society, under a powerful king. To help him govern, he had officials – soldiers and priests of high rank – drawn from the rich land-owning aristocracy. Next in the social scale were the professional people and farmers, and at the bottom were the slaves, drawn from prisoners of war and from the ranks of poor citizens who had

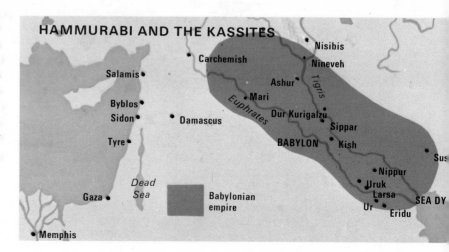

HAMMURABI AND THE KASSITES

to sell themselves to meet debts or in times of famine.

The international situation during the first 30 years of Hammurabi's reign is well documented, thanks to an illuminating series of letters from the royal archives at Mari. In the west, the nomads were still giving trouble, while in the east, Eshnunna and its Elamite allies were causing anxiety. The uncertainties of international relations in the world around Babylon during this period are well illustrated by one particular letter:

No king is powerful by himself. 10 or 15 kings follow Hammurabi, King of Babylon, as many follow Rim-sin, King of Larsa, as many follow Ibalpiel, King of Eshnunna, as many follow Amutpiel, King of Qatna. 20 kings follow Iarimlim, King of Iamkhad [Aleppo] . . .

These 'kings' were, in general, no more than small-city rulers. But Hammurabi was about to upset the balance of power. In a series of campaigns he reunited the whole of Sumer and Akkad once more; turned on his old ally Mari, attacked it, and left it in ruins; and defeated Eshnunna and Ashur. After this, Hammurabi felt entitled to call himself 'Mighty king, King of Babylon, King of the whole country of Amurru, King of Sumer and Akkad, King of the Four Quarters of the World'.

The end of an empire

The glories of Mari were destroyed by Hammurabi, but within a few years of his own death, his city of Babylon was

A wall-painting from the palace of King Zimrilin at Mari. The palace covered 3 hectares (7 acres), with royal apartments, reception rooms, vast open courtyards, and impressive throne-rooms to receive embassies. Here, in the top panel, Zimrilin receives a measuring-stick and string (symbols of justice) from the goddess Ishtar, depicted in her war-like aspect with her foot resting on a lion. Below, goddesses hold vases from which life-giving waters pour.

itself threatened with destruction. One by one its dependant cities broke away, until the kingdom had shrunk to its original, restricted boundaries. The final blow came in about 1600 BC, when the Hittites from Anatolia sacked Babylon.

About the middle of the 18th century BC texts recording economic transactions, found in south Mesopotamia, reveal the presence there of a people of obscure origin called the Kassites. At that time the horse and chariot were beginning to revolutionize warfare throughout the Near East and the status and influence of the Kassites, who appear to have been expert handlers of horses, must have increased correspondingly. One of their chieftains managed to take advantage of the political vacuum created by the Hittite raid and the downfall of the dynasty of Hammurabi to seize the throne of Babylonia. The occupation was to last about 400 years.

Sadly few documents are available for study from the Kassite period, and the Kassite strategic capital of Dur Kurigalzu has only been partially excavated; so our knowledge of the period is severely limited. Such remains and texts as are available, however, show clearly that it was a time of prosperity, with the Kassite rulers

The inscription on this copper figurine states that it was dedicated to the god Amurru by Luanna, one of Hammurabi's soldiers, to solicit divine protection for his king. The hands and face are gilded.

KASSITE WRITINGS
Although the texts available for study from the Kassite period may be comparatively few, it is not true, as was once thought, that this was a dull, sterile era for literature. In fact evidence shows that it was a time of intense scribal activity. Ancient texts were copied, edited, and arranged in a canonical form from which they never varied later. But scribal activity was not confined to copying old texts. They also composed some of the most interesting and profound philosophical works of Akkadian literature, including one which posed the problem of why a good, pious, god-fearing man should be afflicted with misfortune. This problem most strikingly resembles that later posed in the Book of Job, in the Old Testament. It is particularly interesting to note that, during the Kassite period, the great works of Akkadian literature were being read in other countries. Copies of the Epic of Gilgamesh, for example, have been found in Amarna and Boghazköy, the Egyptian and Hittite capitals.

Part of the facade of the Kassite temple of Inanna at Uruk. The reliefs of mountain gods and water goddesses were built up from moulded bricks. This technique influenced the art of the later Neo-Babylonian and Persian periods.

playing a controlling part in the important lapis lazuli trade. The Amarna letters, part of the 'foreign office' archives of the Egyptian kings Amenhotep III and Akhenaten, reveal that Kassite Babylonia was accepted by its contemporaries as a great world power, on a par with the Egyptians, Mitannians, and Hittites.

In the Kassite period was developed the concept of special deities who acted as 'guardian angels' and were mediators between ordinary people and great gods. These guardians remained personal to their devotees and did not intrude on the official cults of the traditional Babylonian pantheon. The Kassites managed to recover the statue of the great god Marduk, captured by the Hittites, rebuilt many temples, and granted some of them special privileges.

From the evidence of texts and *kudurru* (boundary stones) the number of important cities declined at this time; the small village became the normal unit for community life. The Kassite dynasty ended about 1150 BC, after a disastrous raid by the Elamites from across the Tigris. Cities and sanctuaries were sacked, and many works of art and historical monuments were carried off to Elam.

The native Babylonians, under such leaders as Nebuchadrezzar I, rallied and re-established law and order. The organization of the country remained largely as it had been under the Kassites, but the dynasties changed rapidly and some kings were of foreign (Elamite and Kassite) origin. It was during this time that the final elevation of Marduk to the status of supreme national god was accomplished. The earliest known copies of the Creation Epic date to this time, telling how Marduk accepted the task of overcoming the water monster, Tiamat, in return for supreme authority in heaven.

Land shall not spare land, house shall not spare house, man shall not spare man, brother shall not spare brother. Let them kill one another.

As these words from another epic show, the troubles of Babylon were by no means over. Frequent raids by the semi-nomadic Aramaeans and Chaldaeans caused famines, plagues, and riots in Babylonia. The success of these peoples in penetrating and settling the area is shown by the fact that their language and simpler alphabetic script eventually replaced Babylonian cuneiform, and that the founders of the later Neo-Babylonian dynasty were Chaldaeans.

The Babylonians at this time had to face the threat of imperial Assyria. The long-standing rivalry with their northern

Empire of Nebuchadrezzar

Kingdom of the Lydians

Kingdom of the Medes

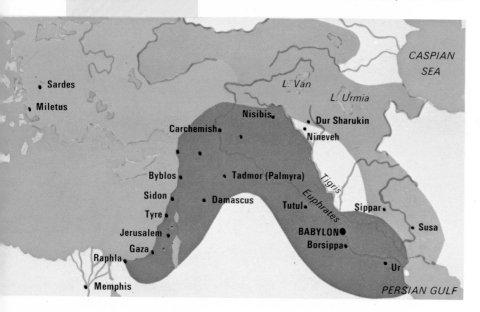

neighbours resulted in the occupation of Babylonia by the Assyrians, but not all Babylonians (and in particular the Aramaean and Chaldaean tribes) were prepared to accept Assyrian rule. The most persistent of the resistance leaders was the man who appears in the Old Testament as Merodachbaladan, King of Babylon, who sent an embassy to King Hezekiah. With treasures taken from the temples, this Chaldaean hired Elamite military aid and constantly harried the Assyrians. It was not he, however, but one of his successors, Nabopolassar, who with the help of the Medes caused the final overthrow of Assyria in 612.

In a series of brilliant campaigns Nabopolassar and his son and successor Nebuchadrezzar II took control of most Assyrian provinces in Syria, Lebanon, and Palestine, creating the great Neo-Babylonian empire and carrying into captivity many of the Jewish nation after the destruction of Jerusalem.

The administration of this empire was in the hands of the governors of the Babylonian provinces, vassal-rulers and high temple officials; the manpower and finance for the immense building programme was provided by prisoners of war, booty, and tribute, while the expenses of maintaining the numerous staff of officials and the court were born by the inhabitants of the country through taxation. Besides normal taxes there were also certain fines paid into the 'King's Basket' which were dispatched to the king. The temples themselves were expected to contribute one tenth of their income to the king. In order to increase the revenue the king interfered more and more in the administration of temple estates. It has been suggested that this policy was responsible for the later disaffection of the Babylonian priesthood, resulting in a peaceful surrender of Babylon to Cyrus of Persia in 539 BC.

The Assyrians

The heartland of Assyria was the area between the cities of Nineveh and Ashur on the Tigris river. Both cities had sanctuaries dating back to about 3000 BC. For roughly the first thousand years of its history Assyria was dominated politically and culturally by Sumer. Both the Agade and Third-Dynasty Ur empires controlled the area, because it lay on the

Under the Neo-Babylonian rulers, particularly Nebuchadrezzar II, the city of Babylon, its temples, and sanctuaries were splendidly rebuilt and extended. In the centre stood the great ziggurat and the temple of Marduk. From there a ceremonial road ran to a huge gate in the city wall — the so-called Ishtar Gate, decorated in brilliantly coloured glazed brick-reliefs. The reconstructed Ishtar Gate shown here is in the Vorderasiatische Museum, Berlin. It uses fragments of the original tiles.

THE KING OF ASSYRIA

. . . the strong king, unrivalled king of the universe, king of the four quarters, king of all princes, lord of lords . . .

The king of Assyria was the representative of the god Ashur on Earth. It was his duty to act on behalf of all the gods of the land for the benefit of the whole community, and the highest responsibilities of government and religion were his. He carried out the daily administration of the kingdom and the empire. 'The god Ashur and the great gods who magnify my sovereignty, who granted as my lot power and strength, commanded me to extend the borders of my land.' As head of the army, it was the king's duty, on divine command, to plan and lead offensive and defensive campaigns.

Because war was a divine duty the king reported on his war achievements to the gods; these reports are usually preserved in the form of 'annals' (see page 37). There is some evidence to suggest that apart from annals, the king at times sent a letter describing a particular campaign which was addressed not only to the gods, but also to the citizens of Ashur, and was read out to them. One such letter that has been preserved is remarkable for the lyrical character of its descriptions of the countryside through which the army was passing:

I passed between Mount Nikippa and Mount Upa, high mountains which are covered with all types of trees, whose surface is chaos, whose passes are dangerous, over whose slopes the shadow stretches like in a cedar forest, where the traveller cannot see the rays of the sun.

As head of the priesthood the king was responsible for temple building and the appointment of priests. He also had to play the leading role in the major religious festivals. Oracles, dreams, and portents were carefully interpreted and faithfully reported to the king. If the omens were appallingly bad, it might be necessary, to save the king's life, to appoint a substitute king for a while, who was later killed when things were looking better.

To run the government efficiently, the king had many officials, generals, priests, provincial governors, and scribes to assist him. The highest positions of state were held by the aristocracy. They owned large estates, which were often enlarged by royal grants and were worked for them by peasants, who might also own small plots of land of their own. Occasionally the king granted these nobles tax exemptions, increasing their wealth even further. The unity and efficiency of the government of Assyria and its empire really depended on the loyalty of these 'Sons of Creation', and the revolutions which broke out when some of them supported a claimant to the throne other than the officially designated heir weakened the state from within.

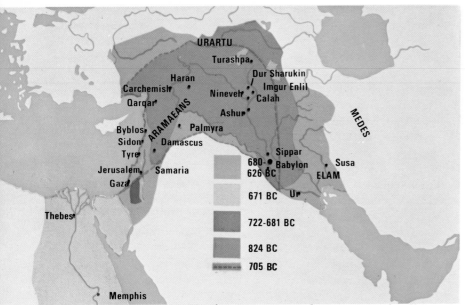

URARTU
Turashpa
Haran
Carchemish
Qarqar
Nineveh
Dur Sharukin
Imgur Enlil
Calah
Ashur
MEDES
ARAMAEANS
Byblos
Sidon
Tyre
Jerusalem
Gaza
Samaria
Palmyra
Damascus
Sippar
Babylon
Susa
ELAM
Ur
Thebes
Memphis

680-
626 BC
671 BC
722-681 BC
824 BC
705 BC

Map of the Assyrian empire. The real centre of Assyria at all times was the city of Ashur which either gave its name to or took it from the national god, Ashur – it is not clear which way round. In the time of the Assyrian empire it served as the religious capital of the country. Three other cities served as royal capitals in this period: Kalhu (modern Nimrud), built up over an older settlement in the 9th century; Dur Sharrukin (now Khorsabad), built and planned entirely by Sargon II and more or less abandoned at his death; and Nineveh, the most famous Assyrian city, which was totally replanned by Sennacherib and remained the royal capital until its fall in 612 BC.

important trade routes leading to Anatolia. But despite the closeness of these and other cultural, linguistic, and religious ties, there were some basic differences between the way of life in Assyria and Sumer. Assyria lies within an area of natural rainfall, so crops could be grown without the aid of artificial irrigation systems, and the peasants were free from the fear of flooding and disputes over water rights. The early sanctuaries may originally have been no more than religious centres for a nomadic people, which would accord well with the tradition preserved in the Assyrian King List that the earliest of the Assyrian rulers 'lived in tents'.

With the fall of the Third Dynasty of Ur Assyria became independent and its merchants became involved in the lucrative trade that passed through their country, dealing especially in metals and textiles. Texts from the Anatolian site of Kültepe show that, for several generations, there were Assyrian merchants living in trading colonies in the principalities of central Anatolia.

About 1814 Shamshi-adad I, an Amorite, became king of Assyria. He was a formidable and tenacious warrior, who built up what is sometimes called the first Assyrian empire. He established Assyrian control over most of north Mesopotamia, including the city of Mari. Many details are known about the life of this monarch, thanks to the royal archive found at Mari. This contained letters written by Shamshi-adad and his two sons – the

warrior Ishme-dagan and the lazy Iasmah-adad, who had been appointed governor of Mari. Iasmah-adad was continually receiving letters from his father, upbraiding him for mistakes and urging him to be more like his brother. The empire of Shamshi-adad did not last long after the death of its founder. Mari was recaptured by its native prince, Zimrilim, and farther south the 'Man of Babylon', Hammurabi, was beginning to assert himself.

After their eclipse by Babylon, the Assyrians had little power and eventually fell under the influence of the newly arrived Mitannians (see page 75); but this domination was short lived.

As the Egyptian and Hittite empires declined as a result of the movements of the 'Sea-Peoples' (see page 70) the political vacuum was filled by the newly emerging state of Assyria in its attempts to control the depredations of the Aramaeans. Many, often successful, expeditions were undertaken against these people. But it is clear from 'Aramaisms' which appear in the language, indicating that the major spoken language by the 8th century

An Assyrian siege-engine, from a bas-relief.

An Assyrian king watches as prisoners of war haul a colossal statue of a winged, human-headed bull from the quarry to the capital. This reconstruction is based on a series of reliefs in Senacherib's palace at Nineveh. Stone statues like this were set up in pairs to guard the entrances of throne-rooms in particular, and to support the massive arches of the doorways. The doors themselves were made of wood (usually imported from north Syria). The doorposts, made of two tree-trunks, were kept in place by the metal sockets shown on the raft in the foreground. Nearly every Assyrian king built himself a palace or extended and embellished an existing one. The walls were built of mud-brick and then covered with frescoes, glazed brick, or more usually (and expensively) with stone reliefs (like the one from which this reconstruction was taken), showing the king at war, hunting, and so on.

BC was Aramaic, that they did penetrate Assyria itself in large numbers.

It was not until the reign of Ashurnasirpal II (883–859) that the Assyrians began steadily to acquire a vast empire, at first moving into the north Syrian area to fight the Aramaean principalities there. This led eventually to conflict with larger, organized states, among which were Urartu and Egypt.

At first the Assyrian army was made up entirely of peasants, but when the empire stretched from the mountains of Armenia to the Nile Valley and from the Mediterranean Sea to the Persian Gulf, it was necessary to use detachments of troops from the provinces of the empire in order to raise large enough numbers. The Assyrian army was a mighty force.

Controlling such a vast empire was a very difficult task. A provincial system was established with each province under a governor responsible for tax-collection; but the garrison armies stationed at fortresses in the provinces were not under his direct control. In order to facilitate the swift movement of troops and royal messengers, roads were maintained and grain-storage depots established. Vassals had to swear obedience and to pay tribute.

The penalties for rebellion were horrible. Cities when taken were looted and might be totally destroyed; even if a city was spared, its citizens were usually deported. The ringleaders faced torture and death. All this was known, yet time and again provinces rebelled and the efforts to subdue them badly stretched Assyrian resources. A combination of pressure from without and civil strife within fatally weakened Assyria. The leader of the Babylonian resistance, Nabopolassar, formed an alliance with the Medes and in a very short time (614–609) they had completely wiped out the Assyrian empire. As the Book of the Prophet Nahun in the Bible says:

And it shall come to pass that all they that look upon thee shall flee from thee, and say: 'Nineveh is laid waste: who shall bemoan her?'

Early Writing

A Sumerian clay tablet, from about 2800 BC. The writing on it clearly derives from pictograms. It is one of the earliest decipherable documents.

Only a relatively small number of writing systems has ever been developed, considering the vast number of different languages spoken in the world. One of the earliest is Egyptian hieroglyphics (used from about 3000 BC), although the undeciphered Elamite script may be earlier. The Indus Valley script, the Cretan Linear A (both undeciphered), and Chinese writing all came later. At least as early as, and far more widespread than, the Egyptian system was the cuneiform script – so-called (from the Latin for wedge, *cuneus*) because of its wedge-shaped symbols, usually impressed on clay tablets. This script originated just before 3000 BC in southern Iraq, and spread throughout the Near East. It was adapted to write languages never spoken in southern Mesopotamia at all, such as Hittite, Eblaite, Hurrian, Elamite, and Urartian. During the second millennium BC the language now most closely associated with cuneiform – Akkadian – was the main diplomatic language of the Near East, used for example in the Amarna letters (page 45).

From pictures to syllables

The wedge shape of cuneiform symbols is the result of the materials first used for writing in southern Iraq, which, poor in most natural resources, has an abundance of clay and reeds. Clay provided an inexhaustible and durable writing material. As a result of its durability, accounts, legal transactions, letters, school exercises, and government directives make up the bulk of surviving cuneiform texts, and allow an insight into even the most mundane preoccupations of the writers at some periods. Cuneiform signs developed from *pictograms* – pictures of the objects they stood for – and these very early texts cannot be read as a language, with sounds and grammar, although their content may be roughly understood. The use of a reed

THE RISE OF THE ALPHABET

Sometime around 1600 BC the notion of an alphabetic system of writing developed in the Levant. Examples of three different types of scripts displaying alphabetic characteristics (the use of a single sign to represent a single isolated sound, which drastically reduces the number of characters required to write) have so far been found. One is the so-called 'pseudo-hieroglyphic' script of Byblos which perhaps represents a development and simplification of the Egyptian consonantal hieroglyph system; but since the Byblose script (of which there are very few examples) has 114 signs it is not generally favoured as the ancestor of the true alphabet. The two strongest candidates for this position are the Ugaritic cuneiform alphabet and the Sinaitic script: both are definitely alphabetic (the Ugaritic script has a total of only 32 signs) and it has been possible to relate some of the signs of both scripts to the fully developed North-West Semitic alphabet from which modern alphabets developed. The Ugaritic developed its letter-forms in imitation of Akkadian cuneiform while Sinaitic used what were originally Egyptian hieroglyph forms.

One of the earliest examples of a fully alphabetic inscription is the Canaanite inscription on the sarcophagus of Ahiram, prince of Tyre, which is generally dated to the early 10th century BC. To this type of Canaanite alphabet the better-known alphabets such as Phoenician and Early Hebrew are related. Whether Greek is directly derived from this alphabet, the Phoenician version, or – as has been suggested – the Phrygian one, is not certain. The Greeks, in adopting the alphabetic system, made a very important innovation: the Canaanite alphabet only represented consonants, but the Greeks used those signs which served no function in their language to represent the main vowels – a feature of all Western alphabets.

A form of the alphabet distinct from, although related to, Canaanite but no less influential was used for Aramaic – the language of a people who settled throughout the Near East in the first millennium BC; this came to be the most widely spoken language in the area. The widespread use of Aramaic sped the adoption of the alphabetic system, and the particular form of the Aramaic alphabet influenced the 'square' classical Hebrew letter-forms. The Arabic script is also closely related to it.

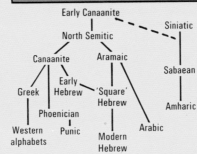

Water									M
Snake									N
Fish									X
Eye									O

Development of the alphabet: left to right Egyptian hieroglyphs; Ugaritic; Proto-Siniatic; South Semitic (Arabian); North Semitic (Phoenician and Aramaic); Hebrew; Archaic Greek; Classical Greek; Roman.

Early Canaanite

North Semitic — Siniatic

Canaanite — Aramaic

Greek — Early Hebrew — 'Square' Hebrew — Sabaean

Western alphabets — Phoenician — Punic — Modern Hebrew — Arabic — Amharic

Some cuneiform texts. Top left: A Babylonian geometry textbook of about 1800 BC. Top right: A dictionary of legal terms in Sumerian and Akkadian, from the 8th century BC. Bottom left: An octagonal prism, recording the deeds of Tiglath-pileser of Assyria (1112-1074 BC). Bottom right: A series of recipes for glassmakers. They are written in a deliberately obscure style for craftsmen only.

stylus (pen) to impress the characters in the soft clay caused the original pictograms to be reduced to a number of wedges. When, approximately two centuries later, the signs can be read as words, the language they represented is Sumerian (related to no other known language). As the script developed the pictograms came to be used for the simple *sound-value* of the word they represented, while retaining their original meanings as well. (For example, if this system were used in writing English, the pictogram for 'pen' – writing implement – could be used for 'pen' – enclosure; Penn – surname; and the syllable 'pen' in 'ha*pen*'.) To help the reader understand how such a sign or sign-group should be read, it became the practice to put a *determinative* before some words – a sign indicating to the reader that the subsequent word meant a city, a god, a man, a woman, or an animal.

All this made the cuneiform system rather complicated, but there is one thing more that created problems. In about 2340 BC Sargon of Agade (see page 28), who had conquered the Sumerian city states, adopted this writing-system for his own language, usually called Akkadian. This belonged to the Semitic language-group (like Hebrew and Arabic). Akkadian came to be the dominant language for which the cuneiform system was used. As Akkadian is utterly different from Sumerian in grammar and vocabulary, many of the signs could only be used to represent single sounds in Akkadian, rather than complete words as before. Strings of signs had to be combined to record one Akkadian word, with each sign representing a syllable. Since this was rather laborious, the Sumerian equivalent word would quite often be written instead, although when read it would be mentally translated into Akkadian! So, in order to write Akkadian, all Mesopotamian scribes had to learn Sumerian.

Main types of text

Why did writing develop at all in this area? The prime reason must have been the need to record the very complicated transactions made by huge land-owning organizations – the temple and the palace. So at first writing was used to keep account of actual daily and annual transactions; but once things are written down and it is possible to refer back to the written word, the existence of the text itself can influence the way people act. This process can be most clearly seen in the realm of Mesopotamian law. The original purpose of writing down law was to codify existing practice and make possible any changes needed, but eventually rulers (usually towards the end of their reigns) composed law-codes so that the gods and their subjects could see that they had ruled well. (Several scholars interpret the famous Code of Hammurabi in this way.) Another important text group is formed by ceremonial and religious texts, whose purpose is to preserve traditional wording and guard it against change. The political structure of Mesopotamian society made the recording of annual events and the succession of kings necessary (to establish border claims or to date events). This material eventually provided the basis for genuine historical writing, particularly the Babylonian chronicles of the first millennium BC (see page 33).

There is one group of texts which we cannot understand so easily. These are the texts which were not really meant to be read by human eyes. Royal accounts of building operations were placed in the foundations or walls of important structures. In the Assyrian empire these were expanded to include accounts of the campaigns of the ruler. Assyriologists usually call these the annals. The annals are now one of the primary historical sources for the period, but were in fact never

DECIPHERMENT

The ancient forms of languages which are still spoken and written, such as Greek and Chinese, present only slight problems to modern scholars; the same applies to those languages which, while no longer spoken, have continued to be studied, such as Latin and Sanskrit. The use of the alphabet for certain less well-known languages – such as Phoenician, Punic, and Aramaic – has made it possible to assign such languages to linguistic families and so to understand them, even if only to a limited extent.

But other ancient languages with non-alphabetic writing systems have presented much greater difficulties. Sometimes bilingual or trilingual texts have given the key to their decipherment. This was the case with Egyptian hieroglyphs: the Rosetta Stone (brought to Europe by Napoleon) has an inscription first in hieroglyphs, then demotic (a later, cursive, and simplified form of Egyptian), and Greek. A long bilingual text from Karatepe in south Turkey made it possible to decipher Hittite hieroglyphs, the known language in this case being Phoenician. Code-breaking techniques have occasionally led to success, as in the decipherment of Mycenaean Linear B, decoded by Michael Ventris in 1952 and shown to be an early form of Greek.

In the case of the cuneiform script, the difficulty facing scholars was immense. Brief trilingual Achaemenid texts from Persepolis (in Old Persian, Elamite, and Akkadian) became available for study in the 18th century, but as they were all in a type of cuneiform and no-one had any idea what kind of language was represented, decipherment seemed impossible. Grotefend, a German schoolmaster, assumed that the first of the cuneiform versions must be Old Persian (and so was related linguistically to other Persian texts then being studied); that it would probably contain the names and titles of Persian rulers, known from Herodotus and the Old Testament; and that because of its relative length it was more or less alphabetic (here he was wrong; Old Persian is in fact a kind of simplified syllabary). He succeeded in deciphering a major part of one of the Old Persian texts. Deciphering the other two versions now seemed feasible, but was still very difficult: not a single Old Persian cuneiform sign corresponds to any Akkadian cuneiform signs. A number of scholars worked for many years on the very complex Akkadian cuneiform and in 1857 the decipherment was officially declared 'achieved', making not only the Akkadian but also the Sumerian, Hittite, Elamite, Urartian, and Eblaite writings accessible to scholars.

intended to be read by living people; they were an account to the gods. Amulets to protect people – especially children – from illness also belong to this category; they were often inscribed with a conjuration to keep evil spirits at bay. Similarly, in treating an illness, its symptoms could be written on a clay tablet which was then ritually broken.

The scribe's work

Trained scribes were indispensable for compiling all these types of text, and, here as in all literate early societies, formed an important professional group. Their training took place in schools (usually attached to the palace or temple) where the main method of teaching was setting the pupils traditional texts to copy. A large number of the literary texts that survive are in fact school exercises. The need for scribes to learn Sumerian led to the preservation of much Sumerian literature by the schools; it also meant that an enormous number of lexical lists (word lists in the two languages) were compiled.

Many cuneiform texts are very long, and it seems impossible to understand how so much could be accommodated on small lumps of clay. In fact little lumps of clay were only used as tags to label collections of large clay tablets. These tablets varied in size but were all roughly pillow-shaped, with thick

edges which could be written on when the scribe ran out of space on the back and front. For very long, formal compositions, the clay could be shaped into prisms or barrels, which would hold much more writing than even the largest tablet. If very beautiful copies were wanted, the tablet was covered with a slip of very fine clay.

One habit of the Mesopotamian scribes that scholars today find useful was leaving a space at the end of a tablet to be filled with the *colophon*. This contained the sort of information given on the title-page of a modern book: the work's title, the names of the owner of the tablet and the scribe, the date, and a description of the original from which this tablet was copied. Occasionally it was followed by curses on anyone who might remove or damage the tablet. If the tablet was part of a very long series the colophon stated the name of whole work, and the opening line of the next tablet.

Later developments

Once the technique of cuneiform writing had evolved there was very little in the way of innovation. Stamps were introduced in the second half of the third millennium to impress the name of a ruler and the building under construction on innumerable mud bricks, and commemorate the achievement. In the first millennium hinged wooden boards with a writing surface of wax were occasionally used in Assyria, instead of tablets. Gradually, in the course of the 8th and 7th centuries BC, Aramaic, written in a much simpler alphabetic script, displaced the cuneiform system. But for certain standard text categories Akkadian cuneiform continued to be used until the end of the 1st century AD.

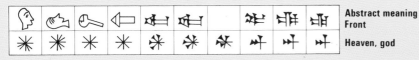

										Abstract meaning
										Front
										Heaven, god

Development of pictograms: left to right Uruk c 3100 BC; c 3000 BC; c 2800 BC; Classical Sumerian (linear and cuneiform); Old Akkadian; Old Assyrian; Old Babylonian; Neo-Assyrian; Neo-Babylonian.

factors – the Egyptian climate, and the Egyptians' unshakable belief that there was a life after death.

The past preserved

Although a few centimetres of rain do fall each year in Lower Egypt (the Delta), places in Upper (south) Egypt may not see rain for several years. But the land watered by the river, and by a complex system of irrigation canals, basins, and dykes, was amazingly fertile. The Egyptians called it the Black Land. The rest is desert, the Red Land. Every metre of land watered by the river was needed for cultivation, and so the desert was the place chosen by the Egyptians for the burial of their dead. Anything buried in the hot desert sand, or in tombs cut in the desert cliffs, is likely to be preserved.

The Egyptians believed not only that there was a life after death, but also that they could take their possessions from this world to the next. Even after thousands of years of robberies, and the depredations of the white ant and other similar pests, large numbers of objects have survived to the present day in the most extraordinary state of preservation.

There were a number of caskets. Carter opened one of these and on the top lay a beautiful ostrich-feather fan. The feathers

Egypt

They tremble when they behold the Nile in full flood. The fields laugh and the river banks are overflowed. The god's offerings descend, the face of man is bright, and the hearts of the gods rejoice.

But for the river Nile, completing the last stages of its journey to the Mediterranean Sea, the north-east corner of the African continent would be a virtually empty desert. Thanks to the river, it is crossed by a thin, fertile strip of land, which was the cradle of one of the earliest, greatest, and longest lasting of all the ancient civilizations. What makes the study of ancient Egypt particularly rewarding is that we have so many actual remains – objects of daily use, texts, buildings, and paintings. For this we have to thank two

This beautifully preserved statue of Ra-Hotep and his wife Nefert was discovered in the statue-chamber (serdab) of the couple's mastaba tomb at Meidum, which dates from about 2700 BC.

The silver coffin of King Psusennes of the Twenty-first Dynasty (around 1000 BC). He carries the crook and flail, the sacred symbols of kingship. On his forehead is a golden cobra, thought to protect the King by spitting fire at his enemies. The coffin was found in the King's tomb, under a temple pavement in the Delta city of Tanis.

Hieroglyphs from the pyramid of the Fifth Dynasty king, Unas. Egyptian hieroglyphic writing is made up out of picture signs; but unlike simple pictograms they do have a sound value. A single sign may represent a whole word, but most words demand two or more. In this text, some signs are enclosed by an oval frame (called a cartouche). This was done to distinguish the name of a royal person — in this case, Unas.

The Giza pyramids, on the west bank of the Nile, viewed across the Cultivation — the narrow strip of fertile land on each bank. The pyramids themselves stand in the desert which begins a few kilometres from the river. Built during the Fourth Dynasty (about 2613 to 2494 BC), the pyramids were designed to ensure immortality for the kings who were buried in them.

were perfect, fluffing out just as if they had recently been plucked. Those feathers completely annihilated the centuries for me. It was just as if the King had been buried a few days before.

The words are those of Sir Alan Gardiner, recalling an incident during the clearing of the tomb of Tutankhamun, but they well describe a sensation that all those who have excavated in Egypt have shared to some degree.

The Egyptian system of hieroglyph writing is hard to master. The modern student may often sympathise with his ancient counterpart, who was always being exhorted to work harder. ('Be not slack, and spend not a day in idleness, or woe betide your limbs!') But the effort was worth it, then and now. 'Fortunate is the scribe who is skilled in his calling . . . persevere every day and you shall obtain mastery over it.' Mastery for the student then meant a good job, with the prospect of advancement. For us, it means we can read the papyrus scrolls, the clay tablets, the ostraca (broken potsherds and pieces of stone, used to write on), and the painted and sculpted inscriptions on statues, stelae, and tomb and temple walls.

So, at first hand, we can hear what the Egyptians had to say about their history, their religious beliefs, and their daily lives. We can learn of their expertise in medicine and mathematics, examine someone's tax return, listen to the wisdom of a sage, or chant a hymn to the Sun.

The first kings

According to tradition the first ruler of all Egypt was Menes, who may be identified with King Narmer, who appears on monuments of the period. He united Upper (south) and Lower (north) Egypt in about

3120 BC. But not until the beginning of the Old Kingdom (c 2686–2181) do we have much detailed knowledge of Egyptian history. This period saw the first great flowering of Egyptian culture. The first pyramids were built to serve as the burial places of the kings, and these monuments, more than any others, convey the power and majesty that belonged to a king of Egypt – the god Horus incarnate on Earth. And the pyramids, surrounded by the comparatively small graves of their courtiers, symbolize the vast gulf between the ruler and even the greatest of his subjects.

The first pyramid – that of King Zoser, who died in about 2650 BC. It was built in several stages, growing from a simple mastaba under the able supervision of Zoser's brilliant vizier, Imhotep. Its site at Sakkara was originally surrounded by a huge complex of dummy buildings, representing the royal palace. It is among the oldest stone structures standing today.

This winged scarab beetle, which holds the Sun's disc in its forefeet, is a representation of one of the names of the Egyptian king Senusret II. It is made of carnelian, felspar, lapis lazuli, and electrum. The body of the scarab is only one centimetre (0·4 inches) long.

The Old Kingdom saw the longest recorded reign in history – that of Pepi II, who succeeded his brother to the throne at the age of six, and lived to be a hundred. But within a few years of his death, the whole structure of the Old Kingdom had collapsed. One vital contributory factor in this may have been the growing power of the nomarchs (provincial governors). Successive generations of kings had granted them powers, privileges, and lands till they were virtually independent of royal control. They had their own private armies, and their extensive powers and considerable riches are reflected in their impressive tombs, cut into the cliffs of their provinces.

About 2181 began the unhappy period of civil war and anarchy known as the First Intermediate Period. Rival rulers emerged in Upper and Lower Egypt. Eventually the country was reunited by a prince of Thebes who founded the Middle Kingdom (c 2040–1633). Egypt rapidly recovered its prosperity. The government was reorganized by Senusret III, who broke the power of the nomarchs; and all authority from then on was in the hands of the king, his vizier, and the royal departments of state. Trade and art flourished, and the rich land of Nubia to the south was conquered.

In the Thirteenth Dynasty several kings had very short reigns. Royal authority, power and prestige were badly affected by the constant changes, and an independent prince set himself up in the western Delta. Then came real disaster. People

known as the Hyksos ('Rulers of Desert Uplands') crossed the eastern frontier and occupied the Beloved Land. This humiliating Second Intermediate Period lasted from c 1633 to 1567. Then the Thebans, having learned how to use the devastating new weapon introduced by the Hyksos, the horse and chariot, rallied and drove the foreigners from Egypt.

The Thebans founded the New Kingdom (1567–1085). The wave of military enthusiasm which had been aroused by the need to expel the Hyksos was channelled into a drive for imperial conquest. Tuthmosis III

(1504–1450) inherited an empire that had already spread into Nubia and across Palestine into Syria. His mummy shows that he was short in stature, and even his most flattering portraits cannot disguise the fact that he had a large beak of a nose, but he was a general and administrator of genius. In a series of arduous campaigns he pushed the frontiers of his dominions south to the Fourth Cataract of the Nile, and well into Syria – at one time even crossing the Euphrates on a raid into the lands of his rivals the Mitannians (see page 75).

Then followed the time of Egypt's greatest power and glory – reflected in the almost incredible wealth buried with the boy pharaoh Tutankhamun, who reigned a mere eight years or so. But during the second half of the Twentieth Dynasty Egypt began once more to decline. The empire was lost, and during the Third Intermediate Period (c 1085–664) Egypt became divided and weak, with kings of Libyan and Nubian origin. Eventually it was conquered first by the Assyrians, then by the Persians, and in 332 by Alexander the Great. In 30 BC Egypt was finally absorbed into the Roman empire.

A historian of the Ptolemaic period, Manetho, grouped the kings of Egypt into dynasties (ruling families) – a grouping used ever since. We often call the rulers of Egypt pharaohs, but this title, a corruption of two ancient Egyptian words meaning Great House, does not appear in texts until the middle of the New Kingdom. In all official inscriptions and documents the rulers were referred to by their official title – King of Upper and Lower Egypt.

Every king of Upper and Lower Egypt is a god, by whose dealings one lives. He is the father and mother of all men. He is alone, by himself, without equal.

These words were inscribed in the tomb of the vizier Rekhmire in about 1470 BC. They were not intended to be read simply as a flowery compliment, but were to be taken literally. In the king, the god Horus was incarnate on earth. His word was law and to oppose him was both treason and blasphemy. The Egyptians believed that kingship was part of *maat*, the divine order of the universe laid down by the gods at the beginning of time. It was the king's duty to rule Egypt wisely and well, and to defend it. That too was part of the divine plan.

Every aspect of the government was dependent on the king. When he was strong and intelligent Egypt would be well-run and prosperous, but if he was weak, stupid, or lazy the whole system could run down remarkably quickly. Naturally, in order to fulfil his divine obligations, the king needed an army of officials as well as one of soldiers. In the Old Kingdom, all the high officials of state were members of the king's immediate family. It was the rise to power of non-

The Egyptians delighted in turning even functional objects into small works of art. This kohl (eye paint) pot is carried by a young Nubian slave girl – no doubt the pot's owner would have been served by just such a female slave. The pot dates from the Eighteenth Dynasty (about 1567–1320 BC).

Tutankhamun scatters his enemies, the Syrians. This scene from a painted and stuccoed chest found in his tomb shows vividly the effect of the introduction of the chariot on warfare in the New Kingdom.

royal officials and nomarchs (district governors) that helped to cause the collapse of the Old Kingdom. Even after royal authority had been restored with the Middle Kingdom, it was not until the reign of Senusret III (1878–1843) that the power of the nomarchs was completely broken, and the departments of state were reorganized.

In the New Kingdom the pharaoh had two viziers to act as his chief ministers, one resident in Thebes for Upper Egypt, and one resident in Memphis for Lower Egypt. There was also a viceroy for the southern province of the empire, who was entitled the King's Son of Kush. Under them were the other high officials of state, the heads of government departments, religious foundations, and the royal household. Below them was a hierarchy of lesser officials, and the entire structure was dependent on the work of the scribes. It is thanks to their labours that we know so much about Egypt, its history, and its daily life.

Come, let me tell you how the soldier fares ... while yet a child he is brought to the barracks and locked up ... he is battered and bruised with flogging ... let me tell you how he goes to Syria, and marches over the mountains. His bread and water are borne upon his shoulders like the load of an ass. ...

The army in the Old Kingdom was small and composed entirely of infantry. They were armed with spears, bows and arrows,

Some of the soldiers sent by Queen Hatshepsut on the famous expedition to Punt. The district, probably located in modern Somalia, provided the Egyptian traders with myrrh trees, gold, and ivory. The scene comes from the Queen's funerary temple.

THE LIVING GOD

The king was not only the incarnation of Horus on Earth; he was also held to be descended from Re, the Sun god. An ancient legend tells how Re came down to Earth and fell in love with the wife of his own High Priest. She bore him triplets who became the first three kings of the Fifth Dynasty. This legend reflects the growing power of the cult of Re at that time. Ever afterwards, the kings bore the title Son of Re. One reason for the king marrying his sister was that in this way the blood of the Sun god would be kept pure in the veins of the rulers of Egypt.

In the Eighteenth Dynasty the queens bore the title 'God's Wife', the god in question being Amun-Re. This marked the queen as the head of the female hierarchy of the cult of Amun-Re, but at least two monarchs invested it with a much deeper significance, claiming that they were the bodily sons of Amun-Re by his mortal wife. In the Late Period, the queens ceased to be the God's Wife. Instead the title went to one of the royal princesses, who was expected to pass her life as a virgin priestess, dedicating herself to the service of her divine bridegroom.

daggers, axes, and maces, but their only piece of armour was a wooden framed leather shield. Troops could be raised in larger numbers for special enterprises, such as punitive raids against those who crossed Egypt's frontiers. It was among the king's divinely ordained duties to guard Egypt, but it is doubtful if Old Kingdom kings actually led campaigns in person. In the Twelfth Dynasty, however, both Senusret I and III appear to have led their own troops, and it was during their reigns that Nubia was conquered. They built two groups of massive forts, which were masterpieces of defensive military architecture. One group was on the Second Cataract to protect the southern frontier; these forts were not captured until late in the Middle Kingdom, when the government at home had collapsed. In the New Kingdom they were in use again, but only as cities and trading depots, for the frontier was then much farther upstream at the Fourth Cataract. The second string of forts guarded the eastern frontier and regulated the passage of bedouin in and out of Egypt. These forts too fell when the central government lost control, but they were restored after the expulsion of the Hyksos, and dispatches of the Nineteenth Dynasty show they were still acting as frontier posts:

The scribe Inena communicates to his lord ... we have finished letting the

This impressive head-dress is made from hundreds of small golden rosettes, inlaid with enamel and semi-precious stones. It belonged to a young Syrian woman, one of three found buried together in the same tomb. They were all minor wives in the harem of the Pharaoh Tuthmosis III (1504–1450 BC). Perhaps they were presented to him, as a sign of loyalty, by his newly conquered Syrian subjects. Their tomb was discovered and rifled by modern tomb-robbers, but archaeologists and police fortunately managed to recover a great deal of the treasure.

bedouin tribes of Edom pass the frontiers of Mer-ne-ptah [probably the Pithom of the Old Testament] . . . to keep them alive and to keep their cattle alive.

During the Hyksos occupation a new weapon was introduced that completely changed warfare – the horse and chariot. Once the new weapon had been mastered, a powerful chariot division was introduced into the Egyptian army, and the kings of the Eighteenth Dynasty were accustomed to lead their troops into battle in person. From boyhood, the heir was trained not only to govern, but also in military tactics and the use of weapons.

When not engaged in warfare, the warrior kings enjoyed hunting. Tuthmosis III records the slaughter of rhinoceros, elephants, and lions, and Amenhotep III boasted of bagging 102 lions in the first ten years of his reign. Naturally nobles hastened to follow the royal example. A king might also give displays of his strength and skill to impress his troops. Amenhotep II, for example, shot arrows through thick copper targets while galloping past them in his chariot; it was said that no-one else could draw his great bow.

In battle, all this display might really be put to the practical test. At Kadesh for example, Ramesses II allowed himself, accompanied only by one of the four divisions of the army, to advance too far ahead of the rest of the troops. He then found himself surrounded by a host of the enemy, the Hittites. It needed all the King's courage and skill to lead charge after charge, until he and his men managed to break out of the trap. Even if Kadesh was not the great victory Ramesses always claimed, at least it was due to his leadership that it was not an appalling rout. The last great warrior king was Ramesses III who, in land and sea battles, saved Egypt

from the confederation of tribes known as the Sea Peoples, who had already advanced across Anatolia, Syria, and Palestine, annihilating all who opposed them.

After 1100 BC the Egyptian empire ceased to exist, but the king's role of god on earth was maintained, and, as late as the Roman empire, the emperors were still being shown in Egypt with the traditional titulary and regalia of the god-king.

The itinerant merchant sails downstream to the Delta to get trade for himself. When he has done more than his arms can really do, the gnats have slain him, the sand flies have made him utterly miserable.

Here, the author of the *Satire of Trades* is pouring his usual scorn on a non-scribal profession, but he would have done well to reflect that many of the luxuries the affluent scribe enjoyed were only available because of Egypt's widespread mining and trading network.

From the Old Kingdom onwards, Nubia was an important source of slaves, cattle, copper, diorite (a decorative stone used for statues and vases), and semi-precious

Syrian traders unload their wares at a wharf in one of Egypt's great cities. The Nile was the country's main highway, and such cities drew much of their strength from their positions beside it. Beyond, Egyptian craftsmen are selling their work from stalls, set up outside their houses. Land was valuable so near the river, and houses were built with three or more storeys so as to use as little as possible. The splendid stone temple, home of a god, contrasts with the cramped brick houses of mortals.

Bearers present gold from Nubia to a New Kingdom pharaoh. Egypt's conquests in Nubia brought it great wealth.

Most people think of Egyptian art as rather formal. But Egyptian painters did produce some delightful comic drawings on papyrus, such as this one, which shows a girl putting on lip-paint with a brush.

the war-like Kushites at bay. Similarly, after the disaster of the Hyksos occupation, it was the kings who led the reconquest of Nubia. During the New Kingdom, Nubia's most valuable asset, the gold mines, were intensely exploited. 'Send me gold, gold, and more gold, for in my brother's land, gold is as the dust!' wrote an acquisitive Mitannian king to the king of Egypt. But it was his 'brother's' province of Nubia that supplied the gold.

Turquoise and incense

Mining expeditions were sent regularly to Sinai from the earliest times. The original aim was to mine turquoise and to obtain the raw material for eye paint which was very important to the Egyptians; it may have been regarded as having healing properties – or have been simply for decoration. Later copper was also sought. Recent excavations at Timna have shown that the Egyptian engineers who built these mines possessed an extraordinarily high degree of technical skill and knowledge.

stones, especially amethyst. Besides the produce of Nubia itself, goods from farther south also passed through the province, including incense, ebony, ivory, ostrich eggs and feathers, panther skins, and live animals, especially monkeys.

In the Old Kingdom, trading expeditions to Nubia were sent at first on the express orders of the kings themselves, and they must have been responsible for the construction of the recently discovered trading post at Buhen, near the Second Cataract. Later in the Old Kingdom autobiographies in the tombs of the nomarchs of Aswan show that these men, who bore the proud title of Keeper of the Gate of the South, were then directing trading expeditions of their own. One nomarch had recorded in his tomb the text of a letter he had received from his king, the boy Pepi II. The child was very excited by the news that a dancing dwarf, possibly a pigmy, was being brought back to Egypt. He wrote urging that the little man should be brought to him swiftly and safely because 'My Majesty desires to see this dwarf, more than any gifts of Sinai and of Punt'.

The Egyptian kings took the initiative in the conquest of Nubia in the Middle Kingdom, and they were responsible for the erection of the great forts which guarded the vital trade route, and kept

TRAVEL

The river was Egypt's main highway. Such roads as there were within Egypt ran along its sides, or the sides of the irrigation canals, but land travel was difficult. If a noble wished to travel by land he would be carried in a chair on the shoulders of his servants; after the introduction of the horse and chariot nobles might use them for general transport as well as war and hunting, but no other wheeled vehicles were used. Everyone who could not afford to be carried walked. When heavy loads had to be transported on land they were dragged on sledges. Smaller loads were carried in panniers on donkey-back, or on yokes across the shoulders of men. Camels were not known in Egypt until the Late Period.

Mining and trading expeditions went by water as far as possible, but they often had to branch out over miles of desert. There are records of caravans setting out with 300 donkeys and their handlers. Water supplies were a problem to such huge expeditions – they had to carry their own, even in the western desert, where there were a few oases. The kings ordered wells to be dug where possible to help miners and traders in the desert; elsewhere jars of water were buried along the routes, and refilled for future expeditions.

But inside or out of Egypt, people travelled wherever possible by water. The Egyptians built boats ranging in size from the small papyrus-reed skiffs used on the river to great wooden cargo ships for sea voyages. Water travel was so important in the daily life of the Egyptians that they even pictured the Sun god as sailing across the sky every day in his divine barque.

Incense played an essential part in Egyptian ritual. One of the most important sources of incense was the land of Punt. Its whereabouts are uncertain, though modern Somalia seems the most likely place. Expeditions made the long and dangerous voyage along the Red Sea coast from the Old Kingdom onwards, but the most famous expedition was sent by Hatshepsut, a queen in her own right. The object was to bring back not only processed incense, but also living incense trees, which could be grown in Egypt. Hatshepsut had an account of the expedition recorded on the wall of one of the colonnades of her funerary temple at Deir el Bahari at Thebes.

Products of Minoan Crete began arriving in Egypt at least from the Middle Kingdom onwards, and tombs of the New Kingdom contain scenes with Cretan envoys and traders, carrying their distinctive wares into the presence of the Egyptian king. After the collapse of Cretan power the Mycenaeans traded with Egypt, till they too disappeared.

Trade with the lands that now form Syria and the Lebanon was vitally important to the Egyptians. The Egyptians must have been trading with Byblos, the main port of the area, from a very early period, because wood from the giant cedars of Lebanon has been found in the royal tombs of the First Dynasty. This timber was the main attraction; other valuable commodities included resins, oils, wine, copper, silver, slaves, and goods from even farther afield, such as lapis lazuli from Afghanistan. From the New Kingdom onwards, horses formed another valuable import from the area.

In the great days of the Eighteenth Dynasty, Egypt ruled a vast empire in the east, and could exact tribute, besides trading as usual. During the reign of Akhenaten (1379–1362 BC) much of this empire was lost, and even the efforts of Seti I and Ramesses II did not restore it to its former frontiers. The empire finally broke up during the Twentieth Dynasty, but the Egyptians continued to trade in the area, especially with Byblos. In the first millenium BC this port was the centre of an extensive trade in Egyptian papyrus and ropes. Later still, Egypt was the granary of Rome, supplying the bulk of the grain required in that city.

Hail to you, O Nile, that issues from the earth and comes to keep Egypt alive. . . . He who makes barley and brings emmer into being, that he may make the temples festive. . . . The bringer of food, rich in provisions. . . .

The majority of the Egyptians were peasants, who tilled the rich black soil that was made fertile by the water and silt of the Nile's Inundation. Every year, rains and melting snows in the Ethiopian Highlands sent flood waters surging down the Blue Nile, into the Nile proper at

Part of a wall painting showing the main activities of a farmer's year, from the tomb of the nobleman Menna at Thebes. Such scenes were always included in Egyptian tombs so that the dead man would have a constant supply of food in the next world. Although the subject was a standard one, artists often managed to introduce unique details of their own. Here, for example, two small girls have quarrelled while gleaning and are fighting furiously.

THE AMARNA LETTERS

In 1887 a peasant woman was digging in the ruins of the city of Tell el Amarna, looking for old mudbricks which make good fertilizer. Instead, she found dozens of tablets of baked clay. Thinking these might be very old and therefore valuable, she loaded them into a sack (damaging them badly) and took them to a dealer in antiquities. It was some time before the significance of the woman's discovery was appreciated, but gradually scholars realized that what she had unearthed was no less than letters from the archive of the 'foreign office' of King Akhenaten.

The tablets, though broken and incomplete, tell a clear and sad story. The Hittites of Anatolia had broken the power of the Mitannians (see page 75) and were intriguing with Egypt's vassals, in particular Abdi-ashirta of Amurru and his son Aziru. They were encouraged to attack their neighbours and to swear allegiance to the Hittite king. Loyal vassals like Rib-addi of Byblos sent impassioned pleas for help to Akhenaten, but they all seem to have been ignored: 'Beneath the feet of the king, my lord, seven times, and seven times, I fall. I have written repeatedly for garrison troops, but they were not given.'

It is possible that someone, perhaps even bribed by the Hittites, was hiding the true gravity of the situation from the King, but it is also possible that Akhenaten was too engrossed in his religious revolution in Egypt to pay much attention to what was happening in his empire. By the end of his reign, the empire in Syria had disintegrated, never to recover.

Khartoum. Before the building of modern dams, the Inundation flooded the land right down into the Delta.

The life of the peasant was undeniably hard, involving hours of back-breaking toil in the fields. There was always a fear that the water of the Inundation might not rise as high as usual, thus causing a famine, or perhaps there would be too much water, sweeping houses away and drowning men and cattle. But the soil was so fertile that, in some places, two crops could be grown in one season, and there were far fewer people in Egypt than there are today; so most of them must have enjoyed a very fair standard of living.

The Egyptians grew wheat for bread and barley for making beer, the staple items in the diet. They also raised a variety of fruit and vegetables, and made wine from locally grown grapes. Flax was an important crop, because it provided both linseed oil and linen thread.

Most of the land watered by the Inundation was used to grow crops. Only in the Delta was there much pasture, so in Upper Egypt cattle to be fattened for the table were kept in their stalls. Other animals kept in Egypt included sheep, goats, pigs, geese and ducks (but *not*

A prosperous country estate somewhere in the thin ribbon of fertile land bordering the Nile. In the foreground a labourer uses a shaduf to transfer water from the main irrigation channel to a subsidiary system of ditches surrounding the fields. The owner lives comfortably in a substantial mud brick house. Like all Egyptian buildings, it has small windows set high in the wall to keep the interior as cool as possible. It is surrounded by a private garden and shaded by tall palm trees. In the hot season, the people in the house will spend as much time as possible on the roof, shaded by an awning, in order to catch any cool breeze.

Above: A nobleman of the Eighteenth Dynasty hunting wildfowl in the marshes, a scene from the tomb of Nebamun (about 1400 BC). He is using a throwing stick to bring down the birds. With him is his hunting cat, which was probably used to flush out the game, rather than to retrieve it.

chickens until the Ptolemaic period), and donkeys. Horses were introduced in the Hyksos period, but they were used only to draw chariots. Dogs and cats were kept as pets, and some were also trained for hunting. Monkeys were also popular pets. Fish from the river, wild fowl from the marshes, and game from the desert were all useful additions to the diet. Professional fishermen, fowlers, and hunters caught these creatures for the table, while nobles also hunted them for sport.

In Egypt, all dwellings, even palaces, were built of mudbricks. Only temples and tombs were ever built entirely of stone, but in the houses of the rich, stone was used for doorsteps and the bases of the wooden columns. In the country, houses might be of one or two storeys; but models and tomb paintings show that in towns where building land was scarce houses might be of three, four, or five storeys.

Village of craftsmen

The Egyptian habit of building new houses on top of the ruins of the old means

THE FARMER'S YEAR

June: First signs of the river rising.

Inundation: Fields flooded; men work on royal building projects.

September: Waters begin to go down. Sowing takes place.

From November: Weeding and watering. Tax-assessors measure crop while it grows.

March to April: Harvest. Threshing, winnowing, and storage of grain.

April to June: Repairing dykes, canals, and basins ready for the new Inundation.

that few sites can be excavated as modern towns and villages are directly above them. Only when a site was abandoned for some reason does the archaeologist have a chance to excavate. One village that was abandoned in ancient times is Deir el Medinah, on the west bank at Thebes. Lengthy French excavations have revealed a great deal of information about the people who once lived there. This is particularly valuable because its inhabitants were workmen who made the royal tombs. Generations of these skilled men produced statues, jewellery, and furniture, which are now prized exhibits in the world's major museums, yet the men who made them remain virtually unknown to us. They are the anonymous figures shown in tomb paintings toiling in the workshops of the king, the temples, or the nobles. Occasionally an unrobbed grave gives us some insight into their standard of living, but it is little to work on. At Deir el Medinah, however, the houses, tombs, and documents enable us to follow the fortunes and life style of some families for several generations.

The men of Deir el Medinah were all skilled artisans. Much of the unskilled labour used on royal building projects, especially in the Old and Middle Kingdoms, was provided by the peasants, who worked for the king during the Inundation, when they could not work in their flooded fields. During the New Kingdom, the numerous military campaigns brought an influx of foreign captives to Egypt. Some became slaves on building sites, and their lives were probably hard. Other prisoners of war, however, did very well and ended up landowners, perhaps after serving in the royal bodyguard.

You are Amun, the lord of the silent [humble] man, who comes at the voice of the poor man. If I call to you when I am distressed, you come and you rescue me. You give breath to him who is weak. You rescue him who is in prison. You are Amun-Re, Lord of Thebes, who rescues him who is in the underworld. . . .

The Egyptians venerated numerous gods and goddesses. Some of these deities were

Rekhmire was the vizier of Tuthmosis III. His tomb contains paintings showing men at work. This section shows men making mud bricks.

A bronze statuette of the Late Period representing the great mother goddess Bast in the form of a cat with her kittens.

THE TOMB-BUILDERS
Sixty craftsmen usually worked on a royal tomb, divided into two gangs, one on each side of the tomb. Each gang worked under a foreman and his deputy, and there was at least one scribe, who helped organize the work, issued tools and supplies, kept records, and reported progress to the authorities.

While at work the men lived in huts near the tomb in the Valley of the Kings, but they spent their holidays — every tenth day, as well as the many religious festivals — at home with their families, in the special village now called Deir el Medinah. The villagers had a good deal of control over their own affairs, for they had a tribunal to deal with all but the most serious offences. They had their own shrines in which to worship, and when they died were buried in tombs in the cliffs above the village.

On site, the men worked a set number of hours each day, with a rest and a meal at noon. Absenteeism was common, and although some of the excuses recorded by the scribes seem rather thin, no action was apparently taken. The men were paid in goods (money was not used in ancient Egypt): food, drink, oil, cloth, natron, salt, and firewood. The authorities also provided washermen, water-carriers, and women to grind grain for bread, so that all the men's needs were seen to. During the Twentieth Dynasty, failures to pay the men on time provoked strikes and sit-ins.

Isis, wife of Osiris, the god of the dead. She nurses their son Horus. By the Late Period (664–332 BC), Isis had become the greatest of all the Egyptian goddesses.

credited with only limited, local influence, while others were revered throughout the land. Even those deities who enjoyed widespread influence were usually especially connected with one city where they had their principal temple. Hathor, for example, had her chief shrine at Denderah, but she was worshipped throughout Egypt, as a mother goddess and mistress of joy. Re, the Sun god of Heliopolis; Ptah, the great craftsman of Memphis; and Thoth the wise of Hermopolis similarly received universal recognition, while the holy family of Osiris, Isis, and their son, Horus held a special place in the hearts of all pious Egyptians.

The god to whom the Egyptians gave the credit for their victory in the war of liberation against the Hyksos was Amun. In the Old Kingdom he had been of little importance outside his city of Thebes, but he was the patron of Amenemhet I, founder of the Twelfth Dynasty, and of his descendants, which enormously enhanced his prestige. After the expulsion of the Hyksos, Amun was identified with Re and became Amun-Re, King of the Gods. His temple at Karnak was rebuilt many times till it was the largest and richest shrine in Egypt.

An Egyptian temple was thought to be the house of its god, and much as the temples varied in size and wealth each had the same basic plan – an outer, open courtyard, beyond which no ordinary person could pass, a hypostyle (pillared) hall, which priests could enter, and a sanctuary, containing a shrine, in which the statue of the god 'lived'. Each day, the

ANIMAL AND DEITY
The connection between Egyptian gods and goddesses and various animals is puzzling to modern eyes. Most deities had a special relationship with one species of animal or bird. The origin of these relationships is unknown, but certainly dates back to predynastic times. The practice of showing a god either as an animal, or with an animal head on a human body, meant that even an illiterate peasant could immediately identify a statue or relief of any deity. Some large temples kept one specially selected animal of the chosen species of their patron deity. The Egyptians believed that at certain times, when the correct prayers and spells had been said, the spirit of the god would pass into the animal, as indeed it could pass into any object in creation. While the body of the animal was inhabited by the divine spirit, it received homage and could give oracles.

THE ATEN HERESY
About the year 1379 BC, the throne of Egypt was inherited by one of the most fascinating characters ever to be pharaoh – Amenhotep IV. He believed that there was only one god, the Aten, who manifested himself as the disc of the Sun. Aten was not shown as an animal, or in human form, but as the Sun's disc, from which extended several long thin arms ending in tiny hands which presented the Ankh, the symbol of life, to his worshippers. The King changed his name from *Amen*hotep to Akhen*aten*, and moved his capital from Thebes, city of the great god Amun, to an uninhabited site chosen by the Aten, and now known as Tell el Amarna. From the new city rapidly constructed here, Akhenaten waged war on all the old gods of Egypt, banning their worship and even the mention of their names.

Art, religion, and foreign affairs – all were affected by the King's personal beliefs. But the whole experiment died with him. His successor, the young Tutankhamun, returned to Thebes and reinstated the old gods. Amarna was left deserted; Aten worship was banned; the name of the heretic Akhenaten was accursed by future generations, and all his monuments were systematically destroyed.

specially purified priest on duty entered the sanctuary, where part of the act of worship consisted in caring for the bodily needs of the god. The king was the head of each cult but obviously he could not officiate in person, so priests and priestesses were appointed to serve all the gods. The great temples also employed numerous scribes to organize their affairs, craftsmen to labour in their workshops, and peasants to tend their fields, the produce of which helped to provide the offerings. The king and his subjects made gifts to the gods, and taxes had to be paid to them.

Oracles played an important role in Egyptian religious life. They were given by statues of gods as well as by sacred animals. Kings were accustomed to consult the gods, especially Amun, on matters of state policy; appeals in difficult legal cases could be referred to divine judgment; and ordinary men and women went regularly to their local temples to ask for the advice of the gods on all manner of problems affecting their daily lives. Petitions were presented to the statue of the deity by the priest on duty, and the statue 'answered', by nodding, raising an arm, or speaking. Though priests clearly had something to do with these manifestations, it would be wrong to imagine that a cynical priesthood was ruthlessly exploiting a gullible public. All classes of Egyptians, including the priests themselves, really believed in their gods, and in the power of the oracles. It must be remembered that, before going on duty, a priest fasted, purified himself, and prayed. He believed that he was in a state of grace with his god, and that his actions were therefore directly inspired by the deity.

> As for the duration of what is done on
>   earth,
> It is a kind of dream.
> But they say 'Welcome safe and sound',
> To him who reaches the West.

Archaeological evidence shows that from the earliest times the inhabitants of the Nile valley believed there was a life after death, for which they would need food, shelter, and the possessions they had owned on Earth. Since life on earth was only transitory it was wise to plan and make some sacrifices in order to ensure a comfortable eternity. We do not know which god or goddess the Predynastic Egyptians expected to encounter in the Next World; but for a while in the Old Kingdom, the kings at least believed they would join Re, the Sun god, in his daily journey across the heavens in his divine barque. By the end of the Old Kingdom Osiris was replacing Re and, for the rest of the pharaonic period, he was to reign supreme in the Other World. Every Egyptian, from the king downwards, looked to Osiris as their hope for resurrection. Osiris had once ruled on Earth, but had been murdered by his wicked brother, Set. He was then restored to life by the magic of his sister-wife, Isis, and to power by the efforts of their son, Horus.

The first Egyptian graves had only been scoops in the sand, but a body lying a few centimetres below the surface of the

A mummified ibis from the recently discovered galleries at Sakkara. Sacred ibises were kept here in the Late Period. When an ibis died it was embalmed and wrapped in linen bandages. Pious pilgrims would pay for the burial of these birds, which were dedicated in their names.

The body of a New Kingdom pharaoh is taken in procession to his tomb in the Valley of the Kings. Furniture and other things for use in the Next World precede a group of hired women mourners, and the chest containing the pharaoh's inner organs. Last come the mummy and coffin, on their funeral boat.

Part of the decorations in the shrine of the goddess Hathor which stands next to Queen Hatshepsut's mortuary temple at Deir el Bahari. Tuthmosis III is shown making an offering to the god Amun.

baking desert sand dried out rapidly, and so was preserved. Deeper tombs or rock-cut chambers such as developed later did not have this quality. It therefore became necessary to find some artificial means of preserving the body, and, over the years, the Egyptians evolved the process we call mummification. By the New Kingdom the procedure was elaborate. When a nobleman died, his body was immediately collected by the embalmers and taken to their workshop on the west bank of the river. There, after prayers and purifications, the brain was drawn down the nose by a hook, and an incision was made in the side to remove the internal organs, which were preserved separately in canopic jars. The body was packed around with natron, which, over many days, dried all the water out of the body. The dehydrated corpse was then wrapped in many layers of bandages. The whole process took 70 days, though there may have been quicker, less elaborate treatments for the less affluent members of society.

When the embalming was completed a

The tomb of the nobleman Sennefer, keeper of the royal gardens, at Thebes. Its unique feature is the ceiling, which was left rough, then painted to represent bunches of grapes hanging from a vine on a trellis.

Below: The mummy and coffin of a priestess showing the elaborate wrappings.

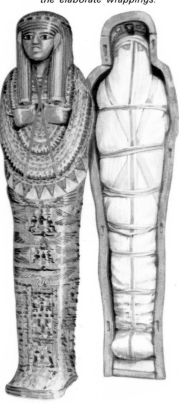

ROYAL TOMBS

Death and the person of their king were so important to the Egyptians that naturally their kings were buried in splendid tombs. The royal tombs of the First Dynasty were rectangular mudbrick structures, known as mastabas. They had elaborate panelled facades, sometimes painted to represent brightly coloured matting. A change came with the tomb of the first king of the Third Dynasty. It began as a stone mastaba, but was altered in plan and enlarged many times. Finally, thanks to the inventive genius of the official Imhotep, it was transformed into the first Step Pyramid. The first straight-sided pyramids were built at the beginning of the Fourth Dynasty. Those at Giza are rightly held to be one of the wonders of the ancient world. From the end of the Fifth Dynasty inscriptions were carved on the walls of the burial chambers, to help the king into the Next World. Old Kingdom pyramids were built of stone throughout, but after the Twelfth Dynasty, mudbricks with a thin outer casing of limestone were used. These later pyramids have not lasted so well as the stone ones.

The monarchs of the New Kingdom had their capital at Thebes, and chose to be buried near there. They had their tombs cut into the cliffs of a hidden valley, now called the Valley of the Kings. The first tomb cut in this remote spot was that of Tuthmosis I. Above the Valley towers a cliff, the top of which is shaped like a pyramid. This is the Western Peak, home of the goddess called the Lover of Silence. One reason for the change from obvious above-ground tombs was the enormous temptation they represented to robbers; but most of the rock-cut tombs were still plundered of their treasures.

Kings of the Late Period, who lived in the Delta, were buried there, sometimes in tombs under the pavements of temple courtyards. Their burials, however rich, can not compete with those of the New Kingdom; but, even so, very few escaped the tomb robbers.

great funeral procession crossed to the west bank, and the body and the funeral goods, accompanied by priests, relatives, and professional mourners, set out for the tomb. This might be a mudbrick or stone mastaba, or a rock-cut tomb, but in either case, the walls would be decorated with many scenes and inscriptions, telling of the deceased's achievements in life, and recording the daily activities on his estates. Thanks to the power of the written word, and the prayers of the priests, these scenes would come to life in the Next World and the nobleman would be able to go on enjoying the same status and comforts he had known on Earth. His bodily needs would be eternally catered for by the food, drink, servants, and possessions shown on the tomb walls. Towards the end of the New Kingdom scenes of daily life were gradually replaced by others showing the deceased in the Next World, overcoming all hazards and passing triumphantly into the Fields of the Blessed.

Before they could enjoy a comfortable eternity, the dead had to prove that they deserved it. Just as the body crossed the Nile to the west, so the soul had to cross the river of death into the Next World. Many dangers and trials awaited the soul. Practical to the last, the Egyptian priests provided the faithful with maps and instructions, explaining the route and the answers to difficult questions.

At last the dead person stood before Osiris for the final test, the Weighing of the Heart. The dead person's heart was weighed against the feather of Truth. A heart free from sin was as light as the feather. A heart heavy with sin outweighed the feather, and a terrible monster devoured the sinner. For the innocent, however, the Fields of the Blessed were open, where the wheat grew seven cubits in height!

Homage is paid to the excellent noble's efficacious soul, now that he is a god, living forever, magnified in the West . . . all our kinsfolk rest in it since the first day of time. They who are to be, millions and millions, will all have to come to it. There exists no-one who may tarry in the land of Egypt. There is no-one who fails to reach that place.

Greece

The first civilization of mainland Europe flourished in the Greek peninsula in the four centuries or so before 1200 BC. We call it Mycenaean. Its rulers spoke Greek and, at least towards its end, kept palace records in that language, using the signs which scholars call Linear B. Its trading connections reached northern Europe and the Baltic Sea. The palace of Mycenae after which this civilization is named was perhaps the centre of one kingdom, the most powerful among many.

The Mycenaean Greeks borrowed a sophisticated art style from the Minoan civilization of Crete. Wall paintings and decorative metalwork often show figures with narrow waists and large-breasted ladies. There is also, in the art of Mycenae itself, something of an obsession with lions. Hunting may have been a favourite way for Mycenaean nobles to prove their strength and courage in peacetime.

But the Mycenaean civilization was not to be the foundation of the great Greek civilization of classical times. For around 1200 Mycenaean power collapsed, in mysterious circumstances. The walls surrounding Mycenae, so impressive that later Greeks thought they must have been built by giants, failed to keep out some powerful enemy. The palaces at Mycenae and Pylos were burned in fires which baked – and so preserved for us to study – many clay tablets inscribed in Linear B. A new people moved into southern and central Greece, perhaps from the north-west. They spoke a form of Greek known as Dorian.

Mycenaean dagger blade inlaid with a scene of a lion hunt, from the 15th century BC. The hunters carry tall shields of the kind described by Homer in the Iliad, *a poem based on ancient memories of Mycenaean culture.*

After the partial collapse of Mycenaean civilization, we enter the period known as the Dark Ages of Greece (c 1200–800 BC). It is so called because very little is now known of what was happening then. Although some Mycenaean techniques lingered on for a while, it seems that in the Dark Ages the life of Greek rulers was much less sophisticated than it was in Mycenaean times. No great palaces or very elaborate dwellings have been found. Little fine jewellery or decorative metalwork seems to have been produced. The art of writing was lost. When people in mainland Greece did start to use writing once again, perhaps a little before 700 BC, it was not the forgotten Linear B signs of the Mycenaean palaces they used, but a form of alphabet probably borrowed from the Phoenicians of the Eastern Mediterranean. Nowadays we take it for granted that technology will improve rather than decline over a long period. But a long decline is what appears to have happened after the fall of the Mycenaean palaces.

Since even the rulers of Dark Age Greece lived in fairly simple surroundings, it is

Above: Galleried passage within the massive walls of the Mycenaean citadel at Tiryns. The fortifications of the Mycenaean period were constructed from huge, roughly squared masonry blocks laid without mortar. To later generations of Greeks, they seemed to be the work of giants (cyclopes). As a result, this type of masonry is often called 'cyclopean'.
Below: A seal ring carved with a finely detailed scene of a stag hunt, found in a shaft grave at Mycenae. The achievements of Aegean craftsmen during the Minoan and Mycenaean Ages remained unsurpassed for almost a thousand years.

Representations of the horse are popular in Greek pottery of the Dark Ages. Probably those Greeks who could afford elegant horses were very proud of the fact. A fine horse was a badge of status, rather like an expensive car nowadays. This 8th-century vase is decorated with a funeral procession of chariots.

likely that the poor were very poor indeed. It has been suggested that by about 1100 BC the population of mainland Greece was only about one tenth of what it had been in Mycenaean times. Perhaps a loss of various skills meant that Dark Age Greece could only produce enough to support a very small population.

Another result of the poverty in post-Mycenaean Greece was that people moved from the Greek mainland to the islands of the Eastern Aegean and to Western Asia Minor. These migrations may have started by 1000 BC and gone on for over two centuries. The Eastern Greeks were later to produce some of the finest thinkers and literary artists of the Greek world. The motives for the original migrations were probably quite primitive – to find new land to farm, or perhaps to plunder.

The most striking material remains from the Dark Ages are pots decorated in the 'geometric' style. At first these decorations are very simple – for example, concentric circles drawn by a multiple brush attached to compasses. In time the abstract designs become more complicated, and after 800 the crudely drawn figures of human beings, horses, and other animals appear.

CHRONOLOGY
BC

1650–1450	Greeks ('Mycenaeans') grow in power at centres such as Mycenae and Pylos.
1220?	Troy destroyed by mainland Greeks.
c 1200–1150	Destruction of Mycenae and Pylos.
c 1150	Dorians (tribes speaking a form of Greek) invade Greece; collapse of Mycenaean civilization. Colonization of coast of Asia Minor.
900–750	Rise of Greek city-states.
776	Traditional date of first Olympic Games.
c 750	Homer's *Iliad* and *Odyssey* composed. Beginning of Greek colonization of Sicily and southern Italy.
c 700–500	Sparta establishes itself as dominant power in the Peloponnese.
546	Persian empire begins to take over Asiatic Greek cities.
507?	Athenian democracy begins.
490–479	Persians threaten Greece in two invasions. The first is defeated by Athens at the battle of Marathon (490). The second is destroyed by allied Greek forces at Salamis (480) and Plataea (479).
477–405	Period of Athenian naval domination of Aegean. Athens enjoys its Golden Age.
431–404	Peloponnesian War between Athens and its rival Sparta end in the defeat of Athens. Sparta now rules Greece.
356–338	Warfare between Greek states allows Philip of Macedon to master Greece.
336–323	After the murder of Philip, his son Alexander the Great invades the Persian empire at the head of a combined Greek and Macedonian army.
323	Alexander dies in Babylon, aged 32.

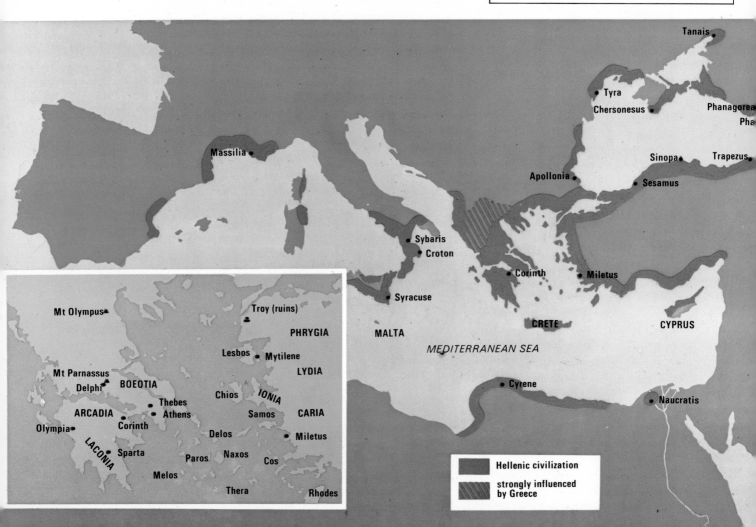

Tanais

Tyra

Chersonesus

Phanagorea
Pha

Massilia

Sinopa

Trapezus

Apollonia

Sesamus

Sybaris

Croton

Corinth

Miletus

Syracuse

MALTA

CRETE

CYPRUS

MEDITERRANEAN SEA

Cyrene

Naucratis

Mt Olympus

Troy (ruins)

PHRYGIA

Lesbos Mytilene

LYDIA

Mt Parnassus

Delphi BOEOTIA

Chios

IONIA

Thebes

Athens

Samos

CARIA

ARCADIA

Olympia

Delos

Miletus

LACONIA

Corinth

Sparta Paros Naxos Cos

Melos

Thera Rhodes

Hellenic civilization

strongly influenced by Greece

It was in the Dark Ages that the *Iliad* and the *Odyssey* were partly formed – poems which the Greeks attributed to Homer. Each poem in translation makes a fair-sized modern book. The *Iliad* and *Odyssey* were probably formed by illiterate bards over many centuries and intended to be recited to the accompaniment of a stringed instrument at several sessions. Archaeological discoveries have shown that even without written records these storytellers preserved with amazing accuracy many details of the long-perished culture of Mycenaean Greece. But probably most of the details of character and plot are fictional.

We do not know whether there actually was a man named 'Homer', responsible for the homeric poetry. If there was, he may have lived on the coast of western Asia Minor, and produced in the 8th century BC an especially good version of the poems inherited from an ancient tradition.

The homeric poems were probably composed to entertain Greek nobles, and they often reflect aristocratic attitudes. In the *Odyssey*, Menelaus says to two impressive strangers 'base men could not produce sons like you: you are no doubt of the family of sceptred kings'. The leading nobles in the poems are usually described in a friendly way; thus Agamemnon and Odysseus are 'excellent', and Menelaus is 'the favourite of the war god'.

The ordinary soldiers get little attention, and when they are mentioned it is usually as a mass rather than as individuals. Modern war poetry often attacks military leaders, and sympathizes instead with the common soldiers. The homeric poems contrast strongly with this approach.

Nobles who listened to these poems would be glad that in them aristocratic characters were at the centre of attention. They would approve too of the way in which the agitator Thersites is portrayed. Thersites complains that King Agamemnon, through greed, has picked a quarrel with Achilles from which the soldiers suffer. He shouts at Agamemnon: 'What do you want now? Your huts are full of bronze, and there are many choice women in them too. You always have first pick of women when we capture a town.' Thersites urges the soldiers not to put up with such leadership, but to go home, 'to show Agamemnon whether we're a help to him

The *Iliad* tells of an episode in the 10 years' war against Troy, a town at the north-western tip of Asia Minor. The war was organized by King Agamemnon of Mycenae. Helen, the beautiful wife of Agamemnon's brother Menelaus, has run away with a Trojan named Paris; and Agamemnon with Menelaus leads a great expedition of revenge against Troy. During the siege of Troy Agamemnon offends the best warrior among his allies, Achilles, by taking from him a captive girl whom Achilles loves. Achilles withdraws himself and his troops. The *Iliad* tells of Achilles's anger, and of how the Trojans exploit his absence: Agamemnon is forced to make amends to Achilles, who rejoins the war and kills the Trojan champion Hector. The poem ends quietly, with Achilles treating sympathetically King Priam of Troy, father of the dead Hector.

War in the *Iliad* is not normally treated as a terrible evil, but rather as an exciting way of winning glory. Descriptions of fighting are vivid and frank, and sometimes seem almost gleeful when dealing with death:

Diomedes threw his spear, and, with the goddess Athene guiding it, it hit his opponent's nose by the side of the eye, and clove through his white teeth. The relentless bronze cut off the tongue at its root, and the point emerged underneath his chin. He fell from his chariot, and his glittering armour crashed down upon him: his swift-footed horses started aside in fear. That was the end of his life and strength. But Aeneas then rushed up and bestrode the corpse, like a lion sure of its strength . . .

The warriors on each side may respect rather than hate each other: 'Ajax,' says his opponent Hector, 'since by god's will you are big and powerful and wise, and the best spearman on your side, let us stop fighting today. We shall fight another time, until god chooses to make one of us the winner. Also, it is getting dark . . . Come, let us give each other fine gifts . . .'

Achilles is fighting for honour, when he does fight: he does not pretend to be making war for the good of his fellow soldiers, or of his country, or for the glory of the gods. He explains his withdrawal from the fighting by claiming that 'a man gets no thanks for fighting unceasingly, but brave man and coward are esteemed alike'. In this way he shows an aristocratic concern for his own prestige.

The *Odyssey* tells how Odysseus returns from Troy to his home in western Greece, after many wanderings and adventures. In his absence, his faithful wife Penelope is pestered by men who wish to marry her, and who use this as an excuse for living in luxury at her – and Odysseus' – expense. For over three years she manages to put them off by saying that she cannot remarry until she has finished a piece of weaving. Each day she weaves, but each night she undoes all the day's work. In the 20th year after his original departure for Troy, Odysseus returns. The suitors try to kill him, but he kills them, and those of his servant girls who have been sleeping with them. The wretched girls are hanged in a row, 'like doves or long-winged thrushes falling into a net'.

or not'. But in the story Thersites does not manage to persuade the army. Instead he is humiliated; Odysseus hits him with a staff and he starts to cry.

Thersites is also portrayed as wretchedly ugly. He is lame, with a pointed head, round shoulders and bandy legs – in fact,

The vast body of Greek legend provided an endless source of subjects for vase-painters. In this episode from Homer's Odyssey the resourceful hero Odysseus and one of his men drive a stake into the eye of their captor, the cyclops (one-eyed giant) Polyphemus.

Olive harvesters, a lively scene from an Athenian black figure vase of the 6th century BC. Three men rattle the branches with long, flexible canes, while a fourth gathers the fallen olives into a basket. As agricultural land in Greece became increasingly impoverished, oil from Athenian olives and silver from Athens's mines were exported and helped to pay for imported corn. In Athens, the olive tree was regarded as the gift of Athene and sacred rites surrounded its cultivation.

'the ugliest man who had come to Troy'. Why is Thersites presented in this way? It is a fair guess that the aristocrats who listened to the *Iliad* suffered from agitators in their own day who criticised *them*. They would want to think that agitators were ridiculous people – like Thersites. They would not enjoy hearing about an agitator who was handsome and a fine orator.

The homeric poems, however, are much too sophisticated to divide characters into purely good and purely bad like a cowboy film. Thersites may lose, but he is given a good argument: Agamemnon does depend on his troops. And Agamemnon, in spite of his nobility, at last admits his treatment of Achilles was wrong.

Poet of rural life

A very different note is struck by Hesiod, a poet of Boeotia in Central Greece, working probably not long before 700 BC. He gives us a picture of rural life as lived by people who were not aristocrats – and the picture is much less cheerful than that of the homeric poems. Unlike the latter Hesiod's poetry talks openly about the poet and his home. He says that his father came to Boeotia to escape poverty, and settled 'in a wretched village, Askra, bad in winter, hard in summer'.

Many country people are cheats, and Hesiod advises how to guard against them. 'When a friend does a job for you, agree beforehand on a fair price. Even if it's your own brother – make a joke and *call a witness*.' Sound advice even today!

Women, Hesiod thinks, need to be treated very cautiously by the farmer. 'Don't be cheated by some woman who flaunts her bottom and says wily things to coax you. What she's really after is your barn.' The idea of cupboard love was evidently in existence by the 700s. 'Get yourself a house first of all, a woman, and an ox to plough – don't marry a woman, buy one, to follow the plough.' As in Greece to this day, women were required to do heavy work in the fields.

Hesiod takes a dim view of aristocrats, whom he several times refers to as 'bribe-devouring judges'. Aristocrats tend to look down on physical work: Hesiod has other ideas. 'There's no shame in working. It's not working which is disgraceful.' While disapproving of warfare, Hesiod insists on the value of competitiveness, 'which stirs even the lazy to work. A man is eager to work when he looks at another who is rich, who is prompt in ploughing and sowing, and in making his house nice. Neighbour competes with neighbour in the hurry to gain wealth'. In the impoverished conditions of 8th-century Greece, keeping up with the Jones's had its positive side.

Resentment of land-owning aristocrats erupted widely in the 7th and 6th centuries, and led to the setting up in several cities of government by one man – a tyrant (*tyrannos* in Greek). Although 'tyrant' became a word of disapproval for later Greeks, tyranny seems at first to have been very popular. Many citizens welcomed a leader who promised to end aristocratic misrule, to abolish the debts people owed the nobles and to share out their estates.

There was a remarkable story told about the infancy of Kypselos, the man who became the first tyrant of Corinth. The story closely resembles the one recorded later in St Matthew's gospel about the attempt of King Herod to kill the infant Christ. When Kypselos was a baby the aristocrats heard a prophecy that he would one day be very powerful, and would punish them. Accordingly a group of nobles went to kill the baby. But as the first man took it up to kill, the baby smiled: the man pitied it, so passed it to the next man. In the same way the baby passed unharmed through the whole group, and Kypselos's mother safely hid her child away. This story probably dates from the time of Kypselos's reign as tyrant, around 650. It is almost certainly untrue, but it is important evidence for his popularity. People are not likely to make up such a story if they hate the person that the baby grew into.

Why were the citizens of many Greek states able to create tyrants and to overthrow the aristocrats? The answer may well be a new technique of fighting which developed soon after 700. Until this period, the nobles, who possessed horses, were extremely important in warfare – cavalry being, until now, the most powerful section in a battle. But there now arose a very effective form of fighting which involved a large body of footsoldiers. These wore heavy armour and advanced in close formation, protecting each other by a wall of shields. They were called *hoplites*, and so long as they kept their formation cavalry could do little against them.

The hoplites were usually citizens less rich than the aristocrats. And so suddenly these citizens became much more important. They knew it, and the aristocrats knew it too. The citizens who owned hoplite equipment must have been encouraged now to resist the nobles, who in turn were demoralized to see their own

A primitive coin made of electrum (an alloy of gold and silver). The invention of coinage is usually credited to the non-Greek kingdom of Lydia some time before 600 BC. The last king of Lydia, Croesus, who reigned in Sardis until 546 BC, is still proverbial for his wealth – 'as rich as Croesus'.

Coinage issued by Greek states was stamped with a symbol indicating its origin. Examples were the turtle of Aegina, the owl of Athens (above), and the sacred stag of Artemis from Ephesus (below).

Below: During the 5th century BC, designs became more sophisticated This beautifully detailed decadrachm from Syracuse shows the head of the nymph Arethusa, surrounded by dolphins.

power and importance decrease. Hoplite-fighting lasted for centuries as the main Greek mode of warfare on land.

Tyrannies became hereditary in some of the city-states, but this normally did not last long. The son or grandson of the original tyrant might be incompetent, and in any case once the power of the aristocracy had been reduced the chief need for tyranny had passed.

During the rule of tyrants, prosperity and artistry in several cities rose impressively. Corinth under the Kypselid tyrants produced very successful pottery: in Athens, under the tyrants Peisistratos and Hippias from the 550s, the Black Figure pottery reached its height, and then was succeeded by the highly successful Red Figure ware. Pottery of all three styles was exported to places from northern Italy to the shores of the Black Sea.

The first historians

In the 500s the Eastern Greeks began the writing of critical history, and philosophic and scientific speculation. Hekataios of Miletus had the courage to reject many of the current myths, and set about reconstructing the past in a way which excluded miracles. He began his history with these words: 'I have followed my own judgement in writing this work. For it seems to me that the stories told by the Greeks are various and ridiculous.' Very little of Hekataios's work survives. In the next century another Eastern Greek, Herodotus of Halikarnassos, wrote a long history of the wars between the Greeks and the Persian empire (see page 56). This work, which includes many stories on other subjects, does survive. It is Herodotus who reports the story about Kypselos.

Herodotus is nowadays respected especially for being fair-minded. Unlike many Greeks, he did not dismiss non-Greek peoples as barbarians, but tried sympathetically to understand them. When different people told conflicting stories, Herodotus sometimes reported each version, letting his readers decide for themselves where the truth lay. He tells a remarkable story about Phoenician navigators who, it was claimed, had sailed right around Africa. The story said that the Phoenicians, while sailing westwards round the south of Africa, had had the Sun to their north. This detail suggests to

GREEK CITY-STATES

In the Classical Period and earlier, Greece was not a political unit: it was divided into many independent city-states. Each was called a *polis* (plural *poleis*); 'politics' meant activities which concerned a polis. Communities with only a few thousand citizens made their own laws and foreign policy, fighting fiercely for their independence. Defeat might mean that a polis was simply wiped off the map — its male citizens executed, its women, children, and slaves sold into slavery elsewhere.

Athens and Sparta, the best-known poleis of the Classical Period, came to control many other city states, and, each leading its great alliance, clashed repeatedly. Other poleis little bigger than villages fought each other ferociously over border disputes and various petty quarrels. If we could ask the ancient Greeks why they did not wish to merge into one great nation-state, they might reply by asking us why all the Americans, Canadians, Australians, and British who speak English don't themselves unite into a single state. The two questions have similar answers. The different Greek-speaking poleis, like different English-speaking countries, had their own separate laws, customs, and ways of speaking the common language, which they were anxious not to lose. And their rulers were unwilling to hand over power to any super-government.

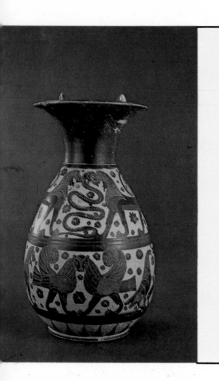

A painted Corinthian vase of the 6th century BC. The stylized beasts and birds with which it is decorated reflect Corinth's trading contacts with Asia through the Greek cities of Asia Minor. From its position on the narrow isthmus connecting northern and southern Greece, Corinth was excellently placed to trade both west and east. By the end of the 5th century BC a level trackway (the diolkos) had been constructed, over which ships were dragged on rollers across the 6000-metre isthmus.

us that the Phoenicians did indeed go south of the Equator. Herodotus himself did not believe the claim about the Sun. He did not, however, suppress it, as many historians might have done. Instead, he rightly recorded it for others to evaluate.

The Eastern Greek philosophers and speculative scientists asked such questions as 'How did the world originate?'; 'How does it keep its position in space?'; 'What was the origin of mankind?'; and 'What is the nature of divinity?' In answering these questions they thought for themselves and, unlike many other people of the time, were not content to accept traditional stories. Although much of their reasoning would not be accepted nowadays, their conclusions are sometimes strikingly like those of modern thinkers. Anaximandros of Miletus believed, like some philosophers today, that time had no beginning or end, but stretched away infinitely backwards and forwards. He is also said to have thought that the human species had developed somehow from fish, or creatures like fish. Xenophanes explained a fossil sea creature found on dry land by saying that in the past the land had been covered by water.

In the early part of the 6th century, and again in the eastern Aegean (on the island of Lesbos), there lived the most famous female poet of the ancient world, Sappho. Sadly, as with so much Greek literature, many of Sappho's poems are lost. The fragments of her work which remain show her to have been an elegant and passionate literary artist. She writes about her little girl: 'I have a beautiful daughter, who looks like the golden flowers, my darling Kleïs: I would not exchange her for all of Lydia or lovely...' – and there the fragment breaks off.

Perhaps as striking as Sappho's talent is the fact that, although a woman, she was enabled to develop it. She was from a rich family: had she not been, probably she would not have had the education, the leisure and the self-confidence needed to compose and publish fine poetry. The Eastern Greeks were perhaps more liberal as regards the education of women than those of mainland Greece. The best-known woman in 5th-century Athens, Aspasia, was again in origin an Eastern Greek – from Miletus. She may have been an expert on the art of public speaking.

A threat from the east

The development of Eastern Greek culture was greatly damaged by the expansion of the Persian empire. The Persians had conquered Croesus's kingdom of Lydia in 546 BC and by the end of the century the Greek cities of western Asia Minor were under Persian domination. After taking part in an unsuccessful revolt against Persian rule, Miletus was captured and made desolate in 494. This city had been the home of many prominent thinkers: its punishment now by Persia may be one reason why so few records survive of Eastern Greek science and philosophy, important though they were. The coasts of the eastern Aegean were only to be freed from Persian control after 479. By then an immense Persian army of invasion had been crushed by Greeks elsewhere.

Athens had aided the unsuccessful revolt of Eastern Greeks in the 490s, and in 490 the Persians sent an expedition to punish the Athenians. This force was defeated by the Athenians less than 50 kilometres (30 miles) from Athens at Marathon. Heavily armed hoplites proved, as so often, superior to the more lightly equipped troops of the non-Greek east.

Persia needed to avenge this defeat. Otherwise, its enemies elsewhere might seek to imitate the Athenians' success. In 480 the Persian King Xerxes led against

Greece a military force of terrifying size. Herodotus, who wrote when many Greeks who had encountered this force were still alive, estimated that it contained over 5 million people, including noncombatants. The true number will probably never be known: modern calculations have reached less than a tenth of this figure. But a force of this size – half a million – was far larger than any the mainland Greeks had met. Its main target was Athens, a city which had well under 50,000 fighting men.

Xerxes assembled his force at Sardis, crossed the Hellespont on a bridge of boats, and brought his army and fleet around the northern coast of the Aegean before descending into central Greece. His Greek opponents formed an alliance under the leadership of Sparta, a small but powerful state of the southern Peloponnese which trained its soldiers to an almost suicidal degree of bravery.

The first serious Greek resistance came at Thermopylae, a narrow pass between mountains and sea, which led into central Greece. Here a small force could oppose a numerous enemy without being surrounded. The Greek fleet, which was also outnumbered, blocked the straits to the east, at Artemision. At Thermopylae the Persians were for a time beaten off by a few thousand Greeks. Prominent in this defence were 300 Spartans. Eventually the Persians were shown – by a Greek – a mountain path which allowed them to surround the Spartan position. It is said that when this was happening the Spartans

THE PERSIAN WARS

ILLYRIA · THRACIA · MACEDONIA · CHALCIDICE · EPIRUS · THESSALY · MYSIA · LESBOS · LEUCAS · Thermopylae · AETOLIA · EUBOEA · CEPHALLENIA · ATTICA · CHIOS · LYDIA · ACHAEA · Salamis · Athens · ZACYNTHUS · ARGOLIS · CYCLADES · CARIA · PELOPONNESUS · Sparta · RHODOS · CRETE · PERSIAN EMPIRE

☐ Under Persian rule
☐ Neutral states
☐ At war with Persia

knew of it, but chose to die at their posts rather than to retreat safely like cowards. And die they did. The Persians passed through Thermopylae towards Athens, and the Greek fleet wisely withdrew from Artemision without a decisive battle.

Greek states commonly resisted a greatly superior enemy by withdrawing their men behind city-walls and standing siege. But in 480 the Athenians chose to evacuate Athens and to resist at sea, off the nearby isle of Salamis. As we shall see later (page

A battle between Spartans and Argives in the 5th century BC; the Spartans are on the right. Some soldiers wear a bell cuirass of bronze, others a tunic made from layer upon layer of gummed linen. Most of them are wearing the Corinthian type of helmet which was made of bronze and covered the entire head except for the eyes, mouth, and chin.

87) there were gloomy religious prophecies which made the Athenians despair of protecting Athens itself. The city was, accordingly, captured and wrecked by the Persians. Without knowing it, the enemies of Athens were helping to clear the way for the famous temples which were later built on the Athenian Acropolis.

At Salamis the Persians made a terrible mistake. They allowed their ships to be drawn into fighting in the narrow water between the island and the mainland. In open water, the Persians could have used their superior numbers to surround the Greeks. And the Persian ships, being more easily manoeuvrable, could have caught their opponents out of position, and sunk the Greek vessels by ramming them amidships. But in the Salamis strait the slow, heavy Greek ships were able to fight the more static battle which suited them while the heavily armed Greek marines could board the enemy's ships. The Persians were badly defeated and withdrew. Aeschylus, an Athenian poet who probably fought in the battle, later wrote of Persian seamen being stabbed in the water 'like tunny fish'.

Xerxes now retreated to Asia Minor; Greece may have been unsafe for him. He left behind only part of his land force. This in turn was defeated in the following

year (479), at Plataea in Boeotia. Now it was Greek hoplites, and especially those of Sparta and its Peloponnesian allies, who proved decisive. The remnants of the Persian fleet were heavily defeated at Mycale, in the eastern Aegean. The failure of Xerxes's expedition was complete.

The Classical Period

The history of Greek mental achievement in the century and a half from 480 is largely the history of thought at Athens. If Xerxes's attack on the Athenians had been successful, much of this achievement would probably never have come about. Athens might have followed Miletus into obscurity. But as things turned out, Athens received an important boost to morale and prosperity. With the Persians driven out of mainland Greece, the great era of Athens, and what is called the Classical Period, begin.

The largest Greek naval force at Salamis had been Athenian, and the Athenians had distinguished themselves also at Mycale. The resulting prestige helped Athens to replace Sparta as leader of the Eastern Greeks who wished to continue the fight against Persia. These Greeks, with Athens, formed a league which held meetings on the island of Delos: its aims were to plunder the Persian empire, and to expel the Persians from those Eastern Greek territories which they still controlled. As the league expanded, it came to include most of the Aegean islands, and very many of the coastal cities to the north and east. Under Athenian leadership, important successes against Persia increased the domination of Athens over the allies. Eventually, in 454, the treasury of the league was moved from Delos to Athens. Contributions to the Delian League by its members turned into a tax paid to Athens by subjects of an empire. And with these contributions were erected the most famous buildings on the Athenian Acropolis – the gateway building, called the Propylaia, and the temple of the goddess Athene, called the Parthenon.

Nowadays we see the Parthenon as the symbol of Greek culture. But many people in Athens thought that it should not have been built. They argued that the citizenry of Athens got itself a bad reputation by taking the money of other Greek states, and said that Athens was 'tarting itself up'

Athene, patron goddess of Athens, carrying a spear and grasping the stern of a ship. The Athenian navy defeated the Persians in 480 BC and formed the basis of the Athenian empire.

Ostraka – pieces of broken pottery on which Athenians inscribed the names of citizens they wished to exile. The custom of ostracism was intended to act as a check against the ambitions of over-powerful citizens. Six thousand votes were necessary to ostracise a citizen. Even Themistokles, the great anti-Persian strategist of 480, was eventually ostracised. Many of the ostraka found bearing his name were written by the same hand. His opponents clearly organized the mass-production of them. The lower ostrakon bears the name of Themistokles.

with gaudy decoration. Many of the richer Athenians probably accepted these arguments; it may have been their wealthy friends in other Greek cities who had provided much of the money.

Most Athenian citizens, however, approved of the plans to build, which were championed by the politician Pericles. Expensive temple-building would please the gods and would provide work for many Athenians. The results would be beautiful for Athenians to contemplate, and the enemies of Athens might hesitate to attack a city so obviously rich, and therefore powerful. In 447 the construction of the Parthenon began; about ten years later work started on the Propylaia.

The big decisions made at Athens during the 400s and 300s (like that to build the Parthenon) were usually taken by a process which nowadays seems both strange and intelligent. This was called *demokratia*. From this comes our word 'democracy', but demokratia was something very different. In a demokratia there was nothing very like a modern president or prime minister. Women citizens, and all slaves, could not vote. Male citizens, however, had far more power than in a modern democracy. They did not vote to choose a government which would take decisions for them. They took their decisions themselves.

The male citizens met several times a month in a general assembly, called an *ekklesia*. There each citizen had one vote. Any man could speak and propose a motion. If a motion received a majority of votes, it normally became law. Only another meeting of the assembly, or the Athenian courts, could overrule it. And the courts were controlled not by professional lawyers but by ordinary Athenians. 'Carpenters, smiths, leather-workers, traders, shipowners, rich men and poor men, noble men and humble' spoke in the assembly, according to Plato.

Many of the administrators at Athens were appointed not, as nowadays, by election or nomination, but by lot. There was a council of 500 men which met on most days, supervised the administration, took minor decisions, and prepared business for the general assemblies. This council, too, was filled by lot. Its members changed every year, by rotation. No one could serve for more than two years in all.

The Athenians realized the importance of listening to experts. Their military commanders were elected every year, and could – like Pericles – serve for year after year. Plato tells us that on a technical matter, such as shipbuilding, the assembly would refuse to listen to anyone who was not an expert, but would laugh at him, and shout him down, 'even if he were very handsome, and rich, and a nobleman'. Why then did the Athenians insist that the man in the street, and the man chosen by lot, should take most of the decisions?

It was probably believed that an expert might know what was best for the community, but might prefer to do what was best for himself – corruption was very common in ancient Greece. Also, an expert might be honest but still, if he was rich, he might not think or know enough about the poor and their needs. The general assembly and the lot made poor men powerful. Permanent officials might plot to increase their own power and wealth at the expense of the public. A man chosen by lot, who served for only a few months, was more likely to act like an ordinary citizen and to take decisions which suited ordinary citizens, because in most cases he *was* an ordinary citizen.

Life in a democracy

Many of the richer Greeks considered that under a demokratia there was too much freedom for the poor. One writer complained that at Athens you could not

The Acropolis at Athens, a sacred enclosure of shrines and temples. For Greeks at the time, the gateway building or Propylaia (left) was perhaps more striking and unusual even than Athene's temple, the Parthenon (right).
A marble bust of Pericles, a Roman copy of a Greek portrait. From the 440s BC to his death in 429, Pericles was the leading statesman of Athens. His vision of Athenian greatness found expression through a splendid programme of public works, financed by money from Athens's allies.

Athenian black-figure lekythos of the 6th century BC. Two women fold a blanket while to either side other women are working wool. One winds the wool on to a distaff, the other spins it into yarn, using a spindle.

This vase-painting from Attica, the region round Athens, shows a woman being dressed by a slave. Above her hangs a mirror of polished bronze.

even hit another man's slave in public, and another that a demokratia was 'saturated with liberty' which 'gets into private houses and ends up infecting the domestic animals with anarchy'. Modern writers too have often disapproved of demokratia, and sympathized rather with those Greek states ruled by oligarchy. (*Oligarchia* meant the rule of a few men and, as the philosopher Aristotle observed, the rulers in an oligarchy were always rich.) We should remember, however, that Athens with its demokratia was in several ways one of the most successful communities which has ever existed.

Little is heard of the thousands of slaves in Athens. Among them were the bowmen who acted as a police force and who were owned by the Athenian community as a whole. Like many slaves in the Greek world, they were not themselves of Greek origin; Athens's policemen were said to come from Scythia, in southern Russia. Occasionally male slaves were freed. They might have grown rich in business, or have been needed to fight in Athens's armed forces. Others, like those forced to work in the silver mines, may have had a dreadful existence. When a good opportunity to escape arose, in a short period from 413, over 20,000 slaves ran away.

Details are also sadly scarce about the lives of Athenian citizen women. Those from rich families seem to have been expected to spend most of their lives at home. They might be too shy to be seen even by male relatives, let alone by other men. It was probably unusual for such women to get much education, or to marry a man of their own choosing. Poorer citizen women might see rather more of the world, through having to go out to work in the fields or, perhaps, in the market.

Even the women at home, however, might take a keen interest in public events. One Athenian speaker in court warns the jury not to give a verdict which their womenfolk will disapprove of, for the women would be sure to find out: 'What would each of you say when you get home, and your wife or daughter or mother asks "Where have you been?"; when you reply "Judging a case", she will immediately ask "Who was on trial?" . . .'

Probably the best-educated women at Athens were not Athenian citizens, but were *hetairai* – slaves and aliens prepared to live with a man outside marriage. Aspasia, who lived with Pericles, was one of these. A man of his intelligence probably felt a need for a companion more educated than an Athenian citizen woman was allowed to be.

The poor at Athens did not use their political power to abolish slavery or other private wealth. They did vote for luxuries, but these were normally for public use. Many elegant buildings were erected for the public to enjoy, such as the porticoes around the market place, and the singing hall (the Odeion). The majority of citizens probably lived in houses with mud walls and earth floors. The Greek word for burglar was 'wall-digger': a house could be burrowed into very quickly indeed!

The Athenian public entertainment best known nowadays is drama. Tragedy and comedy were developed and brought to perfection at Athens. Many Greeks believed that this could not have happened without the confidence and free speech given by demokratia. The tragedies that survive are by three dramatists. Aeschylus, Sophocles, and Euripides usually chose themes from myth, to which they added their own knowledge of human nature.

Greek tragedies often describe the sad consequences of human stupidity or arrogance towards the gods. One play of Euripides, the *Bacchae*, tells of the arrival at the Boeotian town of Thebes of the god Dionysus. He is shown as a handsome

GAMES

The Greeks thought that *arete* – spiritual and physical perfection – was of the greatest importance. To this end, exercise in the gymnasium and athletic contests played a great part in their lives. And the reward for the best athletes was to take part in one of the great athletic festivals, or Games. These took place all over Greece. Some were small local affairs, but others grew into international events attended by people from all over the Greek-speaking world. These festivals were thought so sacred that even states at war would call a truce to be able to compete.

Greatest of all were the Olympic Games, held in honour of Zeus every four years from 776 BC to AD 393. Second in importance were the Pythian Games, held – also every four years – at Delphi, in honour of Apollo. There were horse races and chariot races; the pentathlon of sprint, long-jump, discus, javelin, and wrestling; running races; boxing, wrestling, and a no-holds-barred contest called the pancration.

Prizes at the Games were only wreaths of olive or laurel leaves; but the athletes gained lasting fame, and were almost worshipped in their own cities.

Two boxers engaged in a fierce bout. Blood spurts from the nose of the boxer on the left. Instead of boxing gloves, the Greeks used strips of leather strapped round their fists.

A bronze figure of a cloaked soldier, probably a Spartan, from the 5th century BC.

young man with long hair, and the women of Thebes eagerly follow him – rather as if he were a modern pop star. However, the male ruler of Thebes, Pentheus, perhaps from jealousy as well as from fear that the women will misbehave, tries to stop them. Unable to resist his own fascination, he follows the women, hoping to watch their misbehaviour himself. Inspired by the god, the frenzied women catch him and, led by his own mother, tear him to pieces. The mother is then shown slowly realizing what she has done.

Athenian comedy was very bold indeed. Skilful criticism and wild jokes were made against prominent people of the time, such as Pericles and Aspasia. The best-known comic playwright, Aristophanes, invented the expression 'Cloudcuckoo-land'; he used it to attack Athenian dreams of power in 414, when Athens was trying in vain to conquer Sicily.

Sparta

While the Athenians were at their most powerful and creative, they had to face the deep hostility of Sparta. Historians have not often understood how systematic and deep this hostility was. Between 465 and 404 BC whenever Athens had a difficulty

which made it especially vulnerable, Sparta tried to start, or to spread, a war against Athens. Cunningly, the Spartans never took these aggressive initiatives unless there was a special Athenian weakness to exploit. Why this regular aggression from Sparta?

Sparta had a higher proportion of slaves to citizens than any other Greek state: perhaps as many as seven to every one citizen. In normal times these slaves, called *helots*, had nowhere to escape to. But as Athenian naval power grew, Sparta must have feared that Athens would one

Spartan behaviour to the helots – their land slaves – was often savage. Prominent helots were hunted down and killed. In 424 the helots were tricked into choosing 2000 of their best men, to whom the Spartans promised to give freedom. The chosen 2000 went around the temples, happily celebrating their good fortune. Then the Spartans murdered them all; they had contrived the whole episode to discover which helots were the boldest, and therefore the likeliest to revolt. Such treatment aroused deep hatred in the helots; it was said that they would have been glad to eat the Spartans raw. Just as the Spartans watched for an Athenian weakness, so the helots waited for some Spartan difficulty which would allow them to revolt and gain freedom.

61

A gold stater showing Philip II of Macedon – an idealized portrait in impeccably Greek style. The reverse, with its charioteer and rearing horses, is a reminder that 'Philip' means 'lover of horses' (phil/hippos).

The ruins of the circular Philippeum at Olympia, commissioned by Philip to celebrate his victory over the united Greeks at Khaironeia. Nominally a thank-offering to Zeus, it was in fact a blatant glorification of the House of Macedon. Within were statues of the Macedonian royal family in gold and ivory – materials usually reserved for the images of gods.

day intervene in the Peloponnese to help the helots to run away or to revolt.

It was because of their helots, too, that the Spartans lived 'spartan' lives. They felt that they could only keep the helots in order by turning themselves into supremely tough and well trained soldiers. Sparta itself resembled a permanent armed camp. Soldierly discipline was a cherished ideal. Inquiry and criticism were discouraged. A Spartan king might claim that he and his fellow-citizens were not sufficiently educated to criticize their own laws. Sparta's artistic and intellectual achievement during the Classical Period was virtually nil.

Spartan boys at the age of seven joined a 'herd' of others, and learned to endure physical hardship. At some point a flogging contest was introduced to encourage endurance. The winner was the boy who could stand most flogging; several died while taking part. Spartan girls also underwent tough physical training, so that they should grow up to be strong, healthy mothers.

In their anxiety to keep up the numbers of citizens, the Spartans sometimes allowed men and women to have sex outside marriage so that an infertile person would not prevent his or her spouse from having children. Spartan women were supposed to encourage their sons to be fierce warriors. It was said that a Spartan mother would prefer her son to die in battle than to return safely after running away. But in war Spartan women could disgrace themselves. Shortly after 371, when an enemy force at last penetrated to Sparta,

the women panicked and made more of a din than the enemy. Women in other states made themselves useful on such occasions, sometimes pelting the enemy with stones and roof-tiles.

New conquerors

In 404 BC Athens, weakened by catastrophic losses in Sicily and by the loss of important allies, was forced by Sparta to surrender. Sparta's ally, Corinth, argued that the city of Athens should now be wiped out. Luckily for us, Sparta refused; but it did take over the Athenian empire.

Many people had thought that Sparta's victory was the beginning of freedom for the Greeks. What happened instead was a slaughter of innumerable democrats, as the Spartans persecuted the democratic parties which Athens had protected in the states of its empire. Sparta set up oligarchies in these states, and ran its new empire so unscrupulously that even some of its friends came to condemn Spartan conduct. Probably few people were sorry when, in 371, the Spartan army was smashed at Leuktra in Boeotia, by the forces of Thebes. Shortly afterwards the Thebans invaded Sparta's homeland. By now Sparta had a terrible shortage of citizen soldiers – probably fewer than 1000 remained. The Thebans organized a large and successful revolt of the helots: as a great power in Greece, Sparta was finished for ever.

The Theban domination of Greece was relatively brief. In 356 Phokis, a previously insignificant state of central Greece which was now threatened by Thebes, seized the treasury of the great shrine at Delphi. Melting down the treasure there into coin, the Phocians became rich enough to raise a huge mercenary army which exhausted the Thebans in a long war. Even when allied with Athens, Thebes was unable to stop a new invader from the north, Philip of Macedon.

Operating from the fringes of the Greek world, and financed from his own gold mine, Philip defeated the Greek allies in 338, at Khaironeia in Boeotia. He thus gained control of most of Greece which, on his death two years later, was inherited by his son, Alexander. But Alexander the Great had other ambitions than merely to keep control of Greece. The Persian empire offered far richer prizes.

THRACE
MACEDON
Athens
PHRYGIA
Sardes
Miletus
LYCIA
CILICIA
CAPPADOCIA
ARMENIA
SCYTHIA
SOGDIANA
Oxus
BACTRIA
GANDARIA

Byblos
Damascus
Tyre
PALESTINA
Jerusalem
Royal highway
Arbela
HYRCANIA
Ecbatana
Behistun
BABYLONIA
Babylon
MEDIA
Susa
PERSIS
Pasargadae
Persepolis
SUSIANA
PARTHIA
ARACHOSIA
CARMANIA
GEDROSIA
Indus

LIBYA
Memphis
Heliopolis
Nile
Thebes
ARABIA

	Kingdom of Persia
	Median empire
	Lydian empire
	Babylonian or Chaldean empire
	Egyptian empire conquests of Darius and Xerxes

The Persians

Much of Iran is a high desert plateau, surrounded by mountains, while along the coast of the Persian Gulf in the south the land is scorched by heat. In the valleys of the Zagros Mountains, to the west, people have always lived a semi-nomadic life, for in the great heat of the summer they have to drive their animals up to cooler mountain pastures. In these valleys the inhabitants of ancient Iran grew wheat and barley, vines, figs and pomegranates; the lower slopes of the mountains were then covered with oak forests and with trees that provided food as well as timber such as walnut, wild almond, and pistachio. In the north-west, in Azerbaijan, enough wheat could be grown in the fertile valleys to support many people.

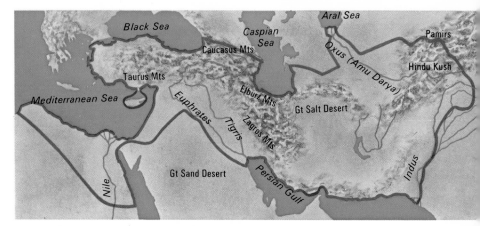

Black Sea
Caspian Sea
Aral Sea
Pamirs
Caucasus Mts
Oxus (Amu Darya)
Hindu Kush
Taurus Mts
Mediterranean Sea
Euphrates
Tigris
Elburz Mts
Gt Salt Desert
Zagros Mts
Nile
Gt Sand Desert
Persian Gulf
Indus

Throughout its history Iran has suffered invasions from nomadic peoples. Some came through the lower eastern end of the Elburz mountains, east of the Caspian Sea. Others, including the original Medes and Persians, Kurds, Mongols, and Turco-Tatars, probably came across the Caucasus and into Iran from the north-west.

All these peoples, in turn, contributed to the civilization of Iran. They brought with them new languages, new styles of ornament, and new technology, such as the knowledge of working iron.

Elam

The south-west of Iran forms part of the south Mesopotamian plain and in this area an urban civilization developed during the fourth millennium BC: the kingdom of Elam. The best-explored city-site of Elam is Susa which, certainly at times, also functioned as the capital of the state; another site, Tepe Yahya, situated 800 kilometres (500 miles) east of Susa, seems also to have formed part of Elam. The complexity of this early civilization

CHRONOLOGY	
BC	
3000s	Elamite civilization in south-west Iran.
1300	Iranians (Medes and Persians) move into Iran.
549	Persians under Cyrus II (the Great) defeat Medes.
539	Babylon falls to Persians.
526	Cambyses conquers Egypt
490–479	Persians under Darius I and Xerxes I unsuccessfully invade mainland Greece.
464	Egypt revolts unsuccessfully against Persia.
360s	Weakening of empire; revolts in many satrapies.
334	Alexander of Macedon invades Persian empire.
331	Alexander decisively defeats Darius III at Gaugamela and becomes master of the empire.

King Teumann of Elam (left) and his son Tammaritu attempt to flee from Assyrian soldiers after the defeat of Teumann's army at Til-Tuba in 653 BC; part of an Assyrian carved relief from the South-West Palace at Nineveh.

An electrum statue of an offering-bearer, possibly an Elamite king, of the 13th – 12th century BC.

can be realized from the fact that it developed its own pictographic script (as yet undeciphered), totally unrelated to the early Mesopotamian script (see page 36), which it may predate. One of the reasons for the development of such a far-flung and sophisticated state seems to have been trade. Elam was at times in control of the trade in lapis lazuli and metals for the cities of southern Mesopotamia, which had few resources, while Tepe Yahya was the centre of an active trade in worked and raw soapstone (steatite).

Very little is known of the history and organization of Elam – it seems, at times, to have been a confederacy of states rather than a single political unity. From about 2300 BC on it was frequently at war with the states of southern Mesopotamia, coming at times under direct Mesopotamian control politically. One reason for our lack of knowledge is the very small number of decipherable texts in Elamite, and their limited scope. From about 2300 onwards the Elamites used a form of the cuneiform script derived from southern Mesopotamia, but few tablets have survived. Some of the Elamite gods are known and a partial list of kings can be drawn up, but anything more has to be derived from occasional references in Mesopotamian texts. The best-known and largest collection of Elamite tablets are those that were found at Persepolis – but these date to the Achaemenid period and so are no help in understanding the earlier civilization. But it is interesting to note that, until the

A curiously shaped ceremonial bronze axe, found in a grave in Luristan. It dates from 1000–700 BC.

A Luristan bronze horse-bit with elaborate cheek pieces in the form of heraldic beasts. Wear marks show it was made for use.

simpler alphabetic Aramaic was introduced in the early 5th century BC, the Achaemenid Persians used the cuneiform Elamite script for administrative purposes.

The rise of the Persians

About 1300 BC, the Iranians, a branch of the Indo-European people, moved into Iran from the steppes. Among them were the tribes whose names are found in later documents as the Medes and Persians.

Archaeologists have found traces of the arrival of the Iranians in the settlements of the period. Iron tools are found for the first time, and a new red or grey-black polished pottery came into use. As the Iranians found new lands in widely separated areas, their pottery and metal-work began to develop regional styles, and to be influenced by the traditions of neighbouring kingdoms in Elam, Assyria, and Urartu (see pages 33 and 76).

Among the Iranians who had settled in western Iran were the Medes and Persians. They are the *Madai* and *Parsua* mentioned in Assyrian documents of the 9th century BC. Assyrian armies fighting in the Zagros came upon these tribes, and forced them to pay tribute in the reign of their King Shalmaneser III.

By 600 the warring kingdoms of Assyria and Urartu were in decline and the Medes, who were great warriors, had become a leading power in Western Asia. At this time the Parsua in the south were among the subjects of the Medes, but under Cyrus II they defeated the Medes in 549.

Kings who built the Persian empire

Cyrus II – the Great, as he was called – was the first king of the independent Persians. His task of welding the Medes and Persians into a single nation must have been made easier for him by the fact that his mother was the daughter of the last Median king, Astyages.

According to the Greek writer Xenophon Cyrus was outstanding for his clemency – but Xenophon was writing for Cyrus the Younger and so his account may well be biased. After he had defeated the Medes their capital Ecbatana was not sacked by his victorious army, as might have been expected. Instead, it was made the capital of the new state, and the former Median and new Persian officials worked there side by side.

Cyrus began his conquests almost immediately. First he moved into Anatolia, following the trade routes from Persia to the wealthy kingdom of Lydia and the independent Greek cities of the Coast.

The cavalry of Croesus, the king of Lydia whose wealth was legendary, were terrified of Cyrus's camels and the Persians captured Croesus and his capital Sardis. One by one, the Greek cities on the coast were conquered. Having established his north-west frontier on the Bosporus, Cyrus set out to extend and strengthen his eastern borders in Turkestan and Afghanistan, hoping by this to keep at bay the nomads of central Asia. Then he turned west again, to Babylonia. Babylon was at this time a cultural and commercial centre and capital of the Neo-Babylonian empire. Cyrus captured it, characteristically sparing the life of its king, Nabonidus, and took the throne himself. Rather than behaving as a conqueror, he ruled as a Babylonian king and observed the religious customs of the land. Peoples who had been subjects of Babylon now became part of the Persian empire. The Phoenicians came to offer Cyrus their famous ships as his fleet; the many Jews exiled in Babylon asked for release from captivity. Cyrus issued a decree allowing them to return to Jerusalem, and to rebuild their temple there. In 537 over 40,000 Jews, accompanied by a high Persian official, returned to their homeland.

Cyrus planned to conquer Egypt, but before he could embark on this he was killed while campaigning in the east. His body was brought home to rest in a tomb near his palace at Pasargadae.

Three royal tombs carved into a cliff-face at Naqsh-i-Rustam, near Persepolis. Here are buried the Persian kings Artaxerxes I, Xerxes, and Darius I. Each entrance is carved to look like a building, with columns supporting a platform on which stand the subject peoples holding up the throne of the king. On the tomb of Darius the Great is written 'O man, that which Ahura Mazda commands, to that show not thyself opposed. Forsake not the straight way. Sin not!'.

The carved reliefs at Behistun. Above King Darius hovers the winged symbol of Ahura Mazda.

THE BEHISTUN INSCRIPTION

Whoever you are, read this inscription, and know that everything written in it is true, and know that I have achieved many other things that are not recorded here.
Thus ends the inscription commemorating the accession of Darius I in 522 BC carved on the rock of Behistun, 35 kilometres (22 miles) east of Kermanshah. The figure of the king is 1·73 metres (5 foot 8 inches) tall. Behind him are two attendants. He is treading a would-be usurper underfoot, and grovelling before him are nine rebel kings. At the end of the row of figures is a strange being called *Skunka*, wearing a conical hat. Beneath the relief is a cuneiform inscription, written in three languages, now identified as Old Persian, Elamite, and Babylonian. But until the early 19th century AD, no-one could read any cuneiform inscription.

In 1835, Henry Creswicke Rawlinson was posted to Kermanshah as part of a British military mission to the court of the Shah. He was an expert climber. Risking his life, without ropes or ladders, he climbed from the top of the Rock of Behistun down to the inscription, clinging to minute projections 120 metres (400 feet) above the ground. Somehow he managed to make copies of two of the inscriptions, and directed a 'wild Kurdish boy' in making paper 'squeezes' of the Babylonian inscription, which he could not reach himself.

The copies enabled Rawlinson to decipher the Persian inscription, which he published in 1837, becoming known as the 'Father of Cuneiform' (his notebooks are in the British Museum). But the title should properly belong to the German scholar Grotefend, who deciphered other trilingual inscriptions as early as 1802, although his work was not known to Rawlinson when he wrote his paper.

Expedition to Egypt

Cyrus's dream of the conquest of Egypt was accomplished by his son Cambyses. After a fierce but short war in 526 BC, in which Greek mercenaries fought with the Egyptians, Cambyses captured the pharaoh and sent him as an exile to Susa. He set up an Egyptian as governor. From Egypt he campaigned unsuccessfully in North Africa and in Ethiopia; a whole Persian army disappeared, perhaps in a sandstorm. At first he reverenced the Egyptian gods, but later he is said to have committed acts of sacrilege that gave

great offence to the Egyptians. In 522 he set out hurriedly to return home to quell a revolt, but had only got as far as Syria when he died. Just what happened is not known – he may have committed suicide, wounded himself accidentally, or been assassinated.

The commander of Cambyses' royal bodyguard was a man called Darius, who came from a branch of the royal Achaemenid family. He had accompanied the King to Egypt and the army now accepted him as ruler. He hurried back to Persia to establish his position there. Two months after the death of Cambyses, Darius had subdued a revolt in Persia; but there were risings in different parts of the empire for the first two years of his reign. After defeating nine kings in nineteen separate battles he had an inscription recording his victories cut into the rock at Behistun.

Darius never forgot the debt he owed to his army. In his new palace at Susa he had his bodyguard – the Ten Thousand Immortals – portrayed lining the walls in all their splendour.

Organizing the empire

The series of revolts after his accession showed Darius the need to reorganize the empire. Cyrus had established some *satrapies*, provinces governed by a reliable Persian. Darius now extended this system over the whole empire, setting a Persian noble or member of the royal family over each of 20 satrapies. To lessen the possibility of corruption, the Persian satrap did not rule alone. The army in each province was under another noble Persian; yet another was in charge of collecting the huge amount of tribute paid regularly into the royal Treasury. These somewhat cumbersome taxes were paid partly in gold and silver, but also in slaves, cattle, camels, horses or food; from Arabia came incense, from the Ethiopians, elephant tusks. As another safeguard against corruption Darius set up a body of independent inspectors called 'the ears of the king'. They travelled about paying surprise visits to the satrapies.

Darius improved communications and trade within his empire by building a system of roads. The Royal Road from Ephesus in western Anatolia to Susa in Persia was 2700 kilometres (1680 miles) long. Fresh horses were kept at post-

houses along it for the royal couriers who – riding by day and night – could cover the distance in one week. Another road ran from Egypt to Babylon, across the mountains to Hamadan, and to the Indus Valley. When he had subdued the lands as far as the Indus, Darius had a fleet built and sent it down the river and across the Indian Ocean to Egypt – a journey which took it two and a half years. Darius had thought that this sea route might provide easier communication between the far east and west limits of his empire. He followed up this expedition by cutting a canal from the Red Sea to the Nile, to allow his ships into the Mediterranean with its busy commerce.

At this time the Greek cities were the principal traders in the eastern Mediterranean; much of the timber for their ships came from the Scythians of south Russia. In 512 Darius set out on a war against the Scythians, to stop the timber supply and to close the Dardanelles to Greek ships carrying corn from their colonies around the Black Sea. He attacked the Thracians, and crossed the Danube to fight the Scythians. They refused to meet him

Soldiers of the king's body-guard, part of a glazed brick frieze in the great throne room of Artaxerxes II in the palace at Susa. Each wears a long, brightly coloured robe and carries a spear. On his back is slung a bow and a quiver of arrows.

in a pitched battle, and devastated the land so that Darius could not get supplies. He was forced to withdraw with heavy losses, but he had added not only Thrace but also Macedonia to the empire and was in a position to blockade the Dardanelles. He now began to intrigue by bribery among the politicians in the cities of Greece itself, trying to weaken them by setting one against another.

The reign of Darius was the culmination of the Persian empire. He was a great lawgiver who upheld justice and truth; he led his armies in the field, and did not settle down in the luxury of his palaces as later kings did. He treated well the subject peoples who accepted his supremacy. The great achievements of his craftsmen can be seen in the remains of his palaces at Susa and Persepolis.

Less is known about Persia after Darius; and what we do know comes mainly from the Greeks and may well be biased. The great days were over; the later Achaemenid kings were plagued by court intrigues which led to the assassination of many promising princes. Greek historians tell us that in the early 5th century Xerxes took an army of 700,000 men across the Dardanelles on a bridge of boats. But his great expedition against Greece, at first successful, ended in total failure. Under Artaxerxes II (404–359) civil war broke out; Egypt and other provinces threw off Persian control and a number of satraps in the western empire revolted. Artaxerxes III reconquered Egypt and the rebellious provinces but was poisoned in 338. His sons were killed by a scheming eunuch called Bagoas, who placed another member of the Achaemenid family on the throne as Darius III in 336. He lost his empire to Alexander the Great in 331; fleeing after his defeat, he was murdered by one of his own satraps. From now on Persia became absorbed into the Hellenistic world.

Palaces of the Achaemenid kings

Impressive even in their ruined state, the huge palaces are almost the only surviving monuments to the power and achievements of the Achaemenid kings. While stone was used for columns, doorways and window-frames, the main walls were built of mudbrick, and mudbrick towers guarded the main buildings. Only the

foundations of these have survived, since the unfired bricks have long since been washed away. Once the palaces gleamed with colours. Many walls were covered with friezes or inscriptions in glazed bricks. Doorways and window-frames were made of highly polished black stone. In contrast, the wooden ceilings and beams were brilliantly painted. Wooden doors glittered with plates of bronze or gold. Painted stone reliefs of processions decorated walls and staircases, while floors were covered with richly woven carpets.

The oldest palace, at Pasargadae, was begun by Cyrus the Great, possibly while he was still a vassal of the Medes. Like all the palaces, it stood on a vast artificial terrace, approached by two grand staircases. On the terrace have been found the remains of a number of buildings, including a rectangular pillared hall, the forerunner of the huge structures of the later palaces. No traces of any town have been found at the foot of the terrace, so the King's followers may have lived in tents.

The winter palace

Darius I started to build at Pasargadae, but moved his capital to Susa, where the climate was pleasant in winter. Here in

Persian craftsmen of the 4th century BC produced work of the highest quality. This leaping ibex, of partly gilded silver, was one of a pair forming the handles of a bowl. The bearded face with horse's ears on which the hind feet of the ibex rest represents the Egyptian dwarf-god Bes. The treatment of the ibex is generally considered to show the influence of the Greek style on Achaemenid art.

Two objects from the so-called Oxus Treasure, a magnificent hoard of gold and silver objects found near the Oxus river. Top: A gold plaque with a repoussé figure of a bearded nomad carrying a bundle of barsom (a type of reed). Below: A hollow gold head of a man. The hoard, dating from the 7th to 4th centuries BC, may once have belonged to a temple in Bactria, and was probably buried to save it from raiders.

the foundations has been found the King's description of the building of a palace, using craftsmen and materials from many different lands:

The decoration of this palace that I built at Susa was fetched from far away. The earth was dug down to the rock. When the digging was done . . . the rubble was thrown into the pit. It was on this base that the palace was constructed. The bricks were moulded and baked in the sun by Babylonians. The cedar beams were brought from a mountain called Lebanon. The Assyrian people brought them to Babylonia. From Babylon the Carians and Ionians brought them to Susa. The wood called yaka *was brought from Gandhara and Karmana. The gold was brought from Sardis and Bactria and wrought here. The magnificent stone called lapis lazuli and the cornelian were wrought here but were brought from Soghdiana. The precious turquoise was brought from Khwarizmia and wrought on the spot. The silver and ebony were brought from Egypt. The decoration for the walls was brought from Ionia. The ivory, wrought here, was transported from Kussa, Sind and Arachosia. The stone columns, which were wrought here, were transported from . . . Elam. The stone dressers were Ionians and Sards. The goldsmiths who wrought the gold were Medes and Egyptians. The men who worked the sun-baked bricks, they were Egyptians.*

Above: The ruins of the royal palace of Darius the Great at Persepolis, probably begun in 520 BC, showing one of the magnificent double staircases. Below: On the walls beside the staircase, Darius's craftsmen carved processions of soldiers, courtiers, servants, and tribute-bearers, shown (in some cases) as if they were actually walking up the staircase itself. The figures are very life-like, illustrating important details of costume, ornaments, and weapons. Here, one man taps another on the shoulder, while another turns as if in conversation.

The men who decorated the walls were Medes and Egyptians.

City of the Persians

The most famous palace is Persepolis – the 'city of the Persians'. Here the king celebrated the Persian New Year festival. Its vast buildings stood on a huge terrace, 13 hectares (33 acres) in extent. This was partly cut from the mountain behind, and partly built up to a height of 18 metres (60 feet) in places, with colossal blocks of hewn stone. Courtiers climbed 111 steps to reach the top, resting to admire the view over the well-watered plain below.

On the terrace stood two great reception halls or throne-rooms. The great Apadana, 60 metres (200 feet) square internally, was begun by Darius I and finished by his son Xerxes. It covered 0·27 hectares ($\frac{5}{8}$ acre) but the roof was supported by only 36 columns. The secret of this was the use of cedarwood beams; if stone had been used, the columns would have had to stand closer together, and many more would have been required. It has been claimed that 10,000 people could have crowded into the hall to see the king. It is not known where the king's throne stood.

The second great hall, 70 metres (230 feet) square, was built by Xerxes, close to the quarters of the army. It may have been the soldiers' assembly hall, for on the doorway the King on his throne is shown carried by five files of soldiers. It was here that Alexander the Great feasted before he burned down the whole palace complex.

69

Trade and the Phoenicians

The 'Nimrud Ivories' were discovered in 1953, in the north-west palace of King Ashur-nasirpal II of Assyria. Among them were these two plaques, once fixed as ornaments on wooden furniture. The ivory objects were scattered about the rooms during the sack of the palace in about 612 BC. They were made by Phoenician craftsmen and some clearly show the influence of Egyptian art.

The sea linked ancient peoples, through seaborne trade. In the east Mediterranean, Egyptian and Minoan ships plied between the Levant, the Greek islands, and Egypt at the beginning of the second millennium BC. About 1500 BC the Mycenaean civilization, which spread from the mainland of Greece to Crete and the coast of Asia Minor, became one of the dominant Mediterranean sea-powers. The Mycenaeans traded wine, perfumed oils, honey, metal ores, and fine pottery.

About 1200, trade and traders received a series of blows from which the Mycenaeans never recovered. The Sea Peoples, as they are called in Egyptian texts, were perhaps barbarians from central Europe, who took ship across the Mediterranean and were joined by renegades of many nations. They devastated large areas of mainland Greece and the Near East. By the time they met defeat at the hands of Ramesses III of Egypt and were dispersed, they had upset the whole balance of power in the Near East. The economy of the Mycenaean city states was in ruins. The Hittite empire had totally disappeared. Even Egypt was at a low ebb. To replace these great powers, a number of previously insignificant peoples rose to prominence as the first millennium began.

Seaborne trade in the eastern Mediterranean came under the control of the people of the coastal cities of modern Lebanon, Syria, and Israel – the people whom Greeks knew as the Phoenicians – *Phoinikes*, the 'purple men'. This was a reference either to their dark skins, or to the famous Tyrian purple dye used on the cloth that they exported.

The Phoenicians and their homeland

The Phoenicians referred to themselves as Canaanites, *Kinahu* or *Kinana*. They were a Semitic people like the Israelites, who spoke a language akin to Hebrew.

The Phoenician area extended from Tartus in the north perhaps as far south

as Jaffa, some 320 kilometres (200 miles) away. The coastal plain between the sea and the mountains was rarely more than 20 kilometres (12 miles) wide. Because the Phoenicians were confined to this narrow coastal strip of land they took to the sea, using the cedar and fir trees that clad the mountainside to make sturdy boats.

Each Phoenician city was an independent state, sometimes allied with another, usually acting on its own. The four most important cities were Aradus (Ruad), Byblos (Gebeil), Sidon, and Tyre, the southernmost. Aradus was situated on an off-shore island.

Phoenician cities and towns were surrounded by high stone walls with strong towers to protect them from enemies. The wealth that came to them through trade had to be carefully guarded. Houses were of two storeys, built of mudbrick with wooden beams and panelling. High in the

70

PHOENICIANS AT SEA

An Assyrian relief of about 720 BC, showing a Phoenician warship.

When Phoenician sailors departed on a voyage, they knew that they would not return home for months, perhaps even for years, even if they survived storms, rocks, currents, and other perils of the uncharted seas. Navigation was unhurried. The Bible tells how Phoenician ships took three years on the voyage from the Levant to Tarshish in southern Spain.

Ships stayed within sight of land as much as possible. Every night, they were dragged up on shore. Here the crew could drink fresh water, and cook their food over a fire of driftwood. The average day's journey was about 40 kilometres (25 miles).

When autumn gales began, a safe anchorage for the winter would be sought. The sailors would stay there for about six months. The ships would be overhauled and repairs made. The sailors would build huts to live in, and might even sow crops. In early summer, the ships would be launched again. Many particularly favourable sites developed later into colonies where cities were established.

walls were little balconied windows. Stone was used for important buildings and public works such as harbour walls.

An Assyrian king called the Phoenicians:

> *Kings who inhabit the sea, whose fortification walls are the sea, whose outer walls the waves, who ride a ship for a chariot, and have oarsmen harnessed in place of horses.*

As the population of the Levant grew, more land was urgently needed. The Phoenicians looked abroad. In the 11th century BC and later, traders left the

Carthaginians trading with Africans on the island they called 'Cerne', off the coast of Senegal. An island was chosen for these dealings because it was neutral territory. The whole transaction was carried out by a kind of mutually accepted sign language.

THE GREAT VOYAGES

When Hanno set off with 60 ships to sail to the west he probably knew something about the lands beyond the Straits of Gibraltar from accounts of Egyptian voyages 200 years earlier. It was said his expedition carried 30,000 men and women, who were to found new colonies along the Atlantic coasts of Morocco – though no trace has yet been found of the six colonies he claimed to have established.

After Hanno's safe return, he had an account of his travels written on a stele that was set up in the temple of Baal Hammon at Carthage. It was seen and copied down by a Greek traveller before it was destroyed. Hanno sailed from Carthage through the Straits of Gibraltar, and turned south. At 'Soloeis, a Libyan promontory covered with trees' (which must have been near the modern Safi) he had a temple built to the god of the sea. Farther south again, the Carthaginians spent some time at the mouth of the river Draa (near the southern border of Morocco). This was the land of the nomads called Lixitae (pale-skinned Berbers). Inland, Hanno says, there lived 'inhospitable Ethiopians', a term used for Negroes. Taking Berber interpreters on board, Hanno at last sailed on, reaching an island where he established a settlement called Cerne. Hanno's account is unclear but it seems likely that this was near the Senegal River. Hanno sailed up a large river near Cerne. He reached a lake, where 'savages clad in skins of wild beasts' stoned the Carthaginians and stopped them landing. He sailed up another branch of this river, which was 'teeming with crocodiles and hippopotamuses'.

Returning to the sea and sailing farther south along the coast, Hanno came to 'high mountains covered with trees' (probably Cape Verde) and a large gulf (the mouth of the Gambia River). He heard the beating of drums, and saw a great volcano, which he called 'the Chariot of the Gods'. This could be either Kakulima in Guinea (887 metres: 2910 feet) or Mount Cameroon, which at 4075 metres (13,370 feet) is far more impressive. There is at present no means of knowing how far Hanno went; he may have reached Cameroon or Gabon, or have turned back at Sierra Leone.

Somewhere in West Africa, Hanno's ships came to a lake where there was an island full of what the sailors thought were 'savages'.

By far the greater number were women with shaggy bodies, whom our interpreters called gorillas. Chasing them, we were unable to catch any of the men, all of whom got away, defending themselves by throwing stones. But we caught three women, who bit and mangled those who carried them off, being unwilling to follow them. We killed them, however, and flayed them, and brought their skins back to Carthage.

While Hanno was in West Africa, his brother Himilco sailed north from the Straits of Gibraltar for four months. Becalmed in the 'Oestrymnian Islands' (probably Brittany with its rocky inlets), he encountered shallow seas, fog, seaweed, and sea monsters.

Did the Phoenicians or Carthaginians ever reach Cornwall, the source of so much tin? There is no evidence that their ships ever reached Britain, nor have any Carthaginian artefacts ever been found north of Portugal.

Another of the 'Nimrud Ivories'. This head of a young girl had been thrown into a well and was preserved by the wet mud there. It was made (from an exceptionally large tusk) in about 715 BC.

Levant to found colonies in Sicily, North Africa, Sardinia, the Balearic islands, and Spain – even beyond the Straits of Gibraltar on the coasts of Morocco.

Trade

Phoenician traders carried wood to countries such as Egypt which needed timber for building. Glassmaking had been developed in northern Syria during the second millennium BC. From about 600 on the Phoenicians produced almost colourless glass vessels, and beads and little pendants of brilliant colours in the form of human heads. Scarabs and amulets were also made, imitating popular Egyptian goods.

The Phoenicians were renowned for their delicate ivory carving. By the beginning of the first millennium BC, the elephants that had lived in Syria were extinct, and tusks had to be imported from India or Africa. Ivory plaques ornamented wooden furniture (the making of which was another Phoenician speciality) and possibly the inside walls of buildings. Little ivory ornaments and boxes were exported to Assyria, to Greek cities, and to the Etruscan cities in northern Italy.

Metal ore was a particularly important commodity handled by the Phoenicians. It was carried from Tarshish, in southern Spain, to the east Mediterranean lands. How the Phoenicians discovered the rich mineral deposits of southern Spain may never be known, for no Phoenician written documents or histories have survived. Perhaps as early as the 1100s the potential of the area was discovered and a colony was set up at Gades, the modern Cadiz, with its excellent harbour.

The Phoenicians met competition from the Greeks, who founded colonies in southern Italy and eastern Sicily, but the Etruscans (see page 91) were allied with the Phoenicians and kept the Greeks from establishing colonies farther west until 600 BC.

Tyre's greatest colony

The city of Carthage, in Tunisia, was traditionally founded in 814 BC as a staging-post on the long voyage from the Levant to Spain. It was a typical Phoenician choice. A fort to defend the settlement was built on a headland, which also sheltered the area below, where good harbours could be constructed. A spring provided plenty of fresh water. Just inland, there was fertile land where food could be grown.

At first Carthage had very close links with its mother-city, Tyre. In the 600s and 500s it grew into a splendid city, but with few industries of its own. Nearly everything that the Carthaginians used was imported – not only luxury goods but everyday objects as well. From Greek workshops in Rhodes and Samos came little figurines of goddesses holding fans or turtle-doves, and pretty little flasks of perfume. The superstitious could buy amulets from Egypt – little figures of gods from Memphis, and scarabs; glazed unguent flasks shaped like monkeys were imported from Naucratis. There were stalls of glittering and delicate gold jewellery from Phoenician cities. Ships from Tyre called at Carthage on their way home from Spain, laden with metal ores. But the ores went all the way to Tyre, to be made into tools, weapons, and ornaments and shipped out to Carthage again.

There were some workshops at Carthage, but only small objects, of poor workmanship, came from them. The potters of Carthage copied Phoenician forms so faithfully that it is not always possible to distinguish between Carthaginian and imported pots.

At the battle of Himera in Sicily, in 480 BC, the Carthaginians were defeated by their trade rivals the Greeks. After this, links with the east and Tyre (which had lost independence to the Persians) seem to have been cut. Carthage became indeed a 'new capital' which is the literal meaning of *Qart Hadasht*, the Phoenician name of the city. One of the leaders of newly independent Carthage was Hanno,

who was born to a leading Carthaginian family in about 490. He instituted a vigorous policy of action to make Carthage self-sufficient. At home, he declared war against the Berbers of North Africa, and much land was seized in Tunisia. This was divided up among the aristocracy, and farmed to provide food for the growing population – possibly swollen by refugees from Tyre and other Phoenician cities in the east as Persian power forced them to flee. Abroad, great voyages of exploration were undertaken to find new sources of metals, now for Carthage's own use.

The great Atlantic voyages assured Carthaginian supplies of gold from west Africa. Increased amounts of tin and copper were now imported through new links with Portugal and better quality bronze goods, containing more tin, were now made in Carthage. The west was replacing the east as the source of supplies. Carthage seemed set for a rich and prosperous future as a trading power. This, however, was not to be, owing to the rise of a powerful competitor – the city of Rome. The Punic Wars between Carthage and Rome began in 264 BC. They were to end in 146 BC with the total obliteration of Carthage and its people.

The most famous exploit of any Carthaginian is Hannibal's invasion of Italy, especially his crossing of the Alps with his war elephants (see page 90). This silver coin, struck by the Carthaginians in Spain, shows an African elephant – usually regarded in modern times as untameable.

TEMPLES OF SACRIFICED CHILDREN

The Carthaginians offered children as burnt sacrifices to their god Baal Hammon at precincts which are often called *topheths*. This was originally a Phoenician practice, described in the Bible. Josiah destroyed a topheth at Jerusalem, where a man 'might make his son or daughter to pass through the fire to Moloch'. Some scholars think that 'Moloch' was not the name of a god, but referred to the act of sacrifice, as in this inscription on a stele placed with the ashes of a child in Carthage:

That this act be good, agreeable to the gods, and beneficial. To Holy Lord Saturn (Baal Hammon) great sacrifice of night, molchomor; spirit for spirit, blood for blood, life for life.

At Salammbo, close to the harbours in the oldest part of Carthage, a topheth has been excavated. It remained sacred throughout the occupation of Carthage and thousands of children were sacrificed here. Most were under two years of age, although some were as old as twelve years. They were the children of the noblest families – only the best could be offered to the god. They were killed, and the little bodies burned on a funeral pyre. Then the ashes were put into an urn and buried in the precinct. Some were covered with a stone slab, or stele, engraved with cult signs. The custom was said to commemorate Dido.

The Topheth or sacrificial precinct at Salambo.

On the Fringes

On coasts, in mountainous regions, in deserts, and in the cold forests of northern Europe lived peoples with their own distinct ways of life, who were never assimilated by the great civilizations. These peoples are often, to us, rather mysterious. Some had no writing, and for knowledge of their history we must rely on the accounts of more civilized peoples, who may not have understood the people they were writing about; they may even never have met them, but have relied on hearsay. Even where a people left a written record of their own, it may be difficult to fit into the history of the ancient world as a whole.

Though independent – and sometimes fiercely so – these 'fringe peoples' were not isolated. They had contact with others through trade. The constant interaction among these fringe peoples themselves can sometimes be seen in their art; the Thracians and Celts, for example, copied motifs and styles from each other and from many other sources. And the great civiliza-tions could not ignore them; they needed the raw materials – especially metals and minerals – which these people could provide. Luxury goods were an important part of this trade – amber from northern Europe, lapis lazuli and other precious stones from the east. Some fringe peoples also kept up a tenuous contact between the West and the empire it hardly knew – China. The nomadic Scythians were as well known to the Chinese as to the Greeks and Romans. Damascus in Syria was at one time a great market-place to which caravans came, loaded with Chinese silk for sale to Rome.

All the peoples in this chapter (except some of the Celts) eventually succumbed to conquest or disappeared. But although their leaders might be killed by the conquerors the ordinary people often continued to live in much the same way as they had before. They were absorbed into newer nations; but sometimes their traditions live on in surprising ways.

A Scythian electrum vase, from Kul Oba in the USSR. Two men are shown, one trying to extract one of the other's teeth. They are wearing the typical costume of the Scythians, including trousers to keep out the cold.

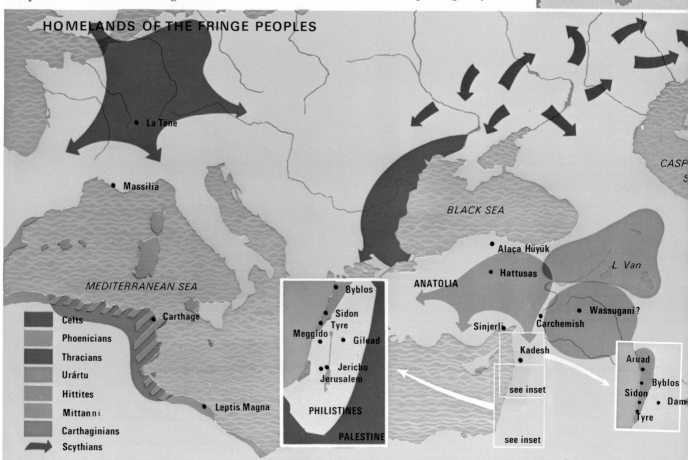

HOMELANDS OF THE FRINGE PEOPLES

Altai Mtns

Lake Balka

La Tène

Massilia

BLACK SEA

MEDITERRANEAN SEA

Alaça Hüyük

Hattusas

L. Van

ANATOLIA

Sinjerli

Wassugani?

Carchemish

CASP

Byblos

Sidon

Tyre

Meggido

Gilead

Kadesh

Aruad

Byblos

Sidon

Dam

Carthage

Jericho

Jerusalem

Tyre

Celts

Phoenicians

Thracians

Urártu

Hittites

Mittanni

Carthaginians

Scythians

Leptis Magna

PHILISTINES

PALESTINE

see inset

see inset

People of Anatolia

The rugged plateau of Anatolia saw the rise of some of the world's first cities. For the period of the Early Bronze Age (c 3000–2000 BC) our knowledge of Anatolian civilization comes almost entirely from artefacts, and the picture that emerges is of a number of different local cultures, sometimes with affinities outside Anatolia. The western area, for instance, is culturally related to the Aegean, while the south-east has much in common with the north Syrian cultures.

After 2000, the archives of the Assyrian merchants in Cappadocia provide a fascinating if incomplete glimpse of the political structure of Central Anatolia: a number of city-states dominating smaller cities in the vicinity, and all recognizing as overlord a 'great prince'.

Around the start of the second millennium the Hittites appeared in Anatolia. As they spoke an Indo-European language (called Nesian) it seems likely that they had migrated from eastern central Europe. But it is not known whether this migration took the form of gradual and peaceful settlement or violent invasion. The Hittite empire was very mixed in population, being made up of several peoples. No less than six languages were spoken at different times, four of them being Indo-European. The group speaking Hurrian must have formed an important part of the population, because Hurrian influence in both Hittite art and religion is very strong.

In Hattusa (Boghazköy), the Hittite capital, were found huge government and temple archives. Here were kept clay tablets, recording in cuneiform treaties with other powers, including Egypt; historical events; and religious practices, including magic and the meaning of omens. These tablets are the oldest known documents in an Indo-European language. The Hittites probably learned cuneiform writing from the north Syrian states, such as Aleppo, adapting the signs for Nesian. They also used a form of hieroglyphic script (not connected with Egyptian hieroglyphics) which was probably used to record one of the other Indo-European languages spoken in Anatolia. These signs were cut into the stones of the entrances to public buildings or beneath figures of gods. Hieroglyphs were also engraved on seal stones.

In the Old Kingdom period (from about 1650 to 1460) the Hittites were constantly at war. They fought the kingdom of Arzawa (probably in south-west Anatolia), conquered north Syria, and invaded Iraq. One

IRON

There is a widespread belief that one of the reasons for the Hittite rise to power was their monopoly of the production of iron. This notion is based on a single passage in a Hittite text, in which a foreign power appears to be asking to be supplied with iron. But this interpretation of the passage is disputed, so in the absence of further and more definite references to iron, or any kind of archaeological evidence, the idea that the Hittites held some kind of secret knowledge of iron-working must be abandoned.

king took Babylon by surprise, entered the city, and removed the statue of the god Marduk. The Hittites owed much of their success in war to the horse and chariot.

In the Empire phase (1460–1180) the Hittites came into contact with the Egyptians in the Levant. Spheres of imperial influence were eventually agreed upon, and the Hittites organized the north Syrian section of their empire by appointing a king at Carchemish who governed the whole of the area. About 1200, the Hittites were overwhelmed by the Phrygians, an Indo-European people from the north. Hittite culture and institutions survived to some extent in their former provinces of Cilicia and north Syria, such as Carchemish and Sinjerli. In the 8th century these Hittite cities became subject to Assyria, and later fell to the Persians.

South of Anatolia lay the Mitannian empire, whose capital was Wassuganni. It was at its height between 1430 and 1350 BC, stretching from the Zagros mountains to the Mediterranean. The population of Mitanni was predominantly Hurrian, but the ruling aristocracy seems to have consisted of Indo-Aryans. One of the reasons for its political predominance in the Near East at this time was the effective use made of the two-wheeled horse-drawn war chariot. Mitanni eventually fell to attacks by the Assyrians (who had been its vassals) and the Hittites.

Palestine and the Israelites

Palestine and the lands around it saw a great deal of movement, as nomads journeyed about the fringes of the Fertile Crescent. But there were also many peoples — mainly Semitic tribes — who had settled down after centuries of intermittent migration. Among these were the Canaanites, the Philistines (after whom Palestine is named), the Aramaeans, the Amorites, the Moabites, and the Israelites. The Phoenicians (see page 70) became a great sea power. The Aramaeans settled in a number of powerful city-states. But most of these peoples were basically farmers — among them the Israelites, the group about whom we know most. The Israelites' passionate belief in the power of their single god above all others led them to preserve their books of history and law (written down from the 8th century BC) through many tribulations. These records have survived to the present day, some as part of the Christian Old Testament. Aided by archaeology, they give us an insight into the lives of people who, apart from the one great difference of their religion, were absolutely typical of the area.

'Israel is ravaged and has no offspring. Palestine is widowed' boasted the Egyptian Pharaoh Merneptah in an inscription recording the success of his wars in Palestine in about 1220 BC. This is the first mention in history of the Israelites. According to the Old Testament, they migrated from Ur in Sumer about 2000, and settled in Palestine. At some time when crops had failed, some of them (like many other tribes) had gone to Egypt, returning after a few generations to Palestine. Merneptah's inscription may indicate that their return happened before 1220.

At the time, the Israelites were farmers. They were stout fighters, carving out a place for themselves among the Canaanite popula-

ALACA HÜYÜK

In 1935 Turkish archaeologists at the site of Alaca Hüyük in central Anatolia found thirteen stone-lined grave pits, dated to about 2200 BC. They contained the burials of men and women, who, to judge from the wealth of the grave-goods, must have been royalty. Diadems, necklaces, and brooches had adorned the dead, and small flat gold plaques had originally been sewn to their garments; around them were placed gold-hilted daggers, copper mirrors, silver cups and boxes. Copper stags, inlaid with gold or silver, originally decorated the wooden bier on which the corpse had rested, and larger disc-shaped standards had marked the corners of the graves. After the body was placed in the pit, wooden beams were positioned over the grave and the whole covered with earth; the remains of oxen found on the burials suggest that a funeral feast was then eaten at the graveside. Unfortunately, nothing of the accompanying settlement site has as yet been found; but the sheer wealth of the burials and the sophisticated metal-working techniques used argue for the presence of a powerful dynasty in the area.

tion in inland Palestine. It was not then the arid land it is today. There were considerable forests on both mountains and plains and wood was an important natural resource, although increasing population led to deforestation. As they became established, the Israelites' villages grew into small walled towns. Water was stored inside the walls in large cisterns, lined with lime mortar. This impervious material was a useful discovery made sometime before 1100 BC.

The greatest time in the Israelites' history was the United Monarchy, from 1000 to 926 BC. About 995, King David captured and refortified Jerusalem, which commands the only north-south route through Palestine.

A late Hittite relief from Aslantepe (Malatya) in Anatolia. A man (left) pours a libation to a god, who stands on a bull. Between the figures are Hittite hieroglyphic signs.

The Scythian Great Goddess seated on a throne, and holding the Tree of Life; part of a wall-hanging in appliqué felt-work, preserved in the frozen tombs of Pazyryk.

The Israelites now came into contact with peoples of the older civilizations. Trade brought exotic goods, and life became more sophisticated. Simple towns grew into cities and foreign ways were adopted. Contact with other lands was encouraged under David's successor, King Solomon, who allied himself with the Phoenicians. He used their ships for his trading expeditions, and skilled Phoenician masons for building his splendid Temple and palace at Jerusalem.

In 926 the Israelite kingdom was divided into Israel (in the north) and Judah (in the south). Omri, King of Israel built himself a new capital at Samaria. On this isolated hill-top he kept the flat summit exclusively for his palace and other royal buildings. A stout wall ran around the summit, supporting a level terrace to increase its area. The palace was decorated and furnished with many ivories carved by Phoenician craftsmen. The town was on the slopes of the hill below the royal buildings, and was surrounded by a wall.

The kingdom of Israel (in the north) lost its independence by becoming an Assyrian province in 720 BC. The southern kingdom of Judah became a vassal of Assyria around the same time, but eventually fell to the Babylonians in 597. The temple at Jerusalem was destroyed and many of the inhabitants were exiled to Babylon.

When the Persians conquered Babylon Cyrus allowed the Israelites to return from exile and to rebuild their Temple at Jerusalem, but they remained under Persian rule. Later, in the time of Alexander the Great and his successors, Persian influence was succeeded by Greek ideas and language. In 64 BC their land became part of the Roman empire.

Urartu

The kingdom of Urartu, or Ararat, flourished between the 800s and 500s BC. Its lands reach from south of the Black Sea in eastern Anatolia, to Tabriz in Azerbaijan. The people were closely related to the Hurrians. The Urartian kings built many cities, each dominated by a citadel on a hill-top to which the people could retreat for safety when the land was invaded from the north by Scythian raiders from the steppes. Within the citadel was the king's palace, a temple and many storerooms. Here, huge jars were set into the floor. Wine, grain, sesame oil, and many other products were stored there, protected by cats.

Metalworkers, potters, and other craftsmen had workshops in the citadel.

Urartian temples were similar to those of classical Greece. Each was built on a platform, and had a pitched roof with a high pediment. In front of the temple was a porch, the roof supported on six columns. Inside the temples were beautiful and precious objects dedicated to the gods. It is not surprising that the doors were secured with elaborate locks. One lock carried off and described by Assyrians weighed about 65 kilograms (145 pounds). Parts were in the shape of winged demons, each holding a curved sword, and trampling on dogs with bared teeth. Three important gods were Haldi, the royal warrior god; Teisheba, a storm god; and Shivini, the sun-god.

Huge engineering works were undertaken to bring water many miles to the fields and an aqueduct 80 kilometres (50 miles) long brought drinking water to Tushpa, a city beside the salty Lake Van. Such irrigation work allowed the Urartian farmers to grow plums, grapes, pomegranates, cherries, apples, and quinces as well as wheat and barley. They kept cattle, and two kinds of sheep. The weaving of linen and woollen cloth was a major industry. Urartians wore long tunics, dyed and embroidered, and long leather boots with laces.

The prosperous kingdom survived many wars. Great horses were bred for the army, and the Urartian archers were famous. But early in the 6th century BC, the Urartian kingdom was destroyed by Scyths and Medes, and became part of the kingdom of the Medes, and later, of the Persians.

The Scyths

The Scyths, or Scythians, were a nomad people of the Asian steppes. In the 8th century BC they were driven westwards by fierce neighbours, and many moved into south Russia. Some crossed the Caucasus and settled in Armenia, bringing about the downfall of the kingdom of Urartu. Some settled in north Iran, fighting the Medes. Tribes of Scyths moved restlessly about the Near East. Some settled in the steppes between the Caspian and Aral Seas, and were the ancestors of the Parthians. In the 4th century BC, Scyths also invaded eastern and south-eastern Europe. Their burials have been found from Prussia to the Balkans.

The Scyths successfully held their lands in south Russia until the 2nd century AD when they were wiped out by the Sarmatians.

The Scyths were an Indo-European people, speaking an Iranian language. They moved swiftly from one grazing ground to another, the men on horseback, riding without stirrups. Women and children travelled in large covered waggons with four to six wheels, roofed with felt. The tops of the waggons may have been made to lift off to serve as tents. These were comfortably furnished with portable belongings: hangings, rugs, and cushions. Felt hangings and saddle-cloths were covered with brightly coloured appliqué embroidery with designs of vigorous birds, stags, and fantastic animals. Fish and meat were cooked in metal cauldrons, and a kind of haggis was eaten. Vegetables included garlic, beans, and onions. Kumis (mares' milk) was drunk and made into cheese.

The Scyths had no temples, but they venerated the burial places of their ancestors. These were visited twice a year, when new burials were made. This meant that when a chief died, his body had to be preserved. The internal organs were removed, and the body cavity filled with herbs and then sewn up. The body was carried in procession, to be buried with a long and splendid ceremony.

The large grave chamber was at the bottom of a shaft up to 13 metres (42 feet) deep. The chief's body was lowered into place, and his head wife and their servants were killed to accompany him. His horses, decked in their finest harness and saddles, were killed and placed outside the burial chamber. Food and drink were left for the chief and his wife.

Some Scythian tombs have by chance survived, wonderfully preserved. They are at Pazyryk, in the Altai Mountains in Siberia. Soon after the burials they were accidentally sealed with a layer of ice, and all the organic remains that would normally decay were frozen. Cushions, hangings, and saddlecloths (one made of Chinese silk) were preserved. But perhaps the most exciting things preserved were the bodies of the dead, their limbs covered with elaborate blue tattoos.

The Thracians

The ancient Greeks had a number of stories about a mysterious people to the north of them, the Thracians. Ancient Thrace covered a huge area of south-east Europe, and there were also some Thracian tribes in Anatolia.

The Thracians never established great cities; their culture suffered a great setback from at least three great invasions about 1200, which impoverished the land. Their tribes were ruled by chiefs, who acknowledged a single king who was also their high priest. The chiefs lived in fortified settlements, surrounded by a warrior aristocracy who, like the Scythians, decorated their bodies with tattoos. They were supported by a farming population. Thracian coastal lands were so rich that a number of Greek city states came to be almost totally dependent on corn supplies from Thrace. The women did all the work in the fields; children were sold as slaves in bad seasons.

At the courts of the king and his chiefs, there were craftsmen who made beautiful vessels in gold, silver, and bronze. (There were rich mineral deposits in the Thracian mountains.) Gifts and loot came to Thracian

The Vulcitran treasure, a Thracian hoard of the 12th or 13th century BC. It is the largest hoard found in Bulgaria. Below: The Thracian Horseman hunting a boar with his dog. Many carvings have been found of this god. His flying cloak suggests the speed of his horse.

Part of the Gundestrop Bowl, a silver ritual vessel found in Denmark. It shows a god (possibly the Celtic 'Lord of the Animals').

courts, from Greece, Persia, and from the Scyths of the Russian steppes. Thracian craftsmen were inspired by the different shapes and patterns of these foreign objects. In the period between 525 and 280 BC, the Thracians traded with the many cities built along the coast by Greek settlers. Chiefs bought Persian cloth and Greek and Persian metalwork, and these valuables were buried with them under mounds of earth.

Chiefs and their warriors went to battle in bronze helmets and cuirasses. Fixed to their chests were silver-gilt plaques; their shins were covered with elaborate greaves. Their wives wore golden ear-rings, necklets, and large bracelets. A gold decorated band, or pectoral, was pinned across the chest by a pair of brooches. From these hung tinkling ornaments on chains.

After the death of the strong King Lysimachus in 280 BC, the Thracians were weakened by internal wars, and their brilliant culture declined. They also suffered at the hands of the Celts, who settled in the country. From the 2nd century BC onwards, the Thracians were to some extent incorporated in the Roman empire.

The Celts

The same Greek traders who knew the Thracians in the 5th century BC were familiar with people in central and western Europe whom they called the Keltoi. This term was applied to a loose grouping of many tribes, whom we now know as Celts. In the 4th century, as the population grew and weather conditions worsened, a number of Celtic tribes migrated south and then east. Many settled in north Italy; they sacked Rome and later invaded Greece, from where they were driven out after prolonged fighting, until Celts were found in Spain in the west and as far east as Anatolia.

The Celts were good farmers, keeping cattle, sheep, and pigs (they were very fond of pork). They grew wheat and barley in small fields. Their farmers invented the balanced sickle, the iron blade curving backwards from the handle. Seed corn was stored in deep sealed pits; grain for daily use was kept in large storage jars, in granaries raised on stilts to keep the grain away from rats. A herb of the mustard family called woad was also grown, for the blue dye that could be extracted from its leaves. This and other vegetable dyes were used to make brightly coloured tunics, trousers, and cloaks for men, and long dresses for women. Some Celts tattooed themselves with woad.

Farmers and their families lived in large wooden farmhouses, constructed of massive tree trunks supporting a thatched roof. Walls were of wattle and daub. The life of chiefs and their warriors was very different. They lived in wooden houses inside hillforts up to 24 hectares (60 acres) in extent, defended by massive timber-framed ramparts and deep ditches. Their days were spent in hunting deer and wild boar, or in raiding the cattle of their neighbours. Sometimes they duelled with warriors from neighbouring tribes. Celts were fearless in battle, and had no dread of death. They considered it better to die young in combat, leaving behind a glorious name to be celebrated by bards, than to live a quiet life and die in inglorious old age by the fire.

Celtic craftsmen in bronze, gold, and iron produced masterpieces in their dark, smoky little workshops. They travelled from one chief to another over the Celtic lands, acquiring new designs as they saw metalwork from Italy, Greece, and Thrace. About 450 BC, Celtic craftsmen in the Rhineland developed the beautiful 'La Tène' art, that quickly spread through Celtic Europe. (This was named after a site in Switzerland where much fine metalwork was discovered.) It was used to ornament armour and the possessions of the rich – it is not found on the humbler goods of the poor farmers.

The Celts did not write. Their laws, stories, and religious rituals were handed down by word of mouth. Their priests and lawgivers were the mysterious druids; a boy who wished to become a druid had to train for 20 years, and much time would have been spent in learning by heart. The Celts worshipped in sacred groves and in sanctuaries which were built of stone and ornamented with skulls and human heads. Some deities, such as the sun-god Lug and the Three Mothers, were worshipped by many tribes, and each tribe worshipped its own local deities. The Celtic year was divided by festivals.

The Celts were never a united people. They quarrelled easily, and tribes were separated by imagined slights and petty feuds. This was a fatal weakness when they were opposed by disciplined Roman armies. Gradually the tribes were brought within the Roman empire. It was only in Britain north of Hadrian's Wall, and in Ireland, that the Celtic way of life went on unaltered.

The Hellenistic Era

Alexander of Macedon inherited a shaky position when his father died in 336 BC. Philip had left huge debts, and little in the royal treasury. What was more, his control of Greece had only been established for two years. Greek opponents of Macedonian rule saw a good chance to revolt: Alexander was only 20, and one of them described him as 'just a boy'. But the performance of this young man, scarcely 150 centimetres (5 feet) tall, was to be a profound shock not only to Greece but to the entire civilized world of the eastern Mediterranean.

The Greek city of Thebes revolted against Macedon. Alexander's troops besieged it and, when Theban soldiers were retreating through a city-gate after a skirmish, the Macedonians followed them in before the gate could be closed. Thebes was captured. After much slaughter, its surviving population, adults and children, was sold as slaves. This official terrorism by Alexander had its effect: it was some time before another important Greek state dared to rebel against him.

But Alexander was not looking for a period of quiet prosperity, in which to pay off his father's debts. Instead, he took on still more debts in order to equip a great new expedition. If it failed, he would be ruined. But if it succeeded, he would become the richest and most powerful man in the known world. He was aiming to conquer the Persian empire.

When Alexander announced his new crusade, many Greeks no doubt thought that they had 'seen it all before'. Earlier in the 4th century Greek hoplites had operated with much success in Asia Minor, but the Persian empire there had managed to remain more or less intact. But Alexander's forces were greater than those of earlier times. His main body of infantry is said to have contained about 12,000 Macedonians and the same number of Greeks. With their heavy armour, carrying pikes about 4 metres (13 feet) long, and guarded by numerous cavalry, they formed one of the most frightening armies of the ancient world. In 334 Alexander led them into north-western Asia Minor.

Alexander leads a charge at the battle of Issos (333), where he defeated the Persian king, Darius. The subject was a popular one in antiquity. This version of it is part of a mosaic at Pompeii, made about 100 BC. The mosaic may reproduce a painting by Philoxenos of Eretria, a Greek artist working not long after Alexander's death.

Gold coin from Egypt showing the head of Ptolemy I Soter, one of Alexander's senior generals. In the wars which followed Alexander's death Ptolemy made himself king of Egypt. His descendants ruled Egypt until it became a Roman province in 30 BC.

Alexander's empire stretched from the Mediterranean to India. On his death it was divided between his generals.

Alexander's soldiers were made more loyal and enthusiastic by the courage of their commander. Unlike many generals, Alexander did not direct his men from a safe position in the rear. In the first great battle of his Asiatic campaign, at the river Granikos, he was in the thick of the fighting, and made himself a clear target to the enemy by wearing white wings on his helmet. Persian noblemen showed great courage too in their attempts to kill this young warrior who was threatening their empire. Alexander was narrowly saved from death at their hands.

After success at the Granikos, the Macedonian army passed into northern Syria. There it first encountered the main force of the Persian empire, under an

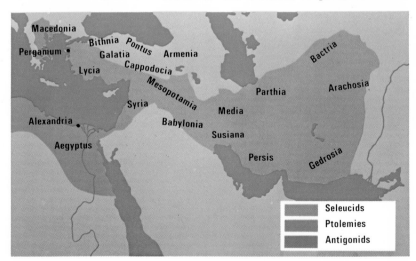

Macedonia
Bithnia Pontus
Pergamum • Galatia Armenia
Lycia Cappodocia
Bactria
Mesopotamia
Syria Parthia Arachosia
Alexandria • Media
Babylonia
Aegyptus Susiana
Persis Gedrosia

Seleucids
Ptolemies
Antigonids

Gold coin showing the head of Arsinoë II (316–271 BC), sister and second wife of Ptolemy II Philadelphos of Egypt. She was perhaps more powerful than her husband, and a province of Egypt was named after her.

inexperienced king, Darius III. At the battle of Issos (333) the Persians fought on ground which did not suit their cavalry, and lost. Alexander, after capturing the enemy's naval base at Tyre, moved into Egypt. Capturing this rich and unstable province of the Persian empire, he founded (in 331) the best-known of his many new cities. There were eventually to be 16 or more of these 'Alexandrias'; and Alexandria-by-Egypt was to become the chief city of the eastern Mediterranean.

Marching east to the heart of the Persian empire, Alexander finally broke the power of Darius at Gaugamela (331). In this battle, the Macedonian army was kept under close control until the Persians, in the course of a manoeuvre, left a gap in their lines. Alexander's cavalry poured through: the Persian forces were split and defeated. King Darius fled, shortly to be murdered by one of his own nobles.

But Alexander could not cease to conquer. Conquest was obviously fascinating to him, and kept adding to his prestige. He must have known that a huge empire would be difficult to govern, yet he pushed his troops as far as north-western India. There, weary and fearing to meet the great herds of war-elephants said to be owned by Indian princes, his men refused to go farther.

As the new master of the Persian empire, Alexander decided to unite Persians, Greeks, and Macedonians in a new ruling race. Many young Persians were recruited to his army. He arranged for thousands of Greek and Macedonian soldiers to marry women from the Persian territories. His commanders were encouraged to do the same. And Alexander himself set an example by marrying Roxane, daughter of a nobleman from Bactria, in the eastern Persian empire. She was said to be the most beautiful woman in Asia. But since her husband was now the most powerful man in Asia, somebody was bound to find this a pleasant thing to say, even if it was obviously untrue!

Anxious to keep the respect of his Persian subjects, Alexander dressed and acted like a Persian monarch, although Macedonian and Greek followers were greatly offended at having to kiss their hand to him in the traditional Persian gesture of obeisance. When he died of illness at Babylon, in 323, eminent Persians mourned his passing as much as any.

The Successor Kingdoms

At the time of her husband's death, Roxane was pregnant. But her child, though male, never inherited the empire of his father.

This mosaic floor at Pella shows the god Dionysus riding a panther, and dates from the end of the 4th century BC. Pella was the home of the Macedonian kings and the birthplace of Alexander the Great. Mosaics like this, made from natural coloured pebbles, have been traced as far back as the 5th century BC.

Like many boy princes in history, he was murdered by ambitious elders. Alexander's domains were split into a number of kingdoms, ruled at first by his former generals. These Successor Kingdoms are called Hellenistic, because in the wake of Alexander's conquests the culture of Greece – Hellas – was spread through much of their population. A dialect of Greek, called the *Koiné* – the 'common language' – became the chief language of the eastern Mediterranean world. It was in this form of Greek that the New Testament of the Christians was written.

The Antigonid rulers became established in Macedonia, while Seleukos, one-time commander of Alexander's shieldbearers, set up a dynasty centred on Mesopotamia and northern Syria. Other kingdoms emerged in Asia Minor and in the far east of Alexander's former domains. But the richest and most powerful Hellenistic kingdom was set up in Egypt – under Ptolemy I, once Alexander's intelligence officer. It was fittingly symbolic that Ptolemy managed to get control of the embalmed body of Alexander, which was displayed for centuries in Alexandria, the Ptolemaic capital. The dynasty of Ptolemy lasted until 30 BC, when its most famous member, Queen Cleopatra, fell to Rome.

Hellenistic history is often difficult and sometimes impossible to reconstruct. The literature of the time has a disappointing shortage of contemporary comment. Perhaps many intelligent persons, who might in other circumstances have written about their own times, were put off by fear of offending their rulers if they spoke frankly. Alexander had his own historian, Kallisthenes, put into prison, where he died. Another Hellenistic writer, resenting his rulers in their royal purple, compared them with the purple marks on the body of a whipped slave: he was crucified for his impertinence. A third man, who made a rude joke in verse about the marriage of a Ptolemy, was drowned by the royal admiral. Blunt comment could be extremely dangerous.

Most of the information we do have about the Hellenistic period is concerned with Egypt. We know that Alexandria under the Ptolemies became for some a place of elegant living, invention, and scholarship. How was the wealth created which made this possible?

This silver Persian dish shows a Parthian archer delivering his famous 'Parthian shot' behind him as his horse wheeled away from the enemy.

THE PARTHIANS
The Seleucid dynasty in Persia was not to last as long as the Ptolemies in Egypt. In about 250 BC the eastern part of their lands fell to the Parthians, a nomadic people from southeast of the Caspian Sea. The Parthians eventually established an empire which stretched from Bactria to the Euphrates and continued despite repeated Roman invasions until AD 226, when they were defeated by the Sassanians, a Persian dynasty.

The Parthian empire was feudal in structure — consisting of provinces governed by vassal princes on behalf of a Parthian 'king of kings' — not as strongly centralized as other empires. It was dominated by a Parthian aristocracy, who amassed great wealth and owned thousands of serfs. These aristocrats led the armies, which were in two divisions, heavy cavalry and mounted archers. The heavy cavalry, horses and riders, wore a complete armour of metal scales, and charged the enemy with long lances. But far more famous were the Parthian mounted archers, whose skill at riding and accuracy of shot became a legend.

The wealth of Egypt

Egypt had an immense and impoverished labour force, which for much of the time worked for its Ptolemaic ruler. Peasants were required to give the Ptolemies fixed amounts of the grain they produced. It has been said that there were two great rivers running through Egypt – the Nile, and a stream of wheat pouring down to the royal granary at Alexandria. Many of the

Reconstruction of the Acropolis at Pergamum in Asia Minor. From the wars that followed Alexander's death Pergamum emerged as the capital of a powerful kingdom and a great centre of Hellenistic culture. The dramatic grouping of the monumental, terraced buildings was the work of a series of architects during the 2nd century BC.

poor were forbidden even to leave their places of work, for fear that the economy would be disrupted. A high official in 3rd-century Egypt wrote that 'no one is allowed to do what he wants, but everything is arranged for the best'.

But hard-pressed workers often did run away. This could be a form of industrial bargaining. A note from some dyke-guardians – workers looking after one of the important waterways built in Egypt for irrigation and transport – complained that they had not been properly paid: 'The canal is full, so you had better pay up. If we are not paid, we shall run away. We are worn out.'

Other producers were even less fortunate. In the Ptolemaic gold-mines slaves, criminals, and prisoners of war worked in dreadful conditions. Young men, wearing lamps on their heads, mined by hand; children dragged out the ore, which was ground at mills worked by women, completely naked and under the lash of armed guards. The guards could not speak the language of their prisoners: the authorities did not want sympathetic communication between them.

Alexandria
The most famous library of the ancient world was founded at Alexandria by Ptolemy I. By the 1st century BC it may have contained about 700,000 rolls of papyrus and parchment. Knowledge of

The writing material papyrus (from which the word 'paper' is derived) was made from an Egyptian water-plant. Much of it has survived in the Egyptian sands – preserving private letters as well as fragments of literary texts. Some inscribed papyrus was reused to encase the embalmed bodies of sacred crocodiles.

A large library of papyrus and parchment rolls like that of Alexandria would be especially helpful to students and authors because of the high cost of producing such texts. Each roll had to be inscribed by hand, by an expensively trained slave. A large private library would have been far beyond the means of most people.

Hellenistic jewellery. The rich materials and craftsmanship of these earrings suggest something of the enormous wealth released into the Greek world as a result of Alexander's conquest of the Persian empire.

earlier culture was greatly respected, and commentaries, both learned and foolish, were produced to elucidate literature of the Classical Period. Hellenistic poets made many references to ancient myths, as they anxiously tried to show how educated they were.

The poet Apollonios of Rhodes, who became Ptolemy's librarian at Alexandria, produced one of the first love-stories in European literature, about the mythical heroine Medea, and her doomed passion for Jason. In this passage from the story thoughts of her love are keeping Medea awake:

Sleep came to her not even for a little while, but her heart was in a whirl of grief. She was like a woman who works wretchedly hard: one who toils at her spindle in the night; who is widowed

ment of 40,091 kilometres (24,901 miles). Such studies, unlike history, could be pursued safely under autocratic government – though one astronomer thought it tactful to name a constellation after Queen Berenike, the wife of Ptolemy III.

The mechanical inventions of Hellenistic times are also impressive. The Alexandrian Ktesibios designed a water-organ: pressure from a hand-pump drove water into a chamber, displacing air which was thus forced up the organ pipes, enabling a tune to be played. Heron of Alexandria designed an underground machine which, by displacing water, caused temple doors to open as if by a miracle. Heron also knew about cogwheels, gears and camshafts. A device called an aeolipile employed the pressure of steam to turn a sphere.

But such machines remained little more than toys. The Alexandrians had no industrial revolution: inventors seem to have felt no great need to devise labour-saving equipment. The cheapness of slave labour may help to explain this. Also, to be concerned with industrial production was thought degrading by intellectuals: such work was fit only for the poorest citizens, and slaves.

Hellenistic art

Hellenistic painting is best illustrated from Pompeii and its neighbouring towns in south-west Italy. Here the volcanic disaster of AD 79 accidentally preserved many delightful works in the Hellenistic style. These paintings show, like Alexandrian literature, an interest in rural landscape and in mythology.

The sculpture of Hellenistic times is famous for its realism and restless

Ruins of the massive funerary monument constructed at Nimrud Dağ, in southern Turkey, by King Antiochos I of Commagene (1st century BC). Of mixed Macedonian and Persian descent, Antiochos consciously blended Persian and Greek elements in the huge figures of gods, of which only the heads remain – Zeus, for example, was identified with Ahura Mazda.
Below: Muse playing a zither, from the 1st century BC. The sinuous and expressive lines of the figure reflect Hellenistic taste for flowing, often dramatic art.

and, with her fatherless children grizzling around her, lets a tear fall at the thought of the harsh fate which has overtaken her. In the same way, Medea's cheeks grew wet . . .

Theokritos of Syracuse, who himself spent time in Alexandria, made famous some highly sentimental poetry about country life. It was from Theokritos that later European literature derived the idea of nymphs and shepherds – happy country folk, idling under the trees and composing love songs.

This fiction is a long way from the reality of the Egyptian dyke-workers, sending the strike notice to their employer. Perhaps it was living in the great city of Alexandria, with its population of several hundred thousand, which made Theokritos and his audience enjoy such extravagant fantasies about the countryside.

Science, and especially mathematics, flourished under the Ptolemies. The geometer Euclid wrote so successfully that until the 20th century the word 'Euclid' *meant* geometry. The astronomer Aristarkhos of Samos argued, against the majority view, that the Earth went round the Sun, rather than *vice versa*. Eratosthenes of Cyrene calculated that the circumference of the Earth was 39,690 kilometres (24,662 miles) – which is strikingly close to the modern measure-

A form of Hellenistic literature much respected nowadays is the epigram — poetry which aimed to communicate, in a very few words, a vivid picture of beauty or sadness. Many such poems were composed in the style of epitaphs, lines upon a tomb:
I am the tomb of a shipwrecked man. But, stranger, sail on.
For the other ships sailed on, when we were lost.
Other epigrams dealt with love and women:
Rose-girl, fair as a rose is, what do you come to sell?
Is it yourself, or your roses? Or them and yourself as well?

character. Earlier, Classical, sculpture had sometimes shown violent scenes, like the battle between Lapiths and Centaurs represented on the Athenian Parthenon. But not even these had always had the same grim detail as in the Hellenistic statue of a Gaulish chief, killing himself over the dead body of his wife.

Encroaching Romans

Gradually the Hellenistic kingdoms were conquered by Rome. Macedonia became a Roman province in 146 BC, after its heavily armed formations had proved too unwieldy in the face of versatile Roman legions. In 133 the western Asiatic kingdom of Pergamum was left to Rome by the will of its deceased ruler. The Seleucid territory dwindled away after Rome, in 163, had forced its monarch to cripple his war-elephants, once the symbol and instrument of Seleucid power.

By 48 BC only Egypt of the great Hellenistic kingdoms remained. In that year Julius Caesar, then the most powerful man in the Mediterranean world, came to Alexandria to extend his power – and very nearly came to grief. He had brought only a small force of soldiers, under-estimating the fierce defence which the people of the city would make for their boy king, Ptolemy XIII. At one point the ruler of Rome had to swim for his life in an Alexandrian waterway.

Ptolemaic Egypt survived for a while. Its last queen, Cleopatra VII, tried to insure herself against Rome by having love affairs with the most powerful Romans. Julius Caesar probably had a child by her. After Caesar's death, Mark Antony gained control of the eastern Roman empire, and Cleopatra formed a partnership with him, military as well as sexual. Cleopatra and Antony gave their children Roman provinces to govern: it was rumoured that they intended to make Alexandria, instead of Rome, the formal capital of the Roman empire.

But Roman forces were divided; and Cleopatra had backed the losing side. In 31 she and Antony were defeated in the naval battle of Actium, off western Greece. Returning to Egypt, they killed themselves, Cleopatra dying by the bite of a small snake which was said to make the soul immortal. Her kingdom, and the whole Roman empire, now belonged to the victorious Octavian – who shortly renamed himself Augustus.

But where Hellenistic military power failed, the culture of Hellenism succeeded. The literature, art, and thought of educated Romans became largely Greek in form. The same Roman poet who, in the age of Augustus, condemned the dead Cleopatra as 'a monster of fate' admitted that the Greeks with their culture had captured the minds of their fierce Roman captors.

In the late 3rd century BC the forces of Pergamum defeated Celtic ('Gaulish') troops in Asia Minor. Rather than be captured, the Celts often preferred suicide. Here a Celtic soldier is shown, with the somewhat horrific realism of Hellenistic art, killing himself over the dead body of his wife.

The walls of Roman villas were often decorated with elaborate paintings in the Hellenistic style – sometimes with the intention of making a small room seem larger. Here is a scene from a Pompeiian wall-painting showing a young woman being initiated, by flagellation, into the cult of the god Dionysus.

83

The Gods of Greece and Rome

Athene, the virgin goddess of wisdom, the arts, and war. Here she bears the snake-wreathed head of the gorgon Medusa, the sight of which turned opponents to stone.

Zeus, as portrayed in the Classical Period on a coin of Elis. Homeric tales of Zeus's wild behaviour were still told at this time, but he was by now often imagined as a more stern and just personality.

Xenophanes, an Eastern Greek of the 6th century, made an impressive observation about religions. He noted that Ethiopians portrayed their gods as being like themselves – 'with black skin and snub noses'. So did the people of Thrace: their gods had blue-grey eyes and red hair. And, said Xenophanes, 'if horses and cows had hands or could draw, they would portray gods in the image of horses and cows'.

The Greeks themselves believed in many divinities: these gods too were formed partly in the image of human rulers. The most powerful of them, Zeus, was male, just as Greek rulers were. He and other divinities were commonly thought to have a human shape. But because Greeks disagreed as to what was good behaviour, they had conflicting ideas about how divinities acted. Some of these ideas were similar to those of Christianity and Judaism. Others would be scandalous nowadays. Xenophanes protested that poets had attributed to the gods 'everything which among men brings blame and disgrace: stealing, adultery, and cheating each other'. God, he said, was 'in no way like mortals, either in body or in thought': 'all of him sees, all thinks, all hears'. But an Athenian, Kritias, wrote that the idea that the gods knew everything was the false invention of a clever man, who wished to deter secret evil-doing.

Several of the best-known Greek divinities are mentioned in the Linear B writings of the late Mycenaean civilization. Oil, honey, wheat and animals are sacrificed to them. But the first very detailed and colourful picture of gods in action comes with the homeric poems. Here Zeus and the other divinities do not live up to present-day notions of god. Their behaviour is more like that of modern comic-strip characters such as Superman and Batman, though perhaps Superman and Batman are rather less selfish!

The gods of Homer

The home of the homeric gods is on Mount Olympus, on the north-eastern Greek mainland. There they live in great luxury. In the Trojan war the gods take different sides. Poseidon, for instance, is opposed to Troy, because he had once done work for the Trojans and been cheated of his wages. When divinities come down to intervene in the fighting they are not always successful. Aphrodite fights the mortal Diomedes, but is wounded: Diomedes threateningly tells her to be off, though he knows she is a goddess. In pain, Aphrodite flies in a chariot back to Olympus, where Zeus smiles and tells her to make love, not war: 'Warlike deeds are not yours to perform, my child. Attend instead to the delightful activities of marriage.'

The goddess Hera, wishing the Trojans to be harder pressed than her husband Zeus will allow, decides to deceive him. Zeus will first be overcome with desire for his wife, then will go to sleep in her arms, leaving the enemies of Troy more free to make progress. The *Iliad* describes how Hera makes herself beautiful for Zeus:

First she cleansed her lovely skin with the substance which brings immortality, and anointed herself with a perfume made from olive oil. As it was stirred in the bronze-floored house of Zeus, its fragrance reached both to heaven and earth. She combed her hair, and plaited the shining locks. Then she put on a richly embroidered robe, made for her by the goddess Athene, and fastened it at the breast with brooches of gold. She put on a belt with a hundred tassels, and in her pierced earlobes put earrings which shone elegantly. Then she donned a fine new headscarf, fair as the sun. And on her feet she fastened beautiful sandals.

Hera succeeds in her plan; although chief god, Zeus can be deceived. In this he is unlike the gods of later religions: even in Classical Greece it was insisted that Zeus 'saw everything'.

The homeric poems were meant to please an aristocratic audience, and the divinities in them seem to reflect aristocratic ideals. The gods have fine food and drink, and live in a splendid palace. They have fighting to intervene in, and females of lower status to court or prey upon. The goddess Circe, like a Greek noblewoman, has servants in her home to attend her. And the beautification of Hera is modelled on that of an aristocratic lady.

The judgement of the gods

In most of the *Iliad* it is not easy to find any sign that Zeus is concerned to enforce justice on Earth. But in later Greek literature the gods, like the supermen in modern comics, are strongly on the side of justice. Such literature seems to reflect the ideals of a poorer section of society, of people who dream of supernatural protection from the injustices of more powerful men. But the aristocrats who listened to the *Iliad were* the more powerful men. They preferred to imagine the gods as like themselves, pleasure-loving individuals not much troubled by conscience.

The unaristocratic Hesiod, who resented the injustice of 'bribe-devouring judges', liked to believe that Zeus did punish the wicked on Earth. He stated that Zeus had 'thrice ten thousand' invisible watchers, to detect injustice. According to Hesiod, it was common for a whole community to be punished by the gods for the sins of only one person.

Centuries after Hesiod's time, in 415 BC, statues of the god Hermes at Athens were mysteriously defaced at night. A terrible panic resulted: several men were executed, as the Athenians tried to prevent Hermes from acting like a jealous mortal ruler, and taking revenge on the whole city. It seemed certain, too, that a god would intervene on Earth to punish a murderer. An accused man argued to an Athenian jury that he could not really be guilty of murder, because if he had been he would have suffered a catastrophe while on a recent voyage.

There were many stories about punishments suffered in an afterlife. One great offender, Tantalus, was afflicted by thirst. Tempting fruit and a lake of water were put close to him, but whenever he moved towards them, they slipped 'tantalizingly' out of reach. Grave goods found from Mycenaean times show that an afterlife was thought by many to be possible, if not certain. However the picture of life in Hades, the underground kingdom of the dead, could be a gloomy one. In the *Odyssey*, the spirit of the dead Achilles announces that it is better even to be a wretchedly poor man on Earth than to have the highest position in Hades. The ghosts of the dead are shown in this poem as feeble, flittering things, needing to drink the blood of sacrificed animals before they can speak.

In Classical Greece it does not seem that there was widespread

A gold krater or wine cup showing <u>Dionysus</u>, god of wine, crowned with vines, with <u>Ariadne</u>. The wild orgies associated with the worship of Dionysus often posed a threat to public order and states took measures to limit the worst excesses.

This figure in relief of the goddess Athene, from about 470 BC, shows the goddess mourning, with her helmet pushed back from her face.

The Venus de Milo *is one of the best known of all classical statues. Found on the island of Melos in 1820, it dates from the late 2nd century BC, and represents the Greek goddess of love Aphrodite, known to the Romans as Venus.*

confidence in an afterlife. Some cults did promise their members favoured treatment beyond the grave. Athenians were proud to have such a cult in their own territory at Eleusis, where the Earth-goddess, Demeter, and her daughter, Persephone, were worshipped. And sacred texts attributed to the legendary singer, Orpheus, spoke of a delightful existence after death. Gold plates inscribed in Greek, and found in a grave in southern Italy, even tell the dead person how to navigate the roads in the underworld. But far more common are signs that the gods were thought to reward and punish people not after death, but while they lived on Earth.

Foretelling the future

To find out what the gods planned to do, and what they knew of the future and past, was a very important part of life in the Classical Period. Impressive and mysterious events, such as eclipses, earthquakes, and plagues, were thought to be the work of divinities: there were many soothsayers who claimed to interpret them. Excessive happiness and prosperity were thought especially likely to provoke the intervention of jealous gods. Shrines which issued, for a fee, prophecies and other statements supposedly from a god, drew visitors from great distances. Lead strips have been found at the shrine of Zeus and Dione, at Dodone in north-west Greece, bearing questions which ordinary people asked the divinities: 'Gerioton asks Zeus whether he should marry'; 'Did Dorkilos steal the cloth?'; 'Shall I be a fisherman?'; 'Lysanias asks Zeus and Dione whether the child with which Annyla is pregnant is his'.

The most famous prophetic shrine was at Delphi in central Greece. Here a priestess called the Pythia became possessed by the god Apollo. Her inspired ravings were supposed to contain a message from Apollo concerning the will of his father, Zeus.

City-states and individuals sent to Delphi for guidance on matters of high importance. And the shrine took care not to issue prophecies which could be proved wrong: if it lost its reputation for truthfulness, and ceased to be visited, priests and attendants would lose their living. Delphic predictions, therefore, were commonly vague. That way if someone followed advice from Delphi, but still came to grief, it could be claimed that the advice had been correct, but had been misinterpreted. Like prophecy in many ages, Delphic prediction was especially vague about *when* the events foretold were to occur.

But visitors would not come to hear pure vagueness. Delphi needed to give some fairly clear statements and hints. Modern scholars have suspected that the Delphic authorities kept a network of good informants in different cities, to help the shrine give sensible and acceptable advice.

These pressures on Delphi can be seen at work on the eve of the great Persian invasion of 480. The Pythia told the Athenians that there would be deaths at Salamis, though she was vague about the timing. They might be at seed time or at harvest. The suggestion was that there would be a battle at Salamis, but no hint was given as to who would win. More helpfully, however, the shrine made clear that the Athenians should flee, and that their city would be captured and wrecked. Delphi said too that only a wooden wall would survive, and this expression pointed fairly clearly to the Athenian fleet.

The Athenians took the advice to evacuate their city, and resisted with almost all their forces by sea. Without divination they might well not have done so: the more dangerous strategy of defending Athens itself was very tempting.

Modern writers have usually thought that the Greeks were too intelligent to let religious prophecy really affect their important actions. This view is wrong. The power of prophecy is shown most clearly in the late 5th century, when the Athenian armada invaded Sicily. The historian Thucydides, who lived through this period, says that men using religious prophecy in 415 made the Athenians hope to conquer Sicily. By 413 the expedition had clearly failed, and most Athenians were eager to sail home. But when they were ready to leave, there was an eclipse of the Moon: the soothsayers interpreted it as a divine indication that to leave immediately would be especially dangerous. Accepting this argument, the majority of Athenians now demanded to delay. It was this delay which allowed them to be trapped and utterly defeated. Religious prophecy had very likely saved the Athenians in 480, but in 413 it made possible the collapse of their empire.

Festivals

Religious festivals were some of the most exciting and colourful occasions of Greek life. The Olympic games were held in honour of Zeus, and Athenian dramatic contests, involving tragedies and comedies, celebrated the god Dionysus. This did not stop Dionysus from being shown in one comedy as a figure of fun, getting a beating. Athenian girls from rich families took part in the great annual procession which wound its way up to the Acropolis and, every fourth year, brought a new robe for a statue of Athene. Wealthy men showed off their fine horses. Musicians went along, too, as did, more reluctantly, animals for sacrifice. Festivals gave Greek women a chance to display their finery in public. There was a joke that at Sybaris, a city famous for luxury, the women needed a whole year to prepare for the big occasion.

The homeric gods were taken over in later centuries by the Romans, who adapted their own divinities to Greek models. The Roman Jupiter, for example, was identified with Zeus, and Juno with Hera. But in Greece itself the Olympian divinities lost something of their hold after the 4th century. As independent city-states became mere units in a huge Hellenistic empire under one ruler, the idea of many independent gods may also have seemed inappropriate. Ideas of divinity, as in earlier times, followed human models. Monotheism spread – belief in only a single god, though he might still be called Zeus. The remote and immensely powerful Hellenistic rulers were also worshipped, while abstract concepts like fate were personified and prayed to.

Eastern religions involving personal dedication were widely adopted in the Hellenistic age. Priests of Cybele, a nature goddess of Asia Minor, had to be castrated. Ministers of the Egyptian goddess Isis faced less severe requirements. They might have to shave their heads, but they could enjoy the physical beauty of their divinity. The Roman novelist Apuleius salutes the beauty and power of Isis: 'the first child of time, and mistress of the spirits: ruler of the heavens, the underworld, and the seas'.

Greeks were quick to adopt the most persuasive of the Eastern cults – Christianity. St Paul in the 1st century AD was writing to Christian communities in Greek cities, like Ephesus and Corinth. The power of Christianity led to the closing of pagan Greek shrines in 391, but some divinities survived in Christian guise. Zeus and Hera perished, but Dionysus and Artemis lived on in the form of 'saints' of the Greek Church.

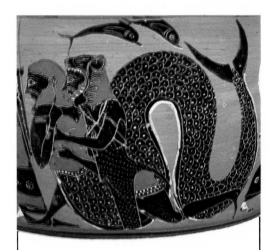

Heracles (Hercules) wrestles with a monster. He wears the skin of the Nemean Lion, which he killed in the first of his 12 Labours for the King Eurystheus of Argos.

THE HEROES

The Greek heroes (such men as Jason of Thessaly, Theseus of Athens, Heracles of Thebes, and Perseus of Argos) formed a link between men and the gods. Strength, courage, and endurance marked them out from other men, as they performed impossible tasks, won great victories, and killed hideous monsters. The Greeks who told the legends about the heroes often explained their superhuman qualities by claiming that a hero was the son of a god and a mortal mother. Heroes were often said to have founded particular cities, and the grave of a hero was always honoured with a sanctuary, to which pilgrimages were made.

The most famous of the heroes was Heracles, son of Zeus (called Hercules by the Romans). To rid himself of the guilt of a crime, he had to perform his 'Twelve Labours': almost impossible tasks, most of which involved killing or taming monstrous creatures. Another of Heracles's exploits was to go on Jason's epic voyage to fetch the Golden Fleece of Colchis, in which many of the great heroes took part.

This altar, discovered in the remains of a Roman fort in the City of London shows Mithras sacrificing a bull. Mithras was the Indo-Iranian god of light, whose cult spread from Persia to Asia Minor and thence to Rome and its empire in the late 1st century AD. Worship of Mithras was especially widespread among the soldiers of the Roman army, many of whom originated from the Near East, and who were attracted to the stern morality that the cult imposed.

The Gods of Greece

Zeus: The king of the Olympian gods and ruler of the weather, especially thunderstorms. Zeus was usually shown armed with a thunderbolt. In some places he was also worshipped as the patron of guests and the home. The eagle was sacred to him.

Hera: The goddess of marriage and childbirth, and wife of Zeus. Stories about her emphasize her justifiable jealousy of and interference in Zeus's many affairs.

Poseidon: The god of the sea, of tidal waves, and of earthquakes. As Poseidon-Hippios, he also ruled horses.

Hades or Pluto: The ruler of the gloomy Underworld (also called Hades), where lived the souls of the dead.

Demeter: The goddess of harvest. A legend tells how her daughter Persephone was kidnapped by Hades and forced to live as queen of the Underworld. Demeter's grief was so frantic that the crops would no longer grow, until the other gods persuaded Hades to let Persephone live above ground for part of the year. Around this were built the secret ceremonies which were known as the Eleusinian Mysteries.

Athene: The goddess of wisdom and courage, and the patron of Athens. Her sacred bird was the owl. She was worshipped in a number of roles, among them Athene Nike, goddess of victory.

Apollo: The god of poetry and the arts, but also the healer and sender of plagues. Son of Zeus, he and his sister Artemis were born on the sacred island of Delos. He was worshipped at Delphi as Apollo Pythios, god of prophecy.

Aphrodite: The goddess of love. She was born out of the sea-foam and carried to her first home, the island of Cythera, on a shell.

Artemis: The virgin sister of Apollo, goddess of hunters. She and her female attendants hunted the deer deep within the forests of Greece. When the hunter Actaeon accidentally came upon Artemis and her nymphs bathing naked, he was turned into a stag and torn to pieces by his own hounds.

Hermes: The messenger of the gods, who escorted the dead down to Hades. He wore a winged helmet and sandals. Hermes was said to have invented the lyre while still only a baby.

Dionysus: The god of wine, revelry, and ecstatic frenzy. He wandered the countryside with a company of excited women.

Moirae, the Fates: More powerful even than the gods themselves, the Fates knew the past, present, and future. They were usually shown as three hideous old hags: Clotho, spinning the thread of life; Lachesis, winding it on her spindle; and Atropos, cutting the thread with shears.

This bronze statue, over 2·5 metres (7 feet) high, dates from about 450 BC and represents Zeus, or possibly his brother Poseidon. It was found on the seabed near Cape Artemisium, in the Aegean Sea.

Stone lions on the island of Delos, one of the Greeks' most sacred sites. Delos was sacred to Apollo as his birthplace, but contained shrines to other gods. These lions were dedicated to Leto by the people of Naxos.

The Gods of Rome

The Romans had an extraordinary variety of gods. They saw the quality they called *numen* (divine power) in almost everything around them. Often they treated an abstract quality (such as Fortune or Plenty) as a god, so that by performing the right ritual a man could get the forces governing it on his side. Another reason for the number of gods they worshipped was the Roman talent for absorbing foreign influences. Religions adopted from the people they encountered as they built their empire sometimes became more important than their own cults. If they thought that a native religion might be a focus for rebellion they might ruthlessly destroy it — as they did with Druidism and sometimes tried to do with Christianity. But more often Romans would see in a foreign religion something their own lacked, and would simply take it over. Minor local gods were sometimes identified with an existing Roman god; thus Sul, the Celtic goddess of the hot springs at Bath in England, became Sul Minerva. The Roman's original gods grew from those worshipped before the city's founding in Italy, and from the gods of Greece. As a result many of the gods of Rome are equivalents of Greek gods. Some of the most important Roman gods were:

Jupiter: The king of the gods — equivalent to Zeus. But he was probably originally an Italian sky god.

Neptune: The Roman Poseidon.

Juno: The equivalent of Hera. With Minerva she shared Jupiter's temple on the Capitol.

Minerva: The Roman Athene.

Mars: The god of war. Mars became important early in Rome's history and figures in the myths of the founding of the city.

The three Roman gods whose shrines were on the Capitoline, the most sacred hill of Rome, as shown on Trajan's Arch, Benevento, built in 114–117 AD. From left to right, Minerva, Jupiter and Juno.

Venus: The Roman Aphrodite.

Diana: The Roman Artemis. Diana absorbed many foreign goddesses, such as the Mesopotamian moon-goddess Astarte, and the Egyptian Isis.

Apollo: The Greek god, also important in the Roman world.

Mercury: Equivalent to Hermes, but also the god of peaceful trade and business.

The Lares and Penates: Gods of the household. Roman homes usually contained a shrine to them. The Penates guarded the family's larder, and the Lares were bound up with respect for one's ancestors. In the *Aeneid* Virgil shows Aeneas, the ancestor of Romulus and Remus, taking the Lares and Penates from his home in burning Troy and bringing them to the new colony which he founds in Italy.

Vesta: The goddess of the hearth. Her temple contained an ever burning flame, tended by the Vestal Virgins.

Saturn: God of agriculture, and weights and measures. He was a gloomy, rather sinister figure, but his annual festival was an occasion of great jollity.

Fortune: Always shown with her oracular wheel, Fortune was perhaps the most important of the abstract gods.

The Deified Emperor: A cult that was useful but sometimes embarrassing to the Romans. In the early days of the empire, emperor-worship was not permitted in Rome itself, only in the provinces. While an emperor lived, worship was only allowed of his *genius*, or protective spirit.

Imported religions
Among the gods and cults imported by the Romans were:

Cybele: A fertility goddess from Phrygia. Her worship was so abandonedly orgiastic that a shocked Senate at one point forbade Roman citizens to take part.

Egyptian gods: The best-known were Isis (see page 49) and Serapis, who had originally been the sacred bull Apis, but was depicted by the Romans as a handsome bearded man.

Mithraism: Mithras was a Persian sun-god. His cult, restricted to males, became very popular in the Roman army.

Christianity: Founded in a Roman province in the early days of the empire, Christianity spread quickly through the Roman world; some emperors persecuted it vigorously, but it eventually became the official religion (see page 115).

A ceremony in a sanctuary of Isis shown in a wall painting from Herculaneum. The worship of Isis was one of many 'mystery' cults which spread throughout the ancient world during the Hellenistic period. Here, a priest bearing a golden vessel steps from the temple door, flanked by a priest and priestess holding sistra — *bronze rattles. At the foot of the steps another priest leads worshippers in prayer, to the music of a flute. In the foreground a fifth priest fans the flames on a small, garlanded altar.*

The forum of Rome was the centre of the business and social life of the city. Under the Republic it served as market-place, a lawcourt, and as a setting for parades, political meetings, and spectacles. Rich citizens and later the emperors erected magnificent public buildings and temples there. Excavations have revealed that the modern ground level is about 15 metres (50 feet) above the original.

Republican Rome

In the great days of the Roman empire it was believed that Rome had been founded in 753 BC. But the true origins of the city, and most of the history of its first centuries, are now unknown. Perhaps by 600 BC a town had developed from a cluster of villages on the site of Rome, 24 kilometres (15 miles) from the sea up the river Tiber. The surrounding district, Latium, gave its name to the language spoken by the Romans – Latin. The speech of this small area, spread across Europe in later years by Rome's empire, became the ancestor of languages nowadays spoken as far apart as Romania and Latin America.

For a time Rome was ruled by kings who came from Etruria in northern Italy. The last of these Etruscan rulers may have been driven out by 510 BC. Then, for almost 500 years, Rome was dominated by a native aristocracy (patricians). This arrangement was known as the Republic: under it there was a long succession of struggles, as the poor of Rome, with some rich allies, sought power and protection against the aristocrats. The poor majority, known as plebeians, eventually created influential officials of their own, tribunes, and in 287 BC the decisions taken by the assembly of the common people were recognized as having the force of law. Violent attacks on the aristocracy, and their central council, the Senate, were to come later. The dual power of the Senate and People of Rome – *Senatus Populus-que Romanus* – gave rise to the famous insignia, SPQR, carried for example on the standards of the legions.

By conquering or allying with its neighbours in Italy, Rome gradually spread its power through the peninsula. External enemies watched this expansion with jealousy or fear. By 272 BC Rome was left clear master of Italy.

Rome's greatest opponent of this era was Hannibal, a Phoenician from Carthage (see page 72). The empire of the Carthaginians had included Sicily, Sardinia, and parts of Spain: driven out of Sicily by the Romans, the forces of Carthage were eventually to invade Italy itself, under Hannibal, in the winter of 218. Hannibal managed to bring war-elephants across the Alps – a frightening feat. Rome suffered heavy defeats, most notably at Cannae in 216: here Hannibal achieved the rare distinction of encircling and destroying an army larger than his own. But far from home, and lacking the

This small altar from the Roman port of Ostia is dedicated to Romulus and Remus. The legend of the founding of Rome tells how these two children were brought up by a she-wolf, and later founded a city. Romulus built walls to surround it, but Remus contemptuously leaped over them. Romulus slew him, with the words 'thus perish any other who leaps over my walls'. He ruled the city alone and it was named Rome, after him.

equipment to take Rome by siege, Hannibal's army achieved no lasting conquest. It withdrew to Africa, where the Romans had in turn invaded Carthaginian land. Carthage was forced to surrender on terms in 202: her Spanish territories, like Sicily before them, became provinces – foreign possessions – of Rome.

In the 2nd century BC Rome expanded her power eastwards, making a province of Greece and Macedonia (in 146), and of the territory in Asia Minor left to her in 133 by the will of King Attalus of Pergamum. Rome's main motive for such empire-building does not appear to have been to exploit the commerce and agriculture of new territories. The Romans chose not to preserve and draw profits from such places as Corinth, an excellently sited commercial city of Greece, destroyed by Rome in 146, or Carthage, captured at last in the same year. Their aggression seems rather to have been aimed at destroying powers which might turn against them.

Politics in Rome

The last century of the Roman Republic, from 133 BC, is nowadays the best known. Many of the important decisions were then in the power of an oligarchy – a group of a few hundred rich families, whose

As Rome extended its power into Italy it came into conflict with the Samnites – the warlike people of the southern mountains. But by 290 BC the Samnites were defeated. This 4th-century painting of a Samnite warrior comes from Paestum, in southern Italy.

The lively movement of a dolphin and the scattering of wild birds disturbed by hunters are captured in this 6th-century Etruscan tomb painting – a pleasant reminder to the dead of their time on Earth. It comes from the necropolis at the Etruscan city of Tarquinia.

CHRONOLOGY

BC

735	Traditional date of the foundation of Rome.
509	Foundation of Republic after expulsion of Etruscan King Tarquinius.
493	Plebians force aristocracy to recognize their tribunes.
343–275	Rome establishes its domination of central Italy.
264–241	First Punic War between Rome and Carthage.
218–201	Second Punic War. Rome eventually defeats Carthage, and gains its territory in Spain, Sicily, Sardinia, and Corsica.
200–145	Rome subjugates Macedonia. Macedonia and Greece eventually incorporated into a single Roman province.
149–146	Third Punic War; ends with the destruction of Carthage.
133–91	Struggles between *Populares* and *Optimates*
113–101	Reform of the Roman army by Popularis general Marius.
91–89	Revolt of Rome's Italian allies ends with Rome granting them full citizenship.
82–80	Dictatorship of Sulla.
83–62	Rise of Pompey.
60–46	Political alliance between Pompey, Crassus, and Julius Caesar ends in civil war between Pompey and Caesar. Caesar emerges victorious as dictator.
44	Assassination of Caesar.
40	Power-struggle between Mark Antony and Octavian ends in a temporary division of the empire between Antony (the east), Octavian (the west), and Octavian's ally Lepidus (Africa).
31	Octavian defeats Antony at Actium.
30–27	Octavian reunifies the empire and nominally restores the Republic. He receives the title Augustus from the Senate. In reality he has become the first Emperor.

THE ETRUSCANS

The Etruscans are one of the more mysterious peoples of history. They have left a wealth of beautiful artefacts – bronzes, terracotta statues, and exquisite tomb paintings – but we cannot say exactly who they were. The Greek historian Herodotus says that they were a people who sailed from Turkey and imposed their rule in Italy, but it seems more likely that they were a mixture of Italians and a few eastern immigrants. They formed a powerful state, and by the 6th century BC controlled most of central Italy. They were probably organized as a league of cities ruled by kings. We have Etruscan inscriptions, in a form of the Greek alphabet, but their language shows no relationship to other languages used in Italy, or indeed to any that are known. It cannot be read and the Etruscans remain silent.

But we do have a little information about them from Roman sources – always hostile. Etruscan kings ruled the infant city of Rome for a while. They were the last kings of Rome, and their foreign arrogance helped to set Rome firmly on the path of republicanism. But Roman civilization retained many Etruscan features, particularly in religion; the reading of divine signs in the entrails of sacrificed animals was an Etruscan practice. Other features of Roman life that were originally Etruscan include gladiatorial combats and the triumphs awarded to victorious generals.

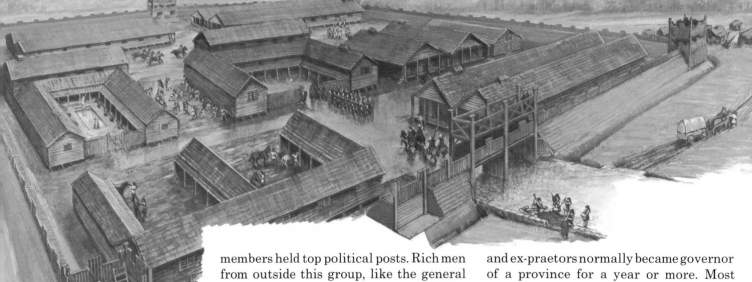

The Romans held on to their military conquests with forts along the frontiers and at likely trouble spots. Skilled military engineers, working to a standard design, produced prefabricated wooden structures which could be transported in sections. With them travelled the tonnes of nails needed to hold them together. The camp above is in the cold forests of Dacia. Large permanent camps of stone were also built, as the headquarters of the legions.

members held top political posts. Rich men from outside this group, like the general Marius and the orator Cicero, needed great talent to gain power: they also needed support from the established families. Such in-comers were called *Novi Homines* – 'New Men', and most Roman aristocrats used the word 'new' as a sign of disapproval. They looked back with reverence to the days of their ancestors. And a New Man was someone with no noble roots in this glorious past.

The chief aim of politically ambitious Romans was to become *consul*. Two consuls were elected for each year: they controlled armies, when necessary, in Italy and the provinces. In the Senate, which might have 300 or more aristocratic members, ex-consuls were listened to with especial attention. Before becoming consul, a man usually needed to hold other, rather less important, administrative posts such as those of *praetor* (a senior magistrate), *aedile* (in charge of public works and welfare), and *quaestor* (in charge of public finance). Like the consulship, they were held only for a year at a time. Ex-consuls

and ex-praetors normally became governor of a province for a year or more. Most quaestors were so ignorant that their junior officials in fact controlled them. Something similar often happens in government today, when a politician is given charge of experienced officials in a department of which he knows little.

In deciding who was elected to these high positions, money was crucial. Consuls, praetors, and the rest had no salary: only the wealthy could spare the time for such work. The election of consuls and praetors was so arranged that the votes of rich citizens counted for much more than those of the poor majority. And many poor men anyway voted according to the instructions of a rich man – their 'patron'. He was a person whose family provided small financial favours, and some protection, for the poor man and his family. In return the poor man, the 'client', gave his patron support at times of political decision – like elections and riots. Money also ruled at elections through simple bribery.

Corruption in the provinces

It seems that in the 2nd century BC many senior officials refrained from evildoing, through fear that the gods would punish them, if they broke the sacred oaths they swore on entering office. Later, standards declined. Many governors of provinces used their positions first to recover the sums they had spent bribing their way to power, and then to make a large profit. There were honest governors, who also tried to prevent other officials from plundering the provincials. But honesty could be dangerous: many Romans resented it.

The rich Greek cities of Asia were a favourite target of greedy Romans. When many of these cities were involved in a

---

THE ARMY

The armies which won Rome's empire owed their success partly to discipline and partly to heavy armour. The foot soldiers, with their shields, breastplates, and helmets, were trained to withstand both superior enemy numbers and setbacks in battle. When conquering Gaul in the 50s BC, the Roman and Italian troops faced soldiers bigger and fiercer than themselves. They were often worsted by the first rush of the Gauls but usually won in the end by keeping their ranks and patiently fighting back against a disorganized enemy. The chief weapons were the two-edged sword and the javelin. The javelin-head was fixed with a wooden rivet which broke on impact, so that the missile could not be thrown back.

Just before 100 BC Marius organized the army into legions of 6000 men, each made up of 10 cohorts of 6 centuries under their centurions. A standard in the form of a silver eagle was given to every legion. It was sacred, its capture by an enemy brought disgrace, and the legionaries were meant to defend it to the death.

The population of the Roman world being far smaller than in the corresponding area today, so were the numbers of troops used to police it. Augustus ruled the empire with about 150,000 legionary soldiers and the same number of auxiliary troops. When Claudius successfully invaded Britain in AD 43, he brought only about 40,000 soldiers — fewer men than in many modern football crowds.

revolt in 88 BC, a captured Roman official was put to death, it was said, by having molten gold poured down his throat. This was meant to seem a fitting punishment for the appetite of Romans for money.

The most notorious of all was Caius Verres, governor of Sicily from 73 to 71 BC. Verres plundered, extorted, and killed. Innocent men were accused so that, on conviction, Verres could acquire their possessions. Governors had the right to order provincials to deliver supplies at stipulated places. Verres accordingly told people to transport goods for great distances across Sicily. The point was *not* to have the transporting done: Verres wanted bribes, in return for excusing the men their 'duty'. Verres's crimes, like those of many other powerful Romans, were immortalized because they were described by Cicero whose lucid and witty writings appealed for centuries. No doubt there were many officials of similar wickedness whose doings are now unknown.

Struggle for power

From the late 2nd century BC until the death of the Republic a struggle between two factions dominated Roman politics. The *Populares*, the Popular Movement, included many of the rich business class, as well as large numbers of the poor and a few prominent aristocrats. They were anxious for efficiency in government, and

A bakery in Pompeii. The typical round loaves are probably being handed out free, as the man behind the counter is wearing a toga (not the garment of a baker), and is likely to be a rich citizen making a gift to the poor.

SLAVES AND THEIR PLACE

People in modern societies which do not have slaves have looked at the ancient world and wondered about the part played by slavery in the societies of Greece and Rome. Slaves did not perform some sort of economic magic in these ancient economies – a slave was merely a person who worked, like almost everyone else, but not where or how he chose. A very poor 'free' peasant farmer might in fact have been just as unfree as any slave, with almost no choice as to what he could do: he had to work for very little, he dared not risk moving anywhere else for work in case he could not find it and starved to death. To be very poor in the Greek and Roman world could mean selling what freedom you had – agreeing to work for someone for 30 years, in the late empire – or having to sell your children as slaves to ensure their survival and the survival of the rest of your family.

Rome first used significant numbers of slaves during the period of her greatest expansion into the Mediterranean world under the Republic. In 167 BC 150,000 people were enslaved by the Romans in the former Greek kingdom of Epirus alone. There was a glut of slaves on the market. The Roman writer Cato, known for the practicality and thrift shown in his treatise on agriculture, maintained that it was good management to work slaves to death and then replace them, rather than to treat them more humanely and give them a longer working life.

The revolt of slaves in 71 BC led by the gladiator Spartacus brought home the desperation of, and the danger from, the slave population of late Republican Italy; and since the Romans had now conquered half the world fresh supplies of cheap slaves began to dwindle. These things prompted a change in attitude. Slaves were treated more kindly because they were now more valuable. Highly literate and gifted Greeks, who could find a place in a Roman home and teach the children – not to say the master – how to read the *Iliad*, were prized indeed. The poet Horace could write at the time of Augustus that captive Greece had taken her conqueror captive.

Imperial legislation obliged people to treat their slaves more reasonably, and eventually the Romans came to realize that slavery was the manufacture of society, not at root in the natural order of things. At the beginning of the 3rd century an outstanding lawyer stated: 'Where Roman law is concerned, slaves are regarded as nothing, but this is not so in natural law, for as far as the law of nature is concerned, all men are equal.'

This realization was demonstrated in the fact that a slave could save to buy his freedom, or it could be given to him by his master. The ties that existed between master and slave or master and freedman were important to both in the world of business, for slaves and freedmen acted as representatives of their masters. Since Roman law (and concern for keeping up appearances) restricted the involvement of the upper classes in business, a stand-in was a necessity. And what was useful to ordinary Romans was also useful to the emperor, who from the time of Claudius on employed freedmen as agents in government.

to get it they were willing to give great power to one or a very few men. They often got their way by the vote of the Popular Assembly, some of their most famous champions being tribunes.

Members of the competing faction called themselves *Optimates* – 'the Best People': Verres was one. They were aristocrats and their followers, anxious to preserve the power of the Senate against that of the Popular Assembly. Power, they believed, should be spread widely among the Senators. They were willing to tolerate scandalous misgovernment, rather than see supreme power slip into the hands of an individual or a tiny group.

In 88 BC the consul Sulla, who claimed to represent the Optimates, lost patience with his opponents at Rome, and used his army to murder several of them. After this, to capture Rome with a Roman army was no longer shockingly new. A pattern was

A small metal figurine of a slave cleaning a boot.

set: the Populares general Marius himself captured the city in the following year, and Sulla retook it in 82. Other civil wars followed, with Roman troops encouraged to join in by large promises of money and land from their commanders. The commanders themselves were made efficient revolutionaries by their confident understanding of politics. Almost every general at this period had already had a successful political career, reaching the post of praetor or consul. In contrast, many states today try to ensure that their army commanders have little or no political experience, in the hope that this will stop them using their troops for revolution.

Rome's problems in the years around 70 BC helped much of the Mediterranean to pass into the control of pirates. In 68 BC two praetors – among Rome's highest officials – were captured by them and carried off. Pirate power became such that even Roman armies dared not sail between Italy and Greece except in the depths of winter. But the Romans most aggrieved were the businessmen, whose sea-trading had become extremely hazardous or impossible, and the poor, who suffered from a shortage of imported corn. The Optimate authorities were not willing to set up the huge military force needed to put down the pirates: they were afraid of the power its commander would have. So the Populares took the matter out of their hands. Amid riotous scenes, the Popular Assembly in 67 appointed its favourite, Pompey 'the Great', as leader of a new force big enough to match the pirates. After a few months' campaigning, Pompey's fleet and army had broken the pirates' strength.

ROMAN LAW

The Romans developed the science and practice of law with such skill and thoroughness that even today the law in most European countries is based on that of Rome – added to and changed over the years but still basically the same system.

Roman law was first written down and organized in the early days of the Republic, in a list of laws called the Twelve Tables (451–450 BC). These early laws were mainly to do with the family and family property, as small groups of relations were still the main unit of society. Over the next 200 years the laws were added to and interpreted by the *pontiffs* – members of leading families who, since the laws were thought of as sacred, were priests.

The actual machinery of legal processes was looked after by a *praetor*, elected annually, who issued an edict or pronouncement each year based on points raised in cases brought to court. In this way Roman law grew year by year as legal solutions were found for the problems of everyday life. Legal experts called *jurisconsults*, who helped people prepare cases for court, became more and more important as the volume of legal writings grew, and the law had constantly to be revised and kept consistent.

The whole government of the empire was in fact held together by Roman law. Strictly local problems could be settled by a community's own law – remember the governor of Judaea, Pontius Pilate, being unwilling to get involved in the problem of Jesus Christ. But anything that concerned Roman citizens (and by 212 AD virtually all the inhabitants of the empire were citizens) had to be dealt with under Roman law, so the same legal principles were used to judge cases in Syria or Gaul.

Roman law was fair and just in theory: but in practice, from the earliest times, when the operation of law had been in the hands of 'the best' families, ordinary people without power or influential friends must have had little chance in the courts.

The codification of Roman law under the Eastern Emperor Justinian (527–535) shaped it into the form used by mediaeval lawyers from the 12th century onwards.

Marcus Tullius Cicero (106–43 BC) was a Roman orator, lawyer, and statesman famous for his eloquence and administrative ability. Amid the chaos and corruption of the last years of the Republic, he embodied the traditional Roman virtues of duty, honesty, and responsibility. In a famous series of orations, the Philippics, *he warned the Roman people against the dangerous ambitions of Mark Antony – who accordingly had Cicero murdered.*

The Roman love of gardens is shown in this delicate painting from the palace of Augustus's wife Livia, with its wild birds and fruit trees. Such paintings were designed to give the impression that the walls of the house had melted away, to reveal the landscape beyond.

Julius Caesar

Pompey went on to extend Rome's power on land in the East, putting down the ancient Seleucid dynasty and setting up the Roman province of Syria. In the process he became inconceivably rich: from 58 another of the Populares, Julius Caesar, sought similar wealth, this time by conquering Gaul (roughly modern France and Belgium). The Gaulish shrines proved an especially rich source of gold. In 55 and 54 Caesar visited Britain, but did not find the silver he sought.

The loot from conquered Gaul was enough to wipe out Caesar's great debts, and allowed him to challenge Pompey for supremacy in the Roman world. In the civil wars between 49 and 45, Caesar defeated Pompey and the Optimates who had at last become his allies. By his victories in Gaul and elsewhere, by his attractive public speaking, and by almost doubling army pay, Caesar built a reputation among the soldiers which lasted long after his own lifetime.

Caesar styled himself 'Permanent Dictator', and may have wished to found a dynasty. However, desperate Optimates, hoping to restore the power of the Senate and of themselves, murdered him in 44 BC, on the Ides (15th) of March. In the ensuing civil wars, the Optimates under Brutus and Cassius were swept aside. Octavian, Caesar's great-nephew, fought it out with Mark Antony (Marcus Antonius), formerly Caesar's henchman. The Queen of Egypt, Cleopatra, once Caesar's mistress and now Antony's, was present with her forces when, in 31 BC, Antony was finally beaten – at the battle of Actium.

The first citizen

After the confusion and bloodshed of the late Republic, the victorious Octavian aimed at a peaceful domination. He promised not a new solution, a 'New Deal' as a modern politician might have done: instead, he claimed to be restoring the old ways. Romans with a sentimental respect for the olden days would approve. Octavian pretended that the Senate still ruled, though in reality the days of government by Senate and People had gone. Renaming himself Augustus ('the August One'), he was officially the first citizen – *Princeps*. In practice he was emperor. The following centuries of monarchic rule are called the Principate.

Virgil and Horace, the empire's great propaganda-poets, encouraged the idea that Augustus was beginning an era of peace – as in fact he was. Augustus may be in some ways an unattractive character to us. But by bringing relative prosperity and freedom from war, he made a majority of Roman voters feel that he was indispensable. The poor of Rome, the business class, and the provincials showed plainly that they much preferred his form of government to the romantic chaos of the late Republic. When Augustus died in AD 14, there was not even any strong attempt to restore the power of Senate and People.

View over Pompeii. A large part of the town remains unexcavated.

Terracotta figure of a gladiator from Tarentum. Gladiators fought to the death for public entertainment, usually in the circular amphitheatres of cities.

A bronze wine- or water-heater from a villa near Pompeii, one of many household objects preserved there by volcanic debris. The liquid flows from the main tank into the semi-circular part, where it is heated by glowing charcoal in the 'grate'.

Even at the beginning of the empire's history in the reign of Augustus, it was difficult to administer. By the time of the emperor Diocletian it was impossible for a single man to rule it. Diocletian established the tetrarchy, or rule of four, with emperors of the East and West helped by caesars, or junior emperors. Here the tetrarchs grasp each other in a gesture of brotherly solidarity in a statue on the corner of St Mark's Cathedral, Venice, Italy.

The Roman Emperors

When Augustus became undisputed master of the Roman empire he faced the immense problem of reorganizing its government – and doing so without either resorting to force or risking another outbreak of civil war. With tact and skill, he achieved a form of government that was to last for some 200 years.

Augustus announced that he was going to restore the Republican system, and even offered to retire. The Senate strongly opposed this – as he had known they would; and they granted him special powers. He was given a special command with proconsular power (*imperium*) over Spain, Gaul, and Syria – three areas containing large and potentially rebellious armies. And until 23 BC he held the office of consul. After this he assumed instead proconsular authority over the *whole* empire (including provinces ruled by the Senate) and over Rome itself, and tribunician authority, with its vague and far-reaching powers of interference with the actions of any other magistrate.

Augustus, though ruler in all but name, avoided outward displays of power. He was careful to give the Senate the appearance of authority, and acted towards them with flattering deference – a policy followed by the wiser of the later emperors. (It is however possible that our judgement of the emperors is influenced by the fact that several historians were senators – so to them an emperor who worked well with the Senate was naturally portrayed as wise!) Augustus gave the Senate the power of passing laws, and control of the main treasury. But the enormous wealth of Augustus and later emperors provided them with an additional source of power.

The Assembly of the People became a mere cypher, but it had a certain amount of public influence and had to be placated. The citizens of Rome were looked after; Augustus continued the free ration of corn (later bread) for all citizens, and there was plenty of public entertainment such as gladiatorial contests and spectacular 'circuses' involving the slaughter of many wild animals imported from the empire.

Below: The empire at its greatest extent, during the reign of Trajan (98–117).

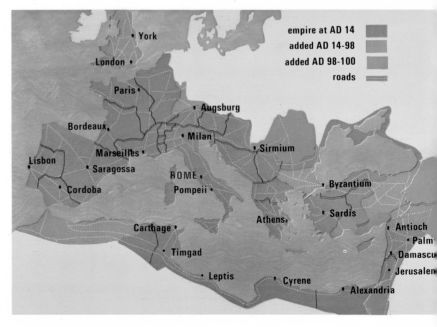

empire at AD 14
added AD 14-98
added AD 98-100
roads

York
London
Paris
Augsburg
Bordeaux
Milan
Marseilles
Sirmium
Lisbon
Saragossa
ROME
Cordoba
Pompeii
Byzantium
Athens
Sardis
Carthage
Antioch
Timgad
Palm
Damascu
Jerusalem
Leptis
Cyrene
Alexandria

and Austria (Noricum). Pannonia (western Hungary), Moesia (Bulgaria), and the client kingdom of Thrace completed the Roman organization south of the Danube. Farther north it seemed economical to take in more barbarian territory and bring the frontier up to the Elbe: a campaign was set in motion to achieve this. But in AD 9 the barbarians struck back, annihilating three legions in the Teutoburger forest. After this the attempt to establish Roman rule beyond the Rhine was abandoned.

The territorial limits of the empire were defined; the administration had been organized, in a manageable if somewhat uneasy partnership with the Senate; the emperor had given himself a legal cloak of acceptable constitutional forms for his power. But one problem had not been solved by Augustus – that of the succession. And this was a problem that was to

The Gemma Augusta, a cameo portrait of Augustus, made during the 1st century AD.

The Emperor Vespasian carrying out a sacrifice in his role as chief priest.

The support of the army was vital to Augustus, as to later emperors. He was their ultimate commander and they took their oath of allegiance to him, rather than to Rome. Emperors were careful to treat soldiers well, giving them generous grants of land and pensions. In fact the soldiers were – perhaps surprisingly – almost always loyal to the emperor; and in general supported the appointed heir, particularly if he were a relation.

To protect the heart of the empire and the emperor himself, Augustus created an imperial guard, the praetorians, who were stationed in Italy. The frontiers were manned by legionaries. Augustus cut down the number of troops on the frontiers, to lessen the cost of the army and to reduce the risk of civil war which large numbers of men under arms obviously entailed. Diplomacy rather than the expense of further conquest was used to settle the problem of Parthia on the eastern frontier, and client kingdoms – states nominally under their own rulers but effectively under the control of Rome – were maintained in Asia Minor.

The biggest problem of territorial organization lay in the European areas of the empire. It was a question of finding the best defensible frontier line that would provide a long-lasting boundary for the empire. Augustus decided to advance to the Danube, and created new provinces in eastern Switzerland (Raetia)

THE ROLE OF THE EMPEROR

All roads led to Rome, and all led to the emperor, for he was the centre of the empire. Petitions – requests for personal intervention by him, from citizens or cities – embassies from natives or foreigners ('royal embassies from India, never previously seen before any Roman general, were often sent to me', boasted Augustus), judgements on appeal cases, queries from provincial officials, all were dealt with, if not by the emperor himself, by one of the members of his secretariat.

An insight into the emperor's involvement in the running of the empire is given by a series of letters written by the younger Pliny, when governor in Bithynia (Asia Minor) to the Emperor Trajan, with replies written by Trajan – or somebody at the palace. 'I was pleased to learn from your letter, my dear Pliny, with what dutifulness and joy my fellow soldiers and the provincials celebrated under your leadership the day of my accession' could be a Jubilee year reply written by a junior secretary – merely protocol, expensively transported by imperial messenger along miles of Roman road. But many real problems of administration were dealt with. 'You observed the correct procedure, my dear Pliny, in going through the cases of those who had been denounced to you as Christians . . . anonymously posted accusations should have no place in any prosecution.' Pliny suggested that an association of firemen might be set up in Nicomedia, which had been ravaged by fire. Trajan advised against it, because the imperial government was always suspicious of organizations that might be a focus for political disturbances – 'the peace of your province, and particularly of these cities, has been repeatedly disturbed by organizations of this kind . . .'

Claudius I (10 BC–AD 54). For years his limp and stammer made him the butt of ridicule among the imperial family. In AD 41, after the assassination of his nephew Caligula, Claudius became emperor and proved to be an admirable ruler.

The traditional Roman country house, or villa, *was a working farm – although, later, rich men built themselves villas which were luxurious country retreats. This medium-sized villa in the Italian countryside is a self-contained agricultural unit. For cash crops, it produces olive oil and grain – some of which is stored in sunken jars in the central courtyard for the winter. Chickens and pigs are reared for meat and goats for milk. To the left, labourers harvest grapes which will supply the villa with wine, using reed baskets. A kitchen garden provides fresh vegetables and fruit.*

dog all the later emperors. Some chose a relation as heir, often with disastrous results; some adopted an able colleague and delegated him as successor. But throughout the history of the empire, civil wars were to break out over the succession problem.

Absolute rulers

In the end it was Tiberius, Augustus's stepson, who took over the government when the first emperor died. Tiberius had been passed over so many times in Augustus's plans for the succession that from the first he was an embittered and suspicious ruler. He felt he had many enemies in the Senate, and by his behaviour made sure that he did. He tried to safeguard his position by appointing an apparently reliable friend, Sejanus, to be prefect of the praetorian guard. But the danger inherent in soldiers at the centre of power materialized: Sejanus plotted to kill Tiberius. The plot was thwarted but now Tiberius could trust no-one. Many completely innocent people were accused of plotting against the state, and killed.

Augustus's programme for ruling the empire had obviously not solved the problem of absolute power: a constitutional ruler governing with the consent of the Senate and army could easily become an autocrat ruling by force. Tiberius's successor, Gaius – known as Caligula after the little soldiers' boots he

wore as a child – was so mad and debauched that people were clearly very relieved when he was murdered by the praetorian guard in AD 47.

The soldiers of the imperial guard then found their own candidate for office, the apparently ineffectual old uncle of Caligula, Claudius. It is possible that they thought that the election of a potential puppet emperor was the best alternative to an autocrat. In fact Claudius turned out to be a very skilful ruler. He was careful not to alienate the most powerful people in Rome. He developed the civil service, giving freedmen (exslaves) whole ministries to run, knowing that they would be working closely with him as his deputies. He speeded up the process of turning conquered enemies into Romans by giving out Roman citizenship more liberally. He himself went to supervise the conquest of south-east Britain and its establishment as a Roman province.

So, for a few years, there was a ruler who was capable of ruling well, who was allowed to rule and improve the running of the empire. But in AD 54 Claudius died, probably poisoned by his fourth wife, the arch-schemer Agrippina, who then gained the throne for her son by a previous marriage, the young Nero.

Tyrant and general

Nero the mad tyrant is one of the stereotypes of history. Accusations that he started the great fire of Rome in AD 64,

which allowed him to clear a great area for his new palace, may be false; but he may well have sung to a lyre while it burned. He certainly had to be awarded the prize for the best singer in rigged competitions, just as it was diplomatic to let him win in chariot races. The false applause may have drowned the sound of screams. The prefect of the praetorian guard was murdered and so was Nero's young wife – killed so that he could marry someone else. His relations with the Senate were disastrous, and he had many senators and senior officials put to death. He spent more and more time on his artistic activities and less on government, disappearing on a prolonged visit to Greece where he collected over 1800 prizes in a series of dramatic festivals and athletic contests. Finally the provincial governors rose against him and even the praetorian guard deserted him. The Senate declared him a public enemy and he committed suicide.

Now the legions guarding the frontiers entered the business of emperor-making. AD 69 was notorious as the year of the four emperors, as each of the frontier armies grouped themselves behind candidates for power. Vespasian, the choice of the eastern and Danubian legions, finally won the day, helped by his control of the grain resources of Egypt.

On his accession Vespasian set out to rebuild the empire, seriously weakened first by Nero's mismanagement and then by the conflict between imperial candidates. His tact and firmness united the army behind him; he worked well with the Senate. His background was modest and his unpretentious way of life was a welcome change after the luxury and dissipation of some of the earlier emperors. He used his own fortune to benefit the state, and increased taxes – for the first time imposing a charge on public lavatories. But he could also be generous, subsidizing poor senators so that they did not lose their rank. He was immensely hard-working, and unlike almost all the other emperors he was able to share the near-impossible burden of rule, having the help of his son and heir Titus. Sadly, Titus died only two years after his father. His brother Domitian was an able administrator but a tyrannical and ruthless autocrat; he was so hated that after his

The remote frontiers of the Roman empire were guarded by a network of forts and defensive walls. Hadrian's Wall across the north of England was part of a general strengthening of defences carried out in the reign of Hadrian. Some 112 kilometres (70 miles) long, it was intended to keep out the fierce northern tribes.

assassination his name was erased from the records and from many monuments.

Pax Romana

The next emperor was the choice of the Senate – Nerva, who was more than 60 when he came to power. His greatest service to Rome was his choice of successor, the Spanish general Trajan, whose reign ushered in a period of unprecedented prosperity and peace in all the empire.

Trajan reigned for 19 years, during which the empire reached its greatest extent with his conquest of the two provinces of Dacia. He was accompanied on campaign by his ward, friend, occasional deputy, and eventual successor Hadrian. Trajan was outstandingly tactful in his relations with the Senate, treating it with deference (though in fact taking all decisions) and earning its backing. He set up a magnificent programme of public building in Rome, which Hadrian continued; and in an effort to halt the decline of Italy built roads and aqueducts, and reclaimed wasteland.

Hadrian was an able successor. His policy was one of consolidating well-established frontier lines rather than of expanding the empire, and at home he ruled wisely. He was immensely popular. As his heir he chose the proconsul Antoninus whose 22-year reign saw the empire more prosperous and contented than ever before. There were only intermittent border problems, as the Picts and the Rhineland barbarians caused sporadic trouble. In the middle of the 2nd century

69 Year of the Four Emperors
69-79 Vespasian
79-81 Titus
81-96 Domitian
96-98 Nerva
98-117 Trajan
117-138 Hadrian
138-161 Antoninus Pius

A coin of the able and popular emperor Hadrian. His extensive travels through the empire, on which he would look into local grievances, repeal unfair taxes, and tighten military discipline, contributed to his reputation among his subjects.

AD the *pax Romana*, the peace of Rome, seemed much more significant than any Roman wars.

The barbarian menace

But the peace that seemed so secure was only fleeting. In the reign of Marcus Aurelius – another just and wise ruler – came the first of the major barbarian invasions which were ultimately to destroy the empire in the West. Across the Danube swarmed the barbarians, threatening the safety of Italy, while in the east major defeats were suffered against the Parthians. And on his death the stable rule which had brought Rome its great prosperity disappeared. His son Commodus was wilful and irresponsible, and became insane; he was murdered by the prefect of his praetorian guard.

Now the army took a hand once more in emperor-making. After an outbreak of civil war Septimius Severus, a tough North African general, emerged supreme. He was the first of a number of soldier emperors who over-ruled the Senate or executed senatorial opposition, and promoted tough soldiers to positions of power. He left the empire to his two sons, with the advice 'Be of one mind, see that the soldiers are well off, and don't bother about the rest'. But his sons quarrelled and the ruthless Caracalla murdered his brother. Perhaps Septimius Severus envisaged a balance of power at the centre of government, with two rulers sharing responsibility. But an actual division of power between two emperors was a solution only attempted after decades of civil war, anarchy, military defeats, barbarian invasions, and economic crises had followed the death of Severus.

The 3rd-century crisis saw the rapid rise of peasants through the ranks of the army to top military posts which could then lead straight to the throne. Several tough soldiers from the Balkan provinces became emperor in this way. Wars on several fronts simultaneously meant there was need for strong commanders in the main areas of trouble.

Rome itself was obviously at risk to barbarian attacks, and in AD 271 Aurelian started to build a wall around it. He could not save Dacia, and Roman armies withdrew behind the Danube. Farther west, the barbarians were whittling away at Roman territories: Saxon pirates menaced the shores of Britain, while Frankish tribes threatened the lower Rhine. Gaul saw much unrest; for ten years it set up a rival empire.

The decline of the Roman empire was reversed at the end of the 3rd century with the reign of Diocletian, a soldier who had risen through the ranks. He reigned for more than 20 years before voluntarily abdicating. He faced the threat of barbarian invasion; the extreme power of the army; the appalling financial difficulties of the empire. And he realized that this was too much for one man. To help him, he chose another soldier, Maximian, who ruled the western part of the empire, while he controlled the East. Maximian was also given the title of Augustus – though in practice Diocletian retained overall authority. Both emperors had junior rulers (*caesars*) under them, to share the burdens of government and, it was hoped, to succeed them automatically – thus circumventing civil wars over the succession.

Diocletian ruled for 21 years, during which he reorganized the empire. Although he set up the tetrarchy (rule of four) he remained the holder of supreme power, and increased the pomp and autocracy of the emperor. For some time emperors had spent less and less time in Rome, which had inevitably decreased the powers of the Senate. Diocletian set up a vast and complicated machinery for the running of the empire. He split up the fifty or so provinces into smaller divisions, and removed them from senatorial control. He strengthened the frontier garrisons, possibly even doubling them, and established a mobile force, the

The 3rd-century emperor Valerian submits to Shapur, one of the aggressive Sassanid kings of Persia. A declining Rome could not be so successful against its enemies as in the past, and Rome's humiliation is boastfully displayed in this rock-carving at Naqsh-i-Rustam.

A 4th-century mosaic from the Basilica of Junius on the Esquiline Hill, Rome. It shows a consul in a racing-chariot. Many of the old offices of the Republic survived into the late empire, but in a very debased form.

284-305 Diocletian
306-337 Constantine I
361-363 Julian the Apostate
379-395 Theodosius I
475-476 Romulus Augustulus
(last Emperor in the West)
527-565 Justinian (East)
1449-1453 Constantine XI
(last Emperor in the East)

A medallion of Diocletian. This efficient emperor's attempt to fix wages and prices throughout the empire failed, but he managed to simplify the tax system and carried out a great census of population and land use.

comitatenses, available – at least in theory – to help out on any front. He also set about financial reforms. For the empire was suffering from appalling inflation – so bad that soldiers and civil servants were being paid in corn instead of money.

Diocletian's system of tetrarchy collapsed after his voluntary retirement; but Constantine, who emerged sole emperor, carried on his reforms and strengthened the empire against the increasing barbarian attacks. Rome itself had ceased to function as imperial capital, though it kept its significance; other cities like Milan and Trier, well placed for administration, became imperial capitals because of the presence of the emperor and his court. Now Constantine, who had adopted Christianity, gave recognition to the strength of this religion and to the political strength of the eastern half of the empire by founding a new, Christian capital for the empire on the site of the old Greek colony of Byzantium. It was called Constantinople.

The halt in the empire's decline under Diocletian and Constantine proved only a momentary check. After Constantine the empire split again. Lack of success against the invaders deepened the division, for clearly the West was weaker than the East. Britain was overrun by the Picts and Scots, joined by the Saxons from north Europe. The Roman armies were formally 'withdrawn' in 410, though the Romanized Celtic resistance kept up the fight against the newcomers and preserved much of Roman administration and culture under skilful leaders like Ambrosius Aurelianus and the great figure, later made into a legend, Arthur. Gaul fell to the Germanic tribe of the Franks and to the Burgundians. The Suebi and the Vandals took Spain; the Vandals then moved across the Mediterranean to North Africa in 429, breaking the important communication line from the provinces which had sent their taxes in grain and gold to Rome. In the year 410 the city of Rome itself was sacked by Alaric and his Gothic warriors (who showed surprising moderation). More terrible was the arrival in Europe of the Huns: Attila 'the Scourge of God' ravaged Gaul and entered Italy. Pope Leo negotiated his withdrawal in 452. But nothing could save Rome from the Vandals, who plundered it in 455. Eventually the barbarians, who had for some time commanded the armies of Rome, claimed the throne as well. The German Odoacer deposed the boy emperor Romulus Augustulus and the nominal existence of the Roman empire in the West was ended.

Life Under Rome

A map of the Roman empire is in some ways as misleading as those maps of the British empire at its height, when almost half the world seemed to be coloured pink. For in both cases alongside the civilization imposed by the conquerors, older cultures still existed in their own right. So each part of the Roman empire had its own, often very ancient, identity. The Punic-speaking farmers of Roman North Africa or the woad-stained Celts of Britain had little in common with a native Latin from Italy. Initially, their subservience to Rome was all that linked them together.

Yet the map of the Roman empire does represent something more than the joining together of vastly different cultures under one label. The areas conquered by Rome were quite definitely changed by the fact of conquest, which in the end meant more than just a change of master. It meant the creation of a different culture – often a fusion of the native and the Roman, but ultimately a new product.

Within the broad spread of Roman civilization over the vast territory of the empire, some things were basically the same almost everywhere. The Roman city, whether on the edge of the Sahara or in the damp lowlands of southern England, had ingredients that would be found more

Every city in the empire had its baths to which the local people could go. Men used the facilities in the mornings and women could go in the afternoons. The baths also functioned as a sort of steamy club where people could lounge around, exchanging the latest gossip, political scandals, and business news. The most luxurious establishments boasted marble walls, but more often (as in Ephesus, below) the rooms were decorated with plaster, sometimes imitating expensive marble.

or less anywhere – baths, market places (*fora*), paved streets with drains, an amphitheatre for entertainment. Naturally the climate caused variations – there would be fewer open-air areas for business and pleasure in a cold climate than under the hot sun – but the basic model was the same in each case.

Just as cities all over the empire had certain obvious things in common, so did the lives of the people in them. For Roman civilization was based on the cities, and Roman government and administration operated chiefly through them. In some ways the biggest gulf was not really between a native of a North African city and a native of a British city, for both would wear the toga, speak Latin, and be subject to the same laws. A bigger gap might exist between the people of the cities and those of the countryside, who kept to their own traditional ways. Yet Roman cities were closely linked to the land around them; the landowners sat on the local town councils and had a town house as well as one in the country. Roman citizens were not just the people who lived inside the built-up area of the city, but those who lived in the territory of the city, which could cover quite a big area.

The granting of citizenship was one of the ways in which Rome extended her power. It could be given to individuals or whole communities, joining them to the community of Rome itself. There were different grades in the structure of political rights. Originally some privileges – mainly the right to fight for Rome – had been given to Rome's allies in Italy during the Republican period. Later such privileges were used to make one

A wall-painting of a harbour, from the Roman sea-port of Stabiae, which was destroyed with Pompeii in the volcano eruption in AD 79. The monument at its entrance may be a lighthouse. Inside the harbour, beyond the pier, is a number of large ships. The surface of the painting is scattered with graffiti — always a sign of widespread literacy, not necessarily put to good use.

cohesive unit of the growing empire. Whole communities in Italy were given the right to go on ruling themselves in local affairs, while being ruled in external affairs by Roman magistrates. These *municipia* would then graduate to being communities with full Roman citizenship. Individuals could be granted citizenship as a special honour – for instance soldiers who fought for Rome could earn it at the end of their service. Citizenship brought many real benefits, including the protection of Roman law particularly in respect of property and inheritance.

Citizens of Rome

It is often pointed out that the basis for a unified culture in and around the Mediterranean was laid by the Greeks with their many independent city states. Rome's conquests, overlying most of the Hellenized areas, joined them politically by force, and then welded them together by the extension of citizenship. Over the centuries outsiders were gradually made insiders until at the beginning of the 3rd century the Emperor Caracalla declared everyone to be a citizen except the *dediticii*, recently conquered foreigners.

The whole process of Romanization (with the darker aspect of the 'selling out' of proud native traditions in favour of the culture of the conquerors) was never better expressed than in the perceptive writing of the great historian Tacitus in the 1st century AD. In the biography of his father-in-law, the general Agricola who conquered Britain, he gives us a double-edged account of Romanization:

Roman goods travelled, by trade or looting, even outside the frontiers of the empire. These painted glass cups found their way to Denmark in the 3rd century AD. The craft of glass-making was highly developed in the Roman empire.

TRADE

The *pax Romana*, the peace and order which came from a well-defended and well-organized empire, allowed trade and commerce to flourish. There were only the natural hazards of the sea itself; and the great cities provided certain markets full of eager consumers. So pottery manufacture, mass-produced from moulds, flourished in the potteries of Gaul; Africa exported millions of gallons of olive oil; Greece could always find a buyer for its best (and maybe even its worst) wine; and in Rome an eighth hill, the Monte Testaccio, grew up from the millions of discarded amphorae (storage jars) which had carried these products to Italy. Everyday trinkets of almost throw-away cheapness were made in the numerous workshops of Alexandria, and still turn up under the farmer's plough or the archaeologist's spade all over the empire. Alexandria also processed the exotic products of the East, spices and perfumes in the 1st century.

Alexandria was the great emporium of the Roman world: Rome was one of the main destinations of all trade. In the 2nd century Aelius Aristides claimed:

You can see here so many cargoes from India or from Arabia that you might think that the trees there have been left permanently bare, and that the inhabitants will have to come here to beg for their own goods whenever they need anything. Clothing from Babylonia and the luxuries from barbarian lands beyond arrive in huge quantities . . . Egypt, Sicily, and the settled parts of Africa are the farms of Rome . . . everything is found here, trade, seafaring, agriculture, the working of metals — all the skills which exist or have ever existed, anything that can be made or grown. If something can't be found here then it simply can't exist.

Rome was indeed the centre of the world.

In order that people who were scattered, uncivilized, and hence prone to war might be accustomed to peace and quiet through comforts, Agricola gave personal encouragement and public assistance to the building of temples, forums, and houses. By praising the energetic and reproving the indolent, he replaced compulsion with competition for honour. He likewise provided a liberal education for the sons of the chiefs. Preferring the native ability of the Britons to the industriousness of the Gauls, he gave them such encouragement that whereas they had previously refused to use Latin, they now took up the learning of rhetoric. The Roman way of dressing came into fashion and togas were worn. Step by step they turned aside to alluring vices, porticoes, baths, and elegant banquets. This in their innocence they called 'culture', whereas it was really only a sign of their enslavement.

Prosperous families in the northerly Roman settlements lived as comfortably as Romans farther south. This man, being groomed by servants at the start of his day, sits in a draught-proof high-backed chair, more suitable for his home in Trier, Germany, than elegant Mediterranean furniture.

The Greeks and Romans have left dramatic statues of Gaulish warriors, whose courage and fierceness impressed them. But this terracotta plaque shows a more humble Gaul, with his strange knotted hairstyle and the rough sheepskin tunic needed in the cold northern climate.

Italy

Rome overshadowed the rest of Italy which was, however, given a privileged position in comparison with the other provinces – it was not, at first, taxed. There were many quite flourishing towns, but from early on there seems to have been concern over the general prosperity of the region. The government pleaded with the rich to keep their money in Italy, and invest in Italian land; for, right at the heart of the empire, the Italians who had been the backbone of Rome's power as it expanded were not finding life easy. Among other problems, people were not bringing up enough children. The Emperor Nerva started a scheme of *alimenta* (aids) to the Italians, by which low-interest loans were made available to farmers and grants were given out for the support of children. Trajan built roads and set up land reclamation schemes.

But Italy continued to decline. Part of the problem was that the other provinces could, between them, provide far more efficiently (and therefore more cheaply) all the things Italy had once provided – grain, wine, and strong soldiers – while investment was more profitable abroad, especially in the potentially rich provinces of North Africa. Italy became a land of rich aristocrats' estates, with poor farmers struggling alongside.

In the late empire Rome lost its position as imperial capital with the division of the empire, power following the emperor to Milan and Ravenna among other cities. Rome functioned merely as the centre of aristocratic and largely pagan senatorial interests, though it retained enough significance for emperors to visit it for specially important festivals. Its grain from Egypt was diverted to the new capital of Constantinople from the early 4th century, as the real centre of gravity of the empire shifted inexorably eastwards. But although its political significance was ended, Rome found a new role as the centre of the Church in the West.

Gaul and the western provinces

Gaul was the name used by the Romans for the main territories of the Celts (see page 77) – Cisalpine Gaul ('Gaul this side of the Alps'), the area they had settled in northern Italy, and Transalpine Gaul, including all of modern France and extending as far as the Rhine. Transalpine Gaul included Narbonensis, the warm southern coast of France, much of which had been colonized by Greeks and which came under Roman influence quite early. Julius Caesar, as governor of Cisalpine Gaul and Narbonensis, turned his attention in 58 BC to the northern tribes, who were becoming a threat as they tried to migrate under pressure from barbarian tribes from farther east. The conquest of Gaul took eight years; but once conquered, its people were rapidly Romanized.

The government of northern Gaul was based on the old tribal territories, which formed three provinces. Lugdunum (Lyons) was joint capital; it saw an annual meeting of tribal leaders. Prosperous lesser towns made pottery for export – mass-produced in imitation of fine Italian ware – and woollen cloth used by the frontier armies for warm cloaks. Baths, theatres, and the fine houses of the rich are evidence of the Gauls' enthusiastic acceptance of Roman ways. In Nar-

A coppersmith's workshop in Pompeii. As the empire grew, Italian craftsmen found it difficult to compete with cheap imported goods.

The Romans' talent for engineering shows in their spectacular system of aqueducts. Miles of water channels were built, with simple machinery such as the treadmill hoist, to take fresh water to cities all over the empire. Tunnels were driven through hills and gravity skilfully exploited so that the spring water came down at just the right speed to keep up the pressure in taps and fountains. But we hear of at least one case where profit-hungry contractors botched a job — tunnels starting from opposite sides of a hill missed each other in its middle.

THE SURVIVAL OF LATIN

One of the best signs of the deep penetration of Roman culture in conquered areas is the fate of the spoken language once Roman power had declined. At the end of the Roman empire, the Roman areas of Gaul and Germany south of the Rhine fell to tribes of the Franks, who spoke a Germanic language. They also settled a large expanse of territory beyond the old frontier, the rest of modern Germany. In those Frankish lands which had been in the empire, the Latin language survived. Modern French is a Romance language (derived from 'Roman'), not a Germanic one, which shows the strength of the Latin culture of the old Roman area of Gaul.

In contrast, Latin did not survive to form the main element in the modern language in the old Roman provinces of Britain. Where the invading Germans established themselves, a Germanic language took over (the basis of modern English), but where the Romanized population held out — in Cornwall and Wales —

against the invader, it was the *Celtic* tongue that survived. This shows that the Romanization of Britain had not penetrated so deeply, nor in quite the same way, as in Gaul. The older native culture of the Celts reasserted itself once the top layer of Roman civilization had gone.

Dacia in the Balkans was officially only part of the Roman empire after its conquest by the Emperor Trajan in AD 106 and until its loss under Aurelian at the end of the 3rd century AD, though obviously Roman influence extended beyond these two points in time. Today Dacia is Romania, whose actual name suggests the land of the Romans: and the language of modern Romania is, like French, Spanish, and Italian, a Romance language, derived from the Latin of the Roman empire. From a Roman occupation that lasted less than 200 years comes a linguistic inheritance that has lasted despite all the turmoil of invasion and settlement of new peoples in the Balkans, now mainly Slavonic-speaking.

bonensis town life had been well established before the Romans, in Greek settlements such as Massilia (Marseilles).

Life in Gaul was the pattern for the other provinces in Europe west of the Rhine, and in Britain. Germania Inferior ('Germany within the empire'), along the northern part of the frontier, became prosperous through serving the soldiers. Towns grew up from settlements of traders near the camps, and many retired soldiers had farms in this fertile area. Britain, visited by Caesar but not conquered until AD 43, had valuable deposits of tin and a little gold; its oysters and slaves were sold in the markets of Rome; and its grain, during the later empire, was shipped across the English Channel to feed the

soldiers of the Rhine. But Britain was not always as easy to govern as Gaul. In AD 60 Boudicca, the Queen of the Iceni, led a revolt and had sacked three cities and ravaged the Ninth Legion before she was defeated. Spain, long colonized by Carthaginians and coming under Roman influence after the Punic Wars, had rich mines of gold and silver which the Romans exploited efficiently.

As the empire declined, western Europe fell to the invading barbarians. But much survived from Roman days: language, the names of towns, buildings, and the road system. Another Roman survival, in some ways, was Christianity – throughout the Middle Ages, and to some extent today, still centered on the city of Rome.

North Africa

The Roman imperium stretched along the Mediterranean coast of Africa, and deep inland to where either mountains or desert formed a natural barrier. Much older civilizations lay within the area of

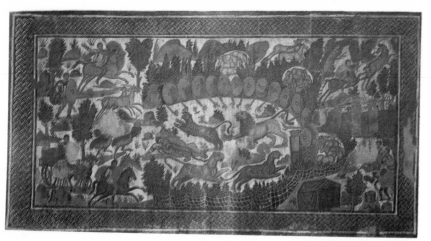

Roman conquests – the Phoenician settlements like Carthage, and former Greek colonies like Cyrene. Under the Roman empire these settled areas became some of the most flourishing areas of urban development. Cities such as Timgad (Thamugadi) in Algeria, which was built as a new city by a Roman legion soon after AD 100, had all the elegance of a Greek city with its porticoes and temples, combined with all the bustling prosperity of a Roman town.

The prosperity of the African provinces came at first from agriculture – vines, olives, good land for growing grain. A huge amount of building activity went on: buildings, streets, and aqueducts were constructed in dozens of thriving towns. The native Africans worked hard for their towns, not just building them, but looking after their poorer inhabitants with low-interest loans, and sometimes making strenuous efforts to improve their political status, since the more 'Roman' a town became, the better everyone's chances within the Roman system, and the prouder they felt.

The 3rd and 4th centuries, disastrous for many areas of the empire, saw a big development in olive production in North Africa. Groves of olives covered the slopes of hills in Tunisia and Algeria. They represented a heavy investment in capital, for the owner of an olive tree has to wait more than twenty years for his tree to bear substantial amounts of fruit. The plantations also needed reliable supplies of water, and miles of irrigation pipes honeycombed whole areas of otherwise rather dry land. Some of these water pipes are still in use in Algeria today – a striking reflection of the intensity and

The North African colonies were a good source of wild animals for the bloodthirsty games which so delighted the Romans. In this mosaic from Timgad hunters trap lions, leopards, ostriches, and antelopes.

The debris of a Roman banquet was thrown to the floor. This unswept floor mosaic is a visual joke. Its gnawed bones, fruit stones, and snail and other shells might confuse a short-sighted slave clearing up after a feast.

long-lived usefulness of the Roman investment in agriculture which brought North Africa greater prosperity than it would ever see again. Today, the ruins of once prosperous cities stand half buried in desert sand.

Eygpt under the Romans

After the Romans conquered Egypt in 31 BC – inheriting the efficient administration of the Ptolemies – Egypt had to pass on most of its wealth to Rome in taxation. (In the early empire one third of the city's grain supply came from Egypt.) Every Egyptian knew this only too well.

Egypt's wealth was grain – fed by the inundation of the Nile (see page 46). The Roman tax officials had to ask for just the right amount to fill the granaries of Rome without crushing the hard-working peasants of Egypt. 'Shear my sheep, don't fleece them', the Emperor Tiberius told an over-zealous administrator of the province.

Egypt had its surplus removed like clockwork every year, without any great boost to its economy. The Egyptians had no chance to drive a hard bargain over

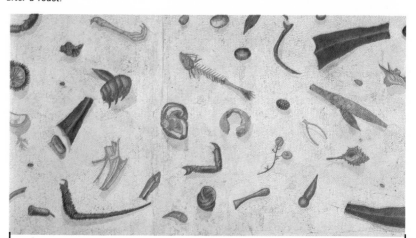

FOOD

In the great cities of the empire, the government took an increasing role in the provision of the grain supply as the years went by – at Rome, all citizens (and this eventually meant most people) were entitled to a basic ration of grain, later bread. Apart from this the diet of city people included meat and poultry, if they could afford it. Fish was something of a delicacy in Rome and Italy, but not in the later capital of Constantinople, which was surrounded by water and on the seasonal route of the great shoals of tunny fish. These were preserved and exported. The rich ate pickles from Spain, and pomegranates from Libya; snails, pigeons, and even dormice were force-fed for their tables.

Fish, in particular their entrails, formed the basis of what sounds like a rather revolting concoction which the Romans used in their cooking – a fermented fish sauce used with meats. Herbs and spices (brought from the Far East) were also used for flavouring, the most important then as now being pepper. Again, what tasted good to them would seem strange to us – wine was used extensively in cooking, often with honey, which gave even main dishes a rather sickly flavour.

prices. So Egypt remained a land of small villages and small towns, rather than cities blossoming on the Roman model as in the provinces of North Africa. The great (and only) city of Egypt was the huge Greek city of Alexandria, where the spoils of the Egyptian harvests were collected for export. In the late empire the city was the focus for much discontent. Centuries of watching the wealth of Egypt being weighed and checked and loaded on to the great convoys of ships taught some of the rebels exactly what their strength was, and they blockaded the grain supply.

But the rebels were the Greeks of Alexandria. For the real Egyptians of the countryside resistance to the harsh demands of the Romans was no simple matter. Anyone caught damaging the dykes along the canals would be buried alive on the spot. We can see why the edict of Caracalla which gave citizenship to virtually all the inhabitants of the empire made an exception of the Egyptians.

The provinces of the east

The eastern half of the Roman empire was made up of territories whose civilizations were in many cases much older than Rome itself. These, the Hellenized areas of the Near East, had for the most part much in common with the Romans, whose civilization was indeed partly a product of Greek culture. There was no question of imposing the Roman way on a group of raw barbarians, as in western Europe. The Romans themselves were happy to imitate the elegance of their eastern subjects. The cities of Asia Minor and the Levant retained their own way of life, their religion, and the Greek language.

There was a wealth of sculpture in the cities of Asia Minor, which the Romans coveted and carried off home in the wake of conquest. Asia Minor was rich in natural resources too; it remained the granary of the eastern empire, with good harvests and a surplus big enough to support the army. The Asclepieion at Pergamum – a sort of combined spa and shrine – was the centre of medical learning.

The Romans used their eastern empire as a base from which to attack the Persians. Trajan at one point pushed the frontier into the Persian lands, but Hadrian wisely let the territory gained revert. But such campaigns brought the

spending power of thousands of soldiers to the eastern empire – especially to Antioch in Syria, where they mustered. Other Syrian cities grew fat on the trade that came overland from the Orient. At Palmyra the caravans from China unloaded their precious bales of silk. Palmyra was the centre of a rebellion in AD 272 by its queen, Zenobia, who briefly ruled the whole of the eastern empire; but she was soon defeated by Aurelian, taken to Rome, and exhibited in his triumphal procession. Syria's textile industry continued to flourish into the Middle Ages.

The great exception among the eastern provinces was Judaea. The Jews, having fought for and won the purity of their own faith against the Seleucids and having been let down in their fight for political independence by Roman allies, were not happy to accept the status of a Roman vassal kingdom, or, after AD 6, that of a Roman province. In AD 66 the Jews rose up and drove the Romans out of Jerusalem. For four years Jerusalem was under siege. In 70 Titus, the new Roman commander, broke into the city and sacked it, destroying the Temple. But despite this defeat, rebellion still smouldered. The siege of the Zealots in Masada in 73 is well known. Sixty years later came the revolt of Simon Bar Kochba, with uprisings throughout all the country. The Romans hit back with extreme cruelty. Even the name Judaea was discarded, and many of the Jews only escaped being sold as slaves by emigrating.

At one point in the Jewish revolt of 132 Simon Bar Kochba took Jerusalem and struck coins, such as this shekel, to celebrate his victory.

The magnificent oval forum of the city of Gerasa (Jerash) in Jordan. Founded by the Seleucid kings, this city had a good position on a trade route and enjoyed great prosperity in Roman times. Most of its buildings, like this, are Roman.

The wealth of the eastern Roman provinces is reflected in the elaborately elegant dress of the woman in this statue, an inhabitant of Palmyra in Syria. Palmyra was one of the greatest and most prosperous cities of the East. Its traders went as far as the Gulf of Arabia.

The Barbarians

Some barbarian chiefs drank from beautiful 'claw beakers', like this one, made of thin glass. Such beakers were made in the Rhineland – whose glass industry was founded in Roman times – in the 6th century AD. They were traded widely. This example comes from a rich 6th-century grave at Mucking, in eastern England; claw beakers were often buried with their owners.

Europe just before the barbarian migrations.

Across the frontiers of the Roman empire, in central and eastern Europe, lived the barbarians. This contemptuous term was used by the Romans for all those who did not come under Graeco-Roman influence; it comes from a Greek word describing the 'bar-bar' sound of the languages of non-Greek peoples. The way of life of the barbarians was still 'prehistoric' in that they had no cities, and used only a very crude form of writing. But their society was not without organization and codes of conduct; their craftsmanship in metals was superb; and the heroic poems recited by their minstrels still ring down the ages.

Just who the barbarians were, and where they came from, is still unclear. Historians have tried to sort out the various names used in Roman accounts, and archaeologists have hoped to use the similarity of remains to identify homelands of particular tribes. Neither has been particularly successful, and one reason for this is that the barbarians would settle in one area for a time – perhaps for several hundred years – and would then migrate to another region.

According to folk tradition, most of the barbarians who harried the north-east frontiers of Rome had their origins in the Baltic area and in Scandinavia. During the last centuries BC and the first centuries AD these peoples moved south and west. As one tribe's territory was invaded it in turn might move into that of its neighbours; some tribes were scattered, others joined

with their conquerors. The period between the mid-3rd and mid-6th centuries AD is known as the Age of Migrations: peoples were constantly shifting around and the pressures on the boundaries of the Roman empire became intolerable.

It is easy to disparage the barbarians if we look at them through the eyes of their enemies. The well-bathed, fastidious Romans described their foes in the worst possible light. 'The long-haired hordes', wrote Bishop Sidonius in the mid-4th century AD, 'the greedy Burgundian who spreads his hair with rancid butter . . . reeking of garlic and foul onions.' Another Roman saw the barbarians as 'continually and at all times covered with filth'. But the habits of the barbarians may well have been exaggerated as propaganda.

Barbarian society

Historians group barbarians into 'peoples' – Goths, Vandals, Gepids, and so on – on the basis of their origins and language. But they themselves had no sense of nationality. Each people was made up of many tribes, and a tribe from one people would ally with a tribe from another people to fight others of the same stock.

Sometimes an outstanding individual, such as Attila the Hun, might bring together a confederacy of different peoples, by means of his own personality and drive. At one time Attila brought nearly half Europe under his sway. But on the chief's death, the different tribes split up. There was no organization capable of administering a large area.

The unit of barbarian society was the tribe. Each was an independent unit, and guarded its rights ferociously and selfishly. The tribe was composed of kindreds – family groups or clans. Girls on marriage joined their husband's kindred. If anyone was murdered, the death was avenged by the kindred as a whole. An elaborate system of compensation existed for death, wounding, or theft; and fines had to be paid by the whole kindred.

Tribal affairs were decided by a council of elders, and an assembly of all men who bore arms. A chief or king was elected by popular acclaim, and a king's son did not automatically succeed him. Some tribes had a royal family, claiming descent from a god, and kings were chosen from among its members. The authority of a king

Picts
Norse
Irish
British
Swedes
Jutes
Angles
Frisians
Saxons
Thuringians
Lombards
Franks
Burgundians
Siling Vandals
Marcomanni
Quadi
Asding Vandals
Ostrogoths
WESTERN ROMAN EMPIRE
Visigoths
EASTERN
Visigoths
ROMAN
EMPIRE
BALTS
FINNS
SLAVS
HUNS
BERBERS
ARABS

depended on his personality, and his skill as warleader and as a warrior. He was not regarded as a god, like the ancient Egyptian pharaohs. His authority was not automatically accepted; sometimes his orders in battle were not obeyed, and he could even be deposed.

Houses and farms

The barbarians lived in wooden houses. They regarded the great stone public buildings erected by the Romans with awe, describing ruined cities as 'the work of giants'. But they were very skilled in the construction of large wooden farmhouses and 'halls' for kings' courts.

Some idea of a 'barbarian' village can be gained from the site of Feddersen Wierde in north Germany. Houses were built on a framework of stout wooden posts, with hurdles plastered over with clay inside and out forming the walls (wattle and daub). Inside the houses were two rows of posts; these supported the roof which was thatched with straw. The family lived in one end of the house, while the other end was divided into stalls for animals. The heat of the animals helped to keep the family warm in the bitterly cold winter. Raising cattle was the chief occupation of the farmers and they also grew some grain. The chief's house was fenced off. Around it were workshops.

A village at Wijster, in Drente, north Holland was occupied from the 2nd to the 5th centuries AD. At first only one or two families lived there, sharing a single large house which was surrounded by out-buildings. They were joined by other

An elaborately decorated belt-buckle, also from Mucking, dating from the early 5th century AD.

families, and a later village on the site was laid out with houses of about 30 by 40 metres (100 by 130 feet), arranged in rows. Water was drawn from wells lined with wood or basketwork. Food was stored in pits, also lined with basketwork, and grain for daily consumption was stored in jars in granaries raised on wooden posts.

Another type of dwelling was the *Grubenhaus*, or sunken-floor hut, found at many sites. This was a poor dwelling compared with the great long-houses that were often side by side with it. To make a *Grubenhaus*, an oval hollow, about 1 metre (3 feet) deep and 3·5 by 2·5 metres

A barbarian chief of the 5th century AD and his court feast in their timbered hall. On the left, a minstrel accompanies himself as he sings a heroic poem. Some of these poems survive to tell us about the life of such warrior courts.

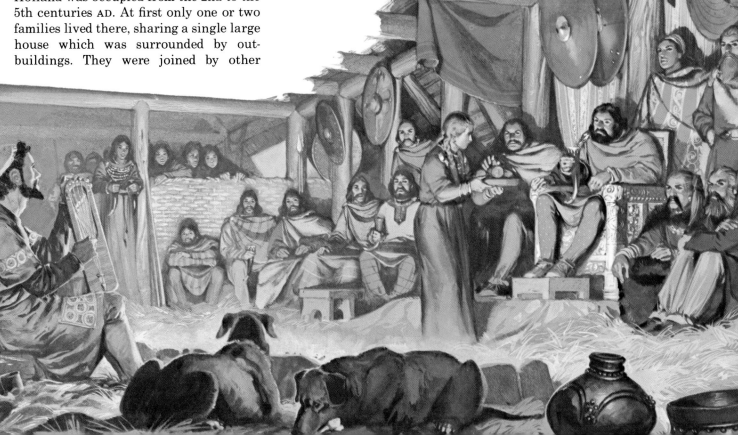

The Nydam boat, found in a peat-bog in northern Germany in the 1860s. It is 21 metres (70 feet) long, and was propelled by 30 rowers. There would be room for nine passengers. At the stern is the heavy steering oar. It is the only surviving example of the type of boat used by the Angles, Saxons, Jutes, and Frisians to cross the North Sea and invade Britain to survive. It is an ancestor of the Viking longships.

Below: Men wore brooches like this to fasten their cloaks on the shoulder. They were cast in bronze, silver, or gold using clay moulds which had to be broken open. Some were inlaid with enamel or semi-precious stones. Different tribes had characteristic brooch-shapes.

Bottom: Three Anglo-Saxon necklaces, of glass, amber, and amethyst beads. Glass beads – clear or opaque – are quite common. Amber from the Baltic was used for beads because of its rich colour and as a charm against witchcraft. Amethyst beads are very rare. Amethyst came from the east Mediterranean but the Anglo-Saxons may have obtained theirs by looting Rome graves.

(12 by 8 feet) was dug. Some had a stout post at each end, to support the roof. This sloped up from the ground surface to a ridge-pole, like a tent.

The Frisians of the coast of Holland and north Germany were forced to build their villages on artificial mounds to escape periodic floods. Some of these mounds or *Terpen* are still occupied by modern villages. The mound was made by heaping up a mixture of animal dung from byres with cart-loads of clay. Some mounds were up to half a hectare (an acre) in extent. The farmhouses and their outbuildings were built on the *Terp*, and at its foot were the cornfields and pastures.

Farm produce

The barbarians kept herds of cattle, for their hides, for meat, and for milk. Cheese was made from the milk. Some tribes kept sheep and goats, and pigs rooted in the forests with little supervision. Crops were less important than cattle in the economy, but rye, wheat, and barley, peas and beans were grown. Flax provided linseed oil.

Wool from the sheep was spun and woven into cloth on upright looms, the warp threads weighted with stones or with thick clay rings. Women wore long skirts. One kind of dress, with sleeves, was made from a rectangular length of cloth folded over at the top to make a cape and hood, pinned on each shoulder with a brooch.

Men wore a short tunic, not reaching the knees, and close-fitting trousers. Sometimes socks were woven in one with the trousers. A short cloak was pinned on the right shoulder with a brooch as elaborate as the owner could afford. Some men wore a short cape of animal fur.

Craftsmen

The barbarians had skilled carpenters who could joint large timbers in house construction, and make benches and indi-

THE HUNS

In the late 4th century AD, the Chinese defeated steppe nomads of Turkish stock whom they called the *Hsiung-nu*. These are probably the people known in Europe as the Huns. Expelled by the Chinese, these nomads rode into south Russia and eastern Europe about AD 370. Grim rumours flew ahead of them: that they were barely human, stunted in growth, beardless, filthy and squalid, drinkers of blood, eating raw food, never getting off their horses even to sleep. These rumours were certainly exaggerated, but it is true that the Huns were aggressive warriors, shooting arrows from horseback with devastating effect. When they erupted into Europe, they overwhelmed the Alans, Ostrogoths, and Visigoths, and settled in Hungary.

The Huns included a number of independent tribes, but about AD 445, a great leader, Attila, murdered his brother and became king over all the Huns. He led them to attack Constantinople, and forced the eastern emperor to buy peace. The Huns then returned to central Europe, where the victorious Attila now ruled over a huge assortment of tribes, occupying nearly half of Europe. Later he moved against the western empire, leading his hordes into Gaul. There, near Troyes, he was defeated by the Emperor Aetius and had to retreat to Hungary.

After Attila's death the great confederacy that he had founded simply broke up into a number of quarrelling tribes. There was no-one of equal stature to succeed him, and he had not been concerned with establishing an empire; he was a warrior, not an administrator.

vidual tables for meal-times, when people sat along the long walls of the house. Kings owned elaborate wooden chairs with carved and turned ornament. The lathe was also used to make plates, flasks, and bowls for food. Specialist wheelwrights made wheels for the waggons and carts that were used on farms, and for transporting women, children, and pos-

A drinking-horn from Gallehus, Denmark, one of a pair that was stolen and melted down in 1802. The decoration (detail) suggests that it was used for ritual purposes.

This splendid armlet was thrown into a lake at Thorsberg, Germany, as an offering to the gods. It is decorated with crudely drawn animals and birds, and borders of human heads.

Runic letters can be made out on the skirt of this mysterious little bronze figure, found in a warrior's grave at Froyhov, Norway. It dates from the 3rd century AD. Runes – an alphabetic form of writing used by the barbarians from about AD 100, formed of straight lines – were often carved on personal possessions, sometimes as spells.

sessions if the tribe had to leave its lands. Leatherworkers made horse-harness, and leather scabbards and soft leather sword-harnesses for warriors. Leather shoes were made for nobles, but most people went bare-foot.

The village blacksmith forged such everyday objects as ploughshares, knives, and waggon tyres but specialist sword-smiths, bronze-workers and jewellers worked at the courts of chiefs. Skilled metalworkers travelled far and wide in barbarian Europe, so that their art style was common to all the tribes – although there were local preferences for some designs. The best work of these craftsmen was not surpassed, it has been said, until the Renaissance. Jewellers worked in bronze, gold, and silver. Their supplies of gold and silver were obtained from the Roman world, either from coins paid to buy off barbarian raiders, or from Roman vessels that were melted down.

The warband
The authority of the kindred and the tribe was increasingly challenged during the 'Age of Migrations' by that of the war-band. Young warriors would break away from the tribal organization, and join a leader (who claimed descent from a god) to fight with a closely knit group. Loyalty was expected of the warriors, and generosity of their leader. At this time, the wealth of the Roman empire, with its villas and towns rich with splendid gold and silver plate and ornaments, acted as a magnet. Any man who was prepared to lead raids could attract a band of followers prepared to cut themselves off from the traditional family loyalties.

An adventurer of this kind could only keep the loyalty of his followers if he led them on raids where much 'treasure' could be won. All the plunder belonged to him – but he was expected to reward his followers with gold and silver arm-rings, fine swords and other weapons.

The rise of the warband and the decline of the old tribal organization with its closely knit kindreds was a consequence of the Age of Migrations. Newcomers from the steppes were forcing their way into the territories of established tribes, forcing them to leave their ancestral

Europe at the time of the fall of Rome, AD 476.

This silver-gilt drinking vessel was buried with a warrior at Himlingoje, Denmark, in the 3rd century AD.

lands. The displaced tribes either attacked a weaker neighbour, or were dispersed, small groups joining different tribes. In these difficult conditions, age-old institutions such as the complex kindred systems were hard to maintain. The warband was much more fluid against the shifting background.

The warrior

Some tribes went into battle wearing only trousers, but most wore tunics as well. Body armour was not worn until after AD 500. Kings were distinguished by their splendid helmets of gilded bronze, with padded linings. It was believed that ornamenting a helmet with a boar would give the wearer the boar's ferocity and courage. Eagles, ravens, and wolves, all symbols of war, were also used to decorate helmets and shields.

Shields were round, made of wood and often covered with leather. In the centre was a recess for the hand-grip, an iron bar. Its front was covered by a projecting boss which could be used to knock a weapon from an enemy's hand.

The main weapon was the spear. The ashwood shafts were about 3 metres (10 feet) long, with an iron blade. Some spearheads were beautifully decorated. The angon, or throwing spear, was copied from the Roman *pilum*. It was designed to bend after it stuck into an enemy shield, so that it could not be thrown back. The way in which the angon was followed up was described by an observer:

Then the Frank rushes in, places his foot on the butt as it trails on the ground, and pulling the shield down, cleaves his unprotected enemy through the head, or pierces his breast with another spear.

Another important weapon was the *franciska*, a throwing axe used not only by the Franks after whom it was named, but also by the Alamanni. It had a weighted iron head, cleverly curved, and a wooden haft.

The warrior's most precious possession was his sword. It might be given to him by his lord, or be a family heirloom. There were legends about the magic qualities of famous swords – that they screamed aloud, or alone could heal the wounds they made.

Some tribes used the bow and arrow. The Huns were famous archers. In north Germany, arrows were kept in wooden quivers, on which patterns were incised. Arrows were tipped with iron or bone heads; on the shafts were marks so that the owner could collect his arrows after a battle, and identify the foes he had slain with his own hand.

Hilt of a sword of the 6th century AD, from a grave in Norway. The ornament on the pommel and at the base of the blade is silver gilt; the grip between is covered with gold sheet. The contorted animal pattern originated in the Scandinavian Iron Age. Such swords were very precious, and were credited with magic powers. They were often handed down from father to son. The purpose of the rings about the hilt is unknown.

BARBARIAN RELIGION

The barbarians worshipped war gods, of whom the greatest was Tiw (after whom Tuesday – 'Tiw's day' – was named). Prisoners of war were offered to him as sacrifices; much of the booty captured from an enemy was broken, to 'kill' it, and thrown into lakes as an offering. Other war gods included Woden or Odin, and Donar or Thor (after whom Wednesday and Thursday were named). Thor may have been a sky god, like the Greek Zeus, for his hammer represented thunder.

Goddesses were worshipped in fertility cults, involving processions to bless the land. In Jutland, the goddess Nerthus was wheeled round the tribal territory in a sacred waggon. Before the goddess was restored to her shrine, the image and the waggon was washed in a sacred lake, and the slaves who had carried out this ritual were afterwards put to death.

The barbarians were very superstitious. They believed that hoards of treasure were guarded by dragons, and that horrible monsters lived at the bottom of deep pools. The movements of birds and animals were interpreted as omens. In AD 454, Attila the Hun was about to give up the siege of a town, when he saw a stork, which had been nesting on one of the towers of the town wall, fly up at sunrise with its young on its back. Attila told his troops that this must mean that the town was about to fall, so they held on to their positions. The very tower where the stork had nested fell down, and the Huns stormed the defences through the gap.

Some barbarians cremated the dead on a funeral pyre; others buried the body unburned. The body of a king might be placed in a ship and pushed out to sea. The dead were buried fully clothed, with their belongings, and food and drink for their new life beyond the grave. A man was given his weapons, a woman her work-box. A gaming board with bone counters was put in, to help pass the time. Some very precious possessions were buried with the dead, such as metal vessels, or glass beakers, imported from the Roman world. This represented a great loss for the heirs. Some barbarians believed in ghosts. To stop the dead walking, the head was cut off and placed at the feet.

The Fall of Rome

Why the Roman empire fell is one of the most argued-over questions in history. Not only might the causes of Rome's decline shed light on the fall of mighty states and the rise of new powers today; the fall of Rome also marks the boundary between the ancient world and the Middle Ages – the end of the ancient civilizations.

Before we begin to look at possible explanations for the fall of the Roman empire, we should remember two things. Firstly, the empire had lasted several hundred years before it distintegrated. Secondly, half of the empire did *not* fall: the eastern provinces survived as the Byzantine empire which lasted for another thousand years. We have to explain the decline of the West and the survival of the East too.

How far back should we look for symptoms of weakness that might lead to collapse? Certainly the earliest wholesale problems of the empire did not take place until the 3rd century, when everything went wrong. Military power was paramount, there were constant civil wars, a rapid turnover of emperors (often with rival emperors ruling simultaneously), appalling inflation that was comparable to the madly spiralling inflation of the Deutschmark before the last world war, and growing oppression of the ordinary people of the empire. This was the 'crisis' of the 3rd century. But several of the weaknesses of the empire which then became glaringly obvious had been there from the start: Augustus and his immediate successors had all found it difficult to maintain a balance of power between emperor, Senate, and army, and to achieve a smooth transfer of power at the centre.

The new element in the 3rd-century crisis was the soaring inflation and financial chaos. Yet for years this had been building up, for emperors in need of money had minted more and more coins to pay their soldiers or buy supplies – and coins of decreasing value. The *denarius*, which had started off as a fine silver coin, ended up as a copper imitation, disguised as silver merely with a thin coating of the precious metal. As with money today, the crunch came when people lost confidence in its worth. Prices rose hourly: traders abandoned the bad money for barter.

The 3rd-century crisis was not the end of the empire, for the decline was halted by two strong and competent emperors, Diocletian and Constantine, who among other measures successfully re-established the coinage.

In many ways, the problems of the 3rd century resulted in a renewal of the structure of the empire. Diocletian thoroughly overhauled the taxation system of the empire – people's taxes were now related directly to the productivity of their land. The government still took much of the supplies it needed for the army and the civil service in kind from taxpayers, so that it would not have to pay high prices for grain purchased through grain-merchants.

Feeding the cities

In the great cities of the empire the problems of the 3rd century had played havoc with the food supply. The government had to intervene more and more to look after citizens who might otherwise have starved. At Rome, people were issued daily with bread in the 3rd century. Then they were also given salt, wine, oil, and pork by the government – the main requirements for a quite substantial diet.

The fall of Rome has sometimes been blamed on the barbarians. But barbarian raids had been a threat to the empire for a long time. A popular and dramatic theme for sarcophagi was a battle between Romans and barbarians; in this sarcophagus, made for one of Marcus Aurelius's generals, cavalry and infantry are fighting a tribe of the middle Danube area. The sarcophagus was made in advance by a workshop; the general's face (centre) is left blank for his portrait to be carved in later.

This was the ultimate development of the issues of free grain to the citizens of Rome that had been started by the Gracchi brothers in the 2nd century BC – not as a 'dole', for the unemployed, but a privilege for citizens. By the late empire the giving out of free food was a way of ensuring the existence of a huge urban population, without starvation – or the dangerous riots that went with a food crisis.

In the face of increasing barbarian attacks, government organization increased. Laws were passed making it an obligation for a baker's son to succeed his father in the bakery business, and many other occupations also became hereditary by law. Many historians have seen this kind of ruthless legislation as a sign of the impending collapse of the empire, which could no longer easily get people to perform jobs that they had once done voluntarily. And certainly many of the efforts of the Roman government to get things done do seem to be born of desperation. On the other hand, we must not exaggerate the symptoms. Most people were in traditionally hereditary occupations anyway; the intervention of the law was a safeguard to a normally stable situation.

Under new legislation peasant farmers were tied to their land or that of their masters. Many were anxious to move because they were simply getting poorer. Many of the peasants' lords were at the same time getting richer, and this increasing gulf between rich and poor distinguishes the late empire from the happier days of the early empire. The poor were at the mercy not only of their powerful landlords, but of the grasping tax-collector, who even with the more efficient tax system of Diocletian, still asked for far too much. As the barbarian pressure increased, Roman rule became so harsh that many people of the empire said they would prefer life under barbarian masters. In Gaul, where conditions seem to have been particularly bad, peasants fled into the forests, finding a living as bandits, or indeed joining the barbarians.

Many of the barbarians had themselves been going over to the Romans – this is another feature that historians have pointed to as a cause of the decline of Rome's power. From the early days of the empire, Rome used barbarian soldiers

This portrait-group of a Christian family dates from the 4th century AD. It is painted on glass and set into the centre of a gold cross, which is studded with precious stones. Realistic portrait painting had been practised in the Roman world since the Republic, and Christians carried this tradition into the Byzantine empire. Some of these glass portraits have been found in the catacombs, underground tunnels where the early Christians met.

in her armies to fight other barbarians; sufficient soldiers were not available from inside the empire itself, although more and more incentives (in the form of generous tax exemptions, offers of land, and the cattle and seed corn necessary to start up farms) were made to army recruits in the 4th century. At first the barbarians were under Roman command; later they provided their own generals. This led in the end to a take-over by the barbarians at the centre of power. The Vandal soldier Stilicho became commander-in-chief of the Roman armies, and married into the royal family. It was only a matter of time before the throne itself was in the hands of non-Romans, and finally the puppet emperor Romulus Augustulus was deposed by his barbarian master and the western empire ended.

It was not only as soldiers that barbarians entered the empire. In the 4th and 5th centuries the 'Age of Migrations' (see page 108) led to refugees from fiercer invading tribes begging, sometimes successfully, to be allowed to settle within the boundaries of the empire.

Even if the Romans had had a vast, all-Roman army, it probably could not in any case have withstood the massive onslaught of the invasions which finally brought down the western part of the empire in the 5th century. The survival of the eastern half of the empire at this stage was due not least to the fact that it sent some barbarian invaders on their way to the West.

Not only do the depredations of the tax-collectors really seem to have hit harder in the West than the East; but more of the cities shrank in size, and lands became deserted, particularly in Italy and

Stilicho, the 4th-century Vandal who became commander-in-chief of Roman army and defeated barbarian armies. In the later empire barbarian power increased within Rome itself.

once-prosperous North Africa. The depopulation of the Roman empire in the West is another explanation that has been suggested as the cause of its collapse. This is perhaps the most difficult 'cause' to discuss, since the overall behaviour of populations in terms of growth and decline is still imperfectly understood. Certainly the more attractively simple explanations of population decline do not work. The suggestion that people were dying off because of lead poisoning from their water pipes or containers for their wine cannot apply to most inhabitants of the empire, who lived in the countryside and did not have piped water!

How far did the growth of Christianity provide an alternative direction for the loyalties of Roman citizens? Driven underground (literally, since many met in underground catacombs – burial vaults – in Rome) for their religious beliefs in the first decades of the Roman empire, Christians were treated by the Roman authorities as dangerous rebels. The wholesale persecution of Christians only started in the 3rd century (although there had been earlier spasmodic outbreaks as under Nero) when the crisis of the Roman state made the authorities look for a scapegoat. The eventual acceptance of Christianity by the Emperor Constantine radically altered the situation and during the 4th century the Christian Church became a huge organization, involving the energies and loyalties of hundreds and thousands of people. Many of them were economically unproductive, and the drain of supporting them must indeed have been great. The 18th-century historian Gibbon in his massive survey of the decline and fall of Rome concluded that Christianity played a major part in the fall of the West. The situation can only have been made worse by a degree of fatalism among churchmen who really believed that the end of the world had come. For some, with the collapse of the Roman power in the West, it had.

The legacy

Many elements of Roman civilization survived the undeniable end of Roman political power. The Latin language remained to form the basis of the new European Romance languages – French, Spanish, Italian, and Romanian. It sur-

vived without great change as the language of the Church and learning, through the Dark and Middle Ages. Educated men could communicate in Latin whether they were Celts or Germans or Italians.

And in the Middle Ages, the old network of Roman roads still formed a basis for communication, when there was communication (and they are still so used today). The vast baths, palaces, and temples of late imperial Rome dwarfed all buildings until the dome of St Peters rose in the 16th century. The Roman way of life cast a long shadow over the succeeding centuries.

The *idea* of Rome and of its empire also survived, in ways that seem curious today. Rome the city, the centre of the civilized world, was transformed from the symbol of imperial power into one of the most powerful symbols in Christian imagery and the centre of the Catholic Church. As for the political legacy, the people of the eastern empire, whom we now call the Byzantines, were still thought of as 'Romans' by their mediaeval colleagues in the eastern Mediterranean. In the west, great leaders claimed to be the successor of the emperors of Rome. Charlemagne, great king of the Franks, extended his power right into the heart of the old Roman empire, into Italy, and the climax of his imperial dream came with his crowning in 800 as Holy Roman emperor. The Holy Roman Empire, made up mainly of the Frankish territories in France and Germany, was a mediaeval institution; but it was a Roman legacy.

A gold mount, from a belt or headdress, from Asia Minor, made in about 350 AD. It shows a woman riding after a lion. The contrast between the formal, abstract border and the lively movement of the realistic figures is typical of its period, when the realism of late Roman art was beginning to give way to the more stylized decoration we associate with the Byzantine empire and the early Middle Ages.

The Eastern Emperor Justinian reconquered part of Italy in the 6th century. The main base of his power there was the city of Ravenna on the Adriatic coast. Here churches were founded, decorated in the Byzantine style with rich mosaics of glass and marble – a continuation of the Roman mosaic tradition. In this mosaic from the church of Sant'Apollinare Nuovo, the Three Magi in their Persian dress bring their gifts.

India

The sub-continent of India is a triangle jutting south from the mainland of Asia. To the north-east lie the Himalayas, to the north-west mountain passes lead to Afghanistan and then to Iran. Much of the peninsula, the Deccan, is a high tableland rimmed by mountains. Between the Deccan and the mountains of the north are vast fertile plains: that of the Ganges to the east, and of the Punjab – the Land of Five Rivers, greatest of which was the Indus – to the west.

The Indus civilization

p. 13

Civilizations grow up in river valleys, where rich soil makes it possible to produce plenty of food. The civilizations of India developed in the northern plains and then spread southwards. The first great civilization grew up in the Indus valley and spread – in a diluted form – to the edge of the Ganges plain. It probably arose about 2500 BC and had three 'capital' cities: Harappa (after which the civilization is often called), Mohenjo-daro, and Kalibangan. Throughout the vast Indus area town planning, house shapes, pottery, stonework, and bronze objects all show an extraordinary standardization, with only minor 'provincial' differences. This can only have been the result of regulation from an authority of some kind, probably located in the 'capitals'.

Gradually this rigid uniformity broke down. Something, or more than one thing, had sent the once strict and authoritarian system of regulation into an irreversible decline. Towards the end of the period objects become more diversified and town planning is lost in a maze of dilapidated buildings.

But not everything was lost when the great cities of the Punjab were finally brought to ruin. In many basic details the Indus civilization was similar to modern Indian culture – a major argument for a continuing Harappan influence. Although the most sophisticated of Indus political and intellectual traditions must have been lost with the end of the cities, traditions of perhaps even greater importance have survived. Houses today, as then, are built around courtyards, the drains emptying through the outside walls into the street just as in the Indus period. Wooden carts drawn by bullocks are built and used today exactly as they were more than 4000 years ago. Aspects of agriculture were much the same. Weights and measures in Harappan times used the ratio of 16 to 1 just as the rupee has until recently been divided into 16 annas. Some gods and goddesses of Harappan India take the same shape, and possibly function in the same way too, in modern Indian religion.

Through all the changes of Indian history life at the lowest level has remained much the same. While the rulers have changed, the peasants have gone on scratching a living from the soil with simple wooden ploughs; growing wheat or rice, and keeping a cow or a buffalo for draught purposes and for a little milk; using plain pottery vessels to carry water from the village well. To the Indian villager the arrival of the annual rains is what matters, not the arrival of a new civilization.

The 'Aryans'

The developments that followed the end of the Harappan civilization are often put down to a race of people called the

Three seals of the Harappan period, made of steatite and baked hard after carving. The bulls, shown in profile, are standing before an object whose use is not known. The writing at the top is in the script of the Indus civilization, which is as yet completely undeciphered. Seals like this were used for commercial purposes such as sealing bales.

This seal, also from the Indus civilization, shows Pashupali, lord of animals, seated in a yogic position. The three faces show that the yogic tradition is in some form very ancient; and they also foreshadow the Hindu trimurti of Shiva, Brahma, and Vishnu.

'Aryans'. The so-called Aryan invasions are seen as a reason for all sorts of things, from the destruction of the Indus cities to the introduction of iron. But this is too simple a picture.

Certainly new peoples did make their way through the north-west mountain passes into India before the beginning of the second millennium BC. Their language belonged to the Indo-European or Aryan family (to which belong not only the most widely spoken languages in modern India and Pakistan, but also most western European languages including English). Movements of these people probably began far to the west and may have coincided with the domestication of the horse.

The _Rigveda_, an enormously long collection of hymns and religious formulae, from which most later Indian religion and philosophy ultimately derives, originates with these same Indo-European speakers. It proves the connections between north India and its western neighbours. The names of the Rigvedic gods Mitra, Indra, and Varuna are specifically mentioned in a treaty between the Hittites and Mitannians in about 1380 BC. Further proof comes from the Indo-European names of the Mitannian kings.

The arrival of people from the north-west is clear from archaeological material as well. Shaft-hole axes of west Asian type, copper stamp seals, and footed and legged bowls of Persian origin are found in the north-west dating from about 1800 BC. Throughout the Indus area there is evidence of new foreign elements, often with Persian or west Asian characteristics.

So the connections between India and regions to the west are indisputable. But this link is not the result of one, or even of a small number, of grand invasions of the sub-continent. The movement of people, languages, and ideas takes place at different rates and over long periods of time. In the case of India these shiftings probably began in the early second millennium BC before the end of the Indus civilization, continuing to as late as the 5th century. And these people must not be thought of as being the authors of everything to appear during this period. Iron-working is undoubtedly a local Indian development as is the growth of the city culture that follows in the middle first millennium BC.

The Iron Age

For years people have said that iron-working was introduced to India by some outside influence. But recent work has shown that in fact iron-smelting developed independently in India on possibly more than one occasion, from about 1000 BC on. The focal point of the Iron Age in north India is the vast area of the Ganges plains, that lie just south of the Himalayas. This is an enormous, fertile region, with rich soil laid down by the hundreds of rivers flowing through it. In ancient times it must have been covered by dry forest, now almost entirely gone.

Early iron objects included arrowheads, knives, spearheads, and axes. Copper was still used for pins and small arrowheads, glass was made into beads and bangles, and there were small objects of ivory.

The beginning of this pre-city Iron Age is put at between 1000 and 800 BC, and it had probably ended by about 500 BC — although it would have overlapped into following periods. At roughly the same time the Iron Age began in South India.

Along the south-east coast of India, near Madras, Iron-Age sites have been found with the usual pottery. Then come objects found together with Roman trade goods. Sir Mortimer Wheeler's discovery of this connection with the ancient western world was of tremendous importance. For the first time the chronology of Indian archaeology could be placed in a well-known time scale.

Indian civilization grew up on river plains. In this landscape, near the caves at Karla in western India, the maze of small fields on the plain is broken only by low granite hills, in some of which are the cave temples for which the area is renowned.

A curious multi-legged sarcophagus with an animal head, found at Sankhavaram in south India and dating from the Iron Age.

The first cities

From about 500 BC, a series of great cities grew up on the sites of Iron-Age villages along the rivers which drain the endless plains of north India. The greatest of these rivers are the Ganges and the Jamuna, and it was in the region of these huge streams that the largest and most important of the cities of the 'Ganges Civilization' grew up.

At the mound known as Atranjikhera on the Kali river, excavators discovered a clear relationship between the earlier Iron-Age settlement and the later fully developed city. The earlier village was surrounded by a wall of mud, possibly acting as protection against flooding of the river. The later city was enclosed by a defensive wall, built by the descendants of the earlier Iron-Age villagers. So the cities of north India are a local development, and owe their origins to no new outside influence. The Ganges cities are often of great size, a kilometre or so across, surrounded by high walls of brick and stone with moats, towers, and other defensive arrangements. Within the walls were large public buildings, temples, palaces, granaries, and so on.

Buddhism and Jainism, the great new religions of north India which grew up at this time, were largely city based. The Buddha and Mahāvira, founder of Jainism, both spent long periods in such cities as Vaishāli, Rājgir, and Shrāvasti. Although many of the great cities of the Ganges plains eventually fell into ruin, overrun by invaders in the early centuries AD, some survived and flourish to this day. Patna and Benares are the most notable.

As in ancient Greece, cities now warred against each other and small states tried

A gigantic statue of the Buddha at Bamiyan in Afghanistan, carved in one piece out of the cliff face. Near it are smaller caves and temples. It was carved by the Gandharans in the early centuries AD, and was an ancient centre of worship.

A bowl of 'painted grey ware', the finest pottery of the early Iron Age of the Upper Gangetic plains. It was made from about 1000 BC to as late as the 6th or 5th century BC.

to overrun their neighbours. Most important of the many states were Magadha, Vatsa, and Kosala. Magadha, where the state of Bihar is today, eventually extended its power far beyond its own borders to form a great kingdom, the basis of the later India-wide Mauryan empire.

The first great king of Magadha was Bimbisara who lived about the time of the Buddha, in the 6th century BC. His capital

Society in India at this time was — as it still is — divided into four main sections or *castes*. This began with the first Indo-European speakers. The four castes are: Brahmins or priests who perform sacrifices and know what is contained in the sacred literature or *Vedas*; the Kshatriyas or warriors and kings; the Vaishyas or the trading class; the Shudras or serfs and labourers. Below all of these castes or *varnas* as they are called, from a Sanskrit word meaning colour, are the outcasts or untouchables. These are people who perform the worst tasks and who have no rights at all. In modern India this last category has been abolished although old ideas, especially when they are as old as this one, are long in dying. Even the introduction of the Buddhist religion had no long term effect on the caste system.

was at Rājgir, a city in a valley formed by high granite hills jutting out of the flat plains. All along the tops of these hills runs an enormous rampart wall, built of huge stones and possibly dating from this early period. Buddhist literature says that Bimbisara was murdered by his son Ajatasatru while in prison. Ajatasatru was responsible for much warfare and greatly extended his kingdom as a result. Later, he repented his former sins and became a Buddhist under the influence of Gautama himself. As the Magadhan empire continued to grow, some of its ruling houses formed separate dynasties, the Shishunagas and then the Nandas.

During the 6th and then the 4th centuries BC India was invaded by forces from the west. The first of these events took place under the leadership of Cyrus the Great, the King of Persia (see page 65).

Among the sacred literature of the Brahmins is the Ramayana of the late centuries BC. It tells the story of the search of the hero Rama for his dutiful wife Sita, who was stolen from him. This illustration shows Rama and Sita enthroned; behind them stand his followers and before them the loyal monkey god Hanuman with his retinue.

A seated Buddha from Mathura, dating from the Gupta period (c 4th–5th century AD). It is made from the typical Sikri standstone of the area, which is pink with white spots. Beside the Buddha stand two attendant bodhisattvas.

HINDUISM

The ancestor of modern Hinduism is the religion of the Indo-European speaking people of the 2nd millennium BC. It is passed down to the present in the form of the sacred *Vedas*, a set of texts from which comes religious authority for the Hindus. These texts are largely collections of hymns and sacrificial formulae dedicated to such deities as Agni the god of fire, Indra the war god, and so on. In this literature the law or *Dharma* is set down. This law provides a set of principles, often very detailed, by which the life of man is ordered. Later texts and commentaries are also used as a basis of this *Dharma*. Embedded in *Dharma* is the notion of the four castes.

The religion of the *Vedas* was shaped and adapted until the early centuries AD, when Hinduism emerged as the chief religion of India, unchanged basically to the present day.

Our knowledge of religion in India before Vedic times is limited to conclusions drawn from the examination of seals and images from Indus Civilization sites, and of mother goddesses, and cult objects from all over India. But a great deal of the religion of the pre-Indo-European peoples of India seems to have remained intact, influenced by the ideas taken from the Brahmins, or embedded in Hinduism itself. For religion in India, and particularly Hinduism, is a patchwork of interconnected sects and sets of beliefs. These may range from the veneration of a tree or curiously shaped stone in a remote village, to the complex philosophy of a Brahmin pandit at the holy city of Benares. The Hindu religion tolerates an almost infinite variety of approaches unified in a very broad framework.

During the early centuries of the first millennium BC the first commentaries on the Vedas were written. These works became known as the *Upanishads*. They examine the nature of the human soul and the universe, and probe into their relationship. In the *Upanishads* the old Vedic gods are accepted but a most important principle is added, that of *Brahman*. Brahman is the idea of a single world spirit from which all gods, people, and other things have developed, and which resides in them always. It is a 'divine essence' and demonstrates the unity that exists in the complex real world. Despite this idea of unity the Brahmanical religion (as it must be called at this stage), remained polytheistic, accepting all gods as manifestations of this single spirit. The relation of Man to this spirit is seen in the idea of *Atman* or soul, an intangible quality of self from which all life proceeds but which cannot be isolated. The absorption of this personal *Atman* into the single spirit is a state of understanding that all men long for. It can be achieved only through a series of births and rebirths, the special *Atman* of the person involved being quite separate from the outward shape of the bodies he inhabits during his various lives.

Three basic principles govern this striving for understanding. The first of these is this cycle of rebirth – the transmigration of souls. The second idea is that of *Karma* or cause and effect, by which means a person leading a good life can hope for better things in his next existence or the opposite if he leads a bad one. *Dharma*, the third idea, is the law stipulating what sort of a life a person must lead according to his place in society – his caste. All these notions are linked. If a person obeys his *Dharma* his *Karma* will be good, making him able to rise in the order of things after death. These basic principles are at the heart of the Hindu religion to this day.

The Hindu religion eventually emerged as a combination of the philosophy of the Brahmins and acceptance of the ancient gods, influenced greatly by the *Ahimsa* or non-violent reverence for life of the Jains, and the ethics of the Buddhists. The Hindu pantheon of gods is enormous but the three most important are Brahma the creator, Vishnu the preserver, and Shiva the destroyer. These gods, and incarnations of them such as Krishna, mother goddesses like Kali or Durga, and thousands of other deities are worshipped in temples all over India just as they have been for countless centuries.

The lion capital from the Ashokan pillar at Sarnath. It was originally mounted high on a polished shaft of marble at the place near Benares where the Buddha preached his first sermon — and set turning 'the wheel of the law' depicted at the lions' feet. Ashoka set up a number of pillars, the inscriptions on which are written in a script known as Brahmi, the earliest decipherable form of writing in India. From it have developed most of the modern alphabets of north India. The capital shows the high finish known as the Mauryan polish.

CHRONOLOGY

BC	
900–700	Iron Age
c 600	Early cities in Ganges valley
c 563	Birth of the Buddha
533	Achaemenid invasion of India
430–364	Shishunagas
364–324	Nandas
326	Alexander the Great in India
324–187	Mauryans
232	Death of Ashoka
187–75	Shungas
AD	
15–300s	Kushans
320–600s	Guptas

THE NANDA ARMY
The Nanda king of Magadha at the time of Alexander's invasion in 326 BC possessed an enormous army. It was said by one writer to have consisted of 20,000 cavalry, 200,000 infantry, 2000 four-horsed chariots, and between 3000 and 6000 elephants. Soldiers were armed with swords and spears, the latter both for throwing and thrusting. Bows were of the composite type (see page 123), and arrows were tipped with iron, copper, or ivory. Indian swords, introduced rather later than the bow, were broad and short, the blade often slightly spoon-shaped towards its point. Soldiers carried round or oblong shields of leather or wood, sometimes reinforced with iron. Body armour is mentioned in the ancient literature but is little known archaeologically. In the 4th century BC King Porus is reported to have worn metal armour in his battles against Alexander.

The Achaemenid empire, as Cyrus's dominions were called, was extended as far as part of the western Punjab. Cities such as Taxila were founded by the Persians, whose influence can sometimes be seen in the decoration of some early Indian sculpture. In 326 BC Alexander the Great reached north-west India. This was the period of the Nanda Dynasty in Magadha but the power of their kingdom did not yet stretch as far as distant parts of the Punjab. Alexander himself did not stay long, but the influence of Greek culture in that part of India remained for centuries in the Indo-Greek cities of Afghanistan and Sind.

Mauryas
The Greeks were driven out of the Punjab not long after the death of Alexander, by Chandragupta Maurya. He founded the Mauryan dynasty, centred in the old kingdom of Magadha, with its capital at Pataliputra on the Ganges. Under the rule of the Mauryas India was unified from nearly one end to the other. The emperor was the highest authority in the land. He ruled with the help of a deputy and a chief minister. Below him was a bureaucracy made up of separate departments of state dealing with trade, forestry, public works, and so on. The heads of these departments were at Pataliputra but local matters were under regional supervisors.

The empire was divided into a number of administrative levels. The lowest level was the village, run by a headman who was responsible to district officials having authority over a number of villages. The governor of a district reported to the officials of a province, made up of a group of districts. At the capitals of these provinces sat a viceroy, usually a member of the royal family, who was responsible directly to the centre. Before his accession to the throne, Ashoka himself had been viceroy at Ujjain and Taxila. The emperor also provided inspectors who travelled to all parts of the empire seeing that the law was being observed.

The greatest of their emperors was Ashoka (273–232 BC), famous not only for his kingly virtue and liberality but for the inscribed, polished stone pillars he set up at important places in his kingdom. One of these great columns, moved later in

SRI LANKA
The recorded history of Sri Lanka begins in the period of Ashoka. In 247 BC, during the reign of Devanampiya-Tissa, Ashoka's son Mahinda came from India and converted the Sinhalese to Buddhism. In those days the great city of Sri Lanka was Anuradhapura, some 145 kilometres (90 miles) north of Kandy, and the chief city of the island for nearly 1500 years. Its Buddhist ruins are among the country's greatest monuments. The collar-bone and food bowl of the Buddha were enshrined there at the Thupa Rama stupa built by King Tissa in 244 BC.

The most interesting aspect of ancient civilization in Sri Lanka is the complex irrigation works found all over the island. They are based upon the construction of huge reservoirs storing water for use in the paddy fields where rice, the staple grain of Sri Lanka, is grown. These reservoirs are surrounded by banks often up to 15 metres (50 feet) high and 14 kilometres (9 miles) long. The earliest identifiable structure in Sri Lanka is the Abhaya Tank covering 91 hectares (225 acres) near Anuradhapura and dating from about 300 BC. Along with these reservoirs, unknown on this scale in ancient India, are dams, sluices, and canals showing the astonishingly high level of the engineering skill of the early Sinhalese.

The dwarf frieze at the Raja Maha Vihare, Kelaniya. This is one of the oldest temples in Sri Lanka and is supposed to have been visited by the Buddha.

history, needed 8400 men pulling a 42-wheeled cart to transport it!

Within only 50 years of the death of Ashoka in 232 BC the great empire of the Mauryas had been broken up. At his death two of Ashoka's grandsons divided the empire between themselves, and many areas broke away to become independent. In 187 BC the last Mauryan ruler was assassinated by his general, Pushyamitra.

The archaeological record does not tell us much about ordinary life during the Mauryan period. The small size of most excavations is at the bottom of this problem. The great wooden palisades surrounding Pataliputra were discovered early in this century, as was the huge pillared hall of the emperor of which now only a few shattered stumps of columns remain. The many beautiful terracotta figurines found at Pataliputra show that the dress of fashionable ladies of the period was elaborate and involved huge headresses and large skirts. Mauryan art comes to us mostly in the form of sculpture. Artists created lifelike and sensitive figures of animals and people, giving the surface of their sculptures a high finish, often called Mauryan polish, unknown in later times. Even the huge stone pillars of Ashoka were polished in this way, and so were the inside walls of caves in the Barabar hills of Bihar, carved out on the orders of the Emperor.

The Shungas

After he murdered his king, Pushyamitra set himself up as ruler and established the Shunga dynasty. It was attached to the old Brahmanical religion of the Vedas but must have tolerated the Buddhists, who continued to construct stupas and excavate the great cave temples of western India known as *chaityas*. They produced the finest artistic creations of this period, and their cave temples are the most famous of all. These caves were carved by hand out of the solid rock, using iron chisels. Their interiors are elaborately decorated in fine stone sculpture and, often, with wall paintings of very great beauty. The paintings in the caves at Ajanta are mostly of a later date, but some few from the Shunga period do indeed remain. These caves provided both a place of worship and a home for the monks who lived there. Cave temples of this type were

sculpted for several centuries, the Hindu motifs in them growing in importance as time passed. Stupa building and decoration also flourished during the Shunga period.

Indo-Greeks

West of Kabul in Afghanistan lay Bactria, whose Indo-Greek rulers were powerful enough by the 2nd century BC to be able to invade India far into the Ganges plains. In the end the Indo-Greeks lost Bactria itself, but they remained rulers of southern Afghanistan and parts of north-west India. The greatest of these kings was Menander, who ruled from about 115 to 90 BC. His kingdom extended as far east as the

The stupa at Sanchi, one of the most famous in India. The stupa was the typical Buddhist monument. In its original form it was a mound of stones covering a relict of the Buddha, whose remains had been dispersed after his cremation. Later stupas became large and elaborate dome-shaped structures. The Sanchi stupa was originally built by Ashoka in the 3rd century BC; it was enlarged in the 2nd century BC and embellished by the Andhras in the late 1st century BC. Its four intricately carved gates show scenes illustrating episodes from the life of the Buddha.

Kushans

The Kushans originally came to India as wandering and warlike tribes from central Asia. In Chinese history they are referred to as the Yueh-chi but may also have been a group called the Tokhari, speaking a language of the same name. The Kushans defeated the Shakas and established a kingdom in their territory. They adopted Buddhism and eventually extended their empire to Bihar in the east, and far into middle India. The first of the important Kushan rulers was Kadphises but the greatest of them all was Kanishka, who ruled at the end of the 1st century AD. The Kushans had close trading links with Rome. Diplomatic contacts between India, Bactria, and Rome usually involved the exchange of valuable presents. Under the Kushans art of all sorts flourished. At Gandhara and Mathura sculptures of the finest quality were produced. Pottery of this period, usually unpainted, is decorated with stamped and applied designs.

By the middle of the 4th century the empire of the Guptas, centred at Pataliputra in the east, had been extended far into Kushan territory to include Mathura. The great Buddhist rule in north-west India and Afghanistan was eventually destroyed forever by the White Hun invasions of the late 5th century.

The Gandharan artists worked mainly in stone but also in gold and precious stones, as in this ruby-set reliquary from Bimaran. It shows the characteristic mixture of Indian and Greek styles and dates from the Kushan period (1st and 2nd centuries AD).

western Ganges plains and south to the Kathiawar peninsula. Although the Indo-Greeks were Indian Buddhists, their importance lies in their extension of Greek cultural influence into India. Its effects can be seen in the use of western styles in Indian art, especially in Gandhara.

Towards the end of the 1st century BC, the Indo-Greeks were overrun by a people known as the Indo-Scythians or Shakas. The Shakas ruled their possessions in India by means of provincial governors called satraps who were based at such cities as Mathura and Taxila, but they were soon swept away in their turn by the Kushans.

China

China is by far the largest country in the Far East. Here, as in other parts of the world, the first civilizations grew up beside the great rivers. The most important of these was the Hwang-Ho or Yellow River, on the plains of which developed a civilization that was to spread throughout China and to a greater or lesser degree influence Japan, Korea, and the rest of South-East Asia.

The Hwang-Ho runs through the north of China; the plains around it are ideal for farming and the river itself provides an easy means of transport. The upper part of the river runs through highlands where *loess* – a fine, fertile soil probably blown down from central Asia during the Ice Ages – is in places up to 60 metres (200 feet) deep. Farther east along the Hwang-Ho lie great alluvial plains where the flooding of the river has deposited yellow loess soil carried down from the highlands. Disastrous floods in this region have caused so much grief to the Chinese throughout their history that the Yellow River is known as China's Sorrow.

The earliest remains of Man in China date back about a million years when a rugged type of *Homo erectus*, the first true man, was living at Lantien in the north west. The most famous of the prehistoric men of China is Peking Man (*c* 500,000 BC) whose remains were found at Choukoutien near Peking. He was a cave-dwelling hunter who used fire and made crude stone tools.

Over thousands of years men learned how to make better and better stone tools, and turned from hunters into farmers. They became skilled potters. This sort of neolithic farming life continued in country parts of China long after the city-dwellers of the Shang period were casting bronze vessels and going to war in chariots.

The Shang period

In the 1st century BC the great Chinese historian Ssu-ma Ch'ien composed his *Records of the Historian*. It is one of the main sources of information on the early history of China. He describes a series of legendary emperors followed by three dynasties – the Hsia, the Shang, and the Chou. No evidence of the Hsia dynasty has yet been discovered; but the Shang and Chou periods are now well known archaeologically.

A busy city street in Han China. The traffic includes a heavy country ox-cart, and the faster and more elegant vehicles of the rich. The buildings are typically Han, without the turned-up eaves of later times.

The Chinese developed a composite bow, of the type shown here unstrung and strung. Before it was strung the bow, which was made of bone and wood, bent right back on itself. The tension when it was strung was considerable, even before the archer drew it. The grip was made of bronze.

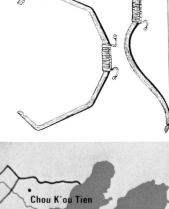

This jade figure of an owl-like bird dates from the Shang dynasty, when jade-carvers were craftsmen of the highest order. It shows the typical Shang dislike for an undecorated surface – designs are carved all over its body. Jade was of particular importance to the Chinese who called it yü, 'the stone that is beautiful'.

An inscribed oracle bone. Such inscriptions have given us most of our knowledge of the Shang dynasty. Modern Chinese writing is the direct descendant of the early Shang script, whose characters are like small pictures. As the centuries passed these have become more and more stylized so that Chinese characters now bear only small resemblance to the objects or ideas they represent.

The Shang period lasted from about 1850 BC to about 1100 BC, although the rule of the Shang dynasty began three hundred years or more later. The Shang kingdom itself may only have been as large as some 450 by 290 kilometres (280 by 180 miles) but objects of Shang manufacture have been found much farther afield. We now know that the area of Shang influence extended not just over the central plain of China but to some degree as far south as the Huai and Yangtse river valleys. The rediscovery of the Shang dynasty began only in 1903 with the decipherment of ancient inscriptions on ox blade-bones and tortoise shells, found in the neighbourhood of the city of Anyang on the river Huan, a small tributary of the Yellow River. These texts, the earliest evidence for writing in China, were in fact the remains of the oracular library of the Shang.

Cities of the plains

Shang cities were all situated on the flat plains of the Yellow River. The capital, Anyang (also called Hsiao-t'un), is on a bend in a river, which acts as a natural moat on nearly three sides of the city. The plains themselves are fertile and treeless. Their flatness was an advantage to the chariots of the Shang in battle, while the mountains, only about 27 kilometres (17 miles) away, provided some protection against attack and were a useful source of wood for building. The upper classes of Shang society hunted in these mountains, and enjoyed their relative coolness as an escape from the heat and dust of the plains in summer.

The Shang kingdom was divided into its capital and four regions named after the four cardinal directions. There were two classes, the warrior nobles and the peasants – the broad outline of a system that has carried on in China until modern times. Feudal rulers reigned over little states, often no larger than a town or two and some farmland.

Local rulers owed allegiance to the king, who had final authority over everything in his domain. They paid him tribute, including manpower for war and for work, and were required to follow him into battle and to protect the borders of the kingdom. In return the king came to the aid of a lord if he were attacked by an

enemy. Feudal nobles of this sort were not always men. Certain powerful women held office as rulers of states and had considerable political influence.

In the cities

Shang cities were generally rectangular in shape, surrounded by high defensive walls. These walls were constructed by the *hang-t'u* method. Earth was poured into a wooden frame and pounded until it was hard enough to support another layer. The walls were so solid that many have survived hard and intact to the present day. This method is still used all over China.

Two main sorts of buildings are found: pits and houses. At Ao, an early capital, round, oval, and oblong pit dwellings have been found which were probably roofed over. Some must have served as store houses but others may have been inhabited. Buildings above ground are long and rectangular. They are built on raised platforms of stamped earth (hang-t'u) and have thatched roofs supported by wooden pillars. At the base of the pillars large round river boulders or bronze hemispheres were placed for stability. At Anyang large halls have been found, one of them 10 by 30 metres (33 by 100 feet). Presumably these grand structures were used by the king and nobles, or for ceremonial purposes. On the city walls

there may have been towers of two or more storeys, but for this we have only the evidence of inscriptions.

Some of the most important Shang buildings were consecrated by animal or human sacrifice. Before the foundations of pressed earth were laid, a series of graves was dug into which were placed a sheep, an ox, and a dog. The consecration of the pillars was completed with a human victim, also buried under the hang-t'u. The consecration of the door involved the sacrifice of six more people, four buried outside and two within. The whole building was then consecrated with the slaughter of several hundred people who, with five chariots, were buried in front of the building. People disposed of in this way were usually war captives, who were also sacrificed at Shang ancestral temples.

Burials at Shang sites are often very elaborate. Kings were buried in large chambers constructed deep in the earth, approached by sloping ramps and filled with hoards of bronze vessels, jade carvings, gold, and pottery. They were accompanied by dozens of sacrificial victims. Charioteers are placed beside their vehicles and their horses, and beheaded attendants lie in rows.

Stone carving
The Shang people possessed a highly developed stone industry. Poor people still used stone tools, including axes, adzes, knives, and arrowheads made from a variety of stones including slate and limestone. Marble was carved by the Shang into sculptures of animals and people, some large enough to be used to support house pillars. Jade carving developed into a significant art form.

Shell and bone carving was also a highly developed art. The inscription of characters on bone was a part of this technique, and much of our knowledge of the Shang period comes from bone texts. These bones tell of wars, hunts, and sacrifices. Some, called 'calendar tablets', are inscribed with the Shang calendar, a system based upon recurring cycles of 60 named dates, days, or years. A bone rule has been found suggesting that a decimal system of measurement was used.

This view is typical of the north China highlands where the fine, fertile soil called loess, blown down from central Asia, is thickly deposited. The land is terraced for cultivation.

Shang dynasty ring discs of the yuan, pi, *and* huan *types (left to right). They are carved from jade and generally formed part of a composite of several jade shapes, suspended one from the other by silk cords. They were often used for ceremonial purposes.*

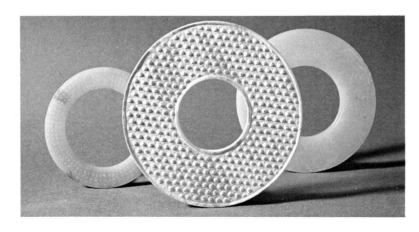

A bronze ku, also of the Shang dynasty. It was used for wine drinking.

A Chou bronze showing a juggler with a tame bear, which has climbed to the top of the pole and is performing tricks there. This would have been a common sight in the streets of any Chinese city of the period.

Daily life

During the Shang period the peasant farmers grew two kinds of millet, wheat, barley, and sorghum. They reared oxen, horses, and water buffalo, sheep, pigs, fowls, and dogs. Although a character for rice exists in the oracle script it cannot have been cultivated, since the watered fields needed to grow rice did not exist at that time. The oracles were used widely for finding out suitable conditions for sowing or reaping. Agriculture seems to have been an organized affair. The sickles used for harvesting were stored by the king who also provided gangs of prisoners for work and organized the people into work groups.

Clothes of the Shang period were of woven material; most people wore loose tailored garments of hemp but the rich wore fine silk. Objects found in Shang tombs show that houses must have contained straw mats and baskets and pottery vessels for cooking. In richer households bronze was probably used for all the usual vessels, washing services, and tools for everyday use such as knives, choppers, and mirrors. Food was often prepared in steamers, much as it is in China today. It included the basic grains produced in the region, as well as the meat of all the domestic animals except the horse, which seems not to have been eaten.

Warfare

Warfare was of great importance to the Shang leaders. Success in battle meant that captives and plunder would be taken, to the enrichment of the king and his followers. Prisoners were always needed for sacrifice and for labour as slaves.

Shang armies consisted of infantry and chariots. These were light and two-wheeled, and drawn by a pair of horses. Sometimes as many as four horses were used. Both horses and chariots were always decorated with elaborate bronzes. The chariot carried three men – an archer, a halberdier, and the driver; in battle it was surrounded by foot soldiers. Chariots were the main offensive weapon of the Shang and of Chinese armies right up to the late Chou period. Soldiers' equipment included knives, shields, helmets, ko-

BRONZE CASTING

Some writers have felt that the origins of bronze-working in China are to be sought in some outside influence. Others have stated that bronze casting in China appears mysteriously and suddenly and in a developed state with no definable origins. Neither of these theories is true. Chinese bronze casting is the end result of a long process of development, beginning in the neolithic period and closely related to the pottery industry. Evidence of early, less well developed work in bronze *does* exist, showing that however quickly the industry may have found its feet in China, it is a native development – and above all else the distinctive hallmark there of ancient civilization.

Bronze was used originally by Shang craftsmen to make objects of traditional form and function. The *li* tripod and *ku* wine cup are among the early bronze vessel shapes of the Shang period; they were previously made in pottery. Objects such as knives and axes were also made in the shapes of their stone predecessors. Later, as Chinese bronze workers became increasingly skilled, they were able to produce a seemingly limitless range of shapes, from everyday tools and weapons to the most elaborately shaped and decorated bronze vessels. The technology these craftsmen developed has never since been surpassed.

Bronze working involved a complicated casting process. The bronze factory excavated at Cheng-chou shows how the metal was first melted in conical pottery crucibles and then poured into two sorts of moulds. All that was needed for such objects as knives and axes (or in later periods, coins) was a flat, two-sided mould. But vessels with their stunningly elaborate surface decoration, knobs, handles, legs and so on had to be cast in compo-

site moulds. Each mould was made of up to dozens of separate clay parts, all fitted together. The inside of the mould was carved and shaped to provide the surface decoration, inscriptions, or projections. In the Chou period the most elaborate vessels were often cast in pieces and then soldered together. In the 6th century BC movable type was invented for casting inscriptions – about a thousand years before its introduction in the West.

Bronze vessels were almost all involved in some way with sacrifices, and are found in great quantities in graves. It is not entirely clear how much household use these vessels served. Some are in the classic pottery shapes, others take the form of monstrous animals. Except for the earliest bronzes of the Shang, the surface of these vessels is invariably entirely covered with decoration – geometric designs, or motifs of stylized animals such as the cicada, dragon, and the *t'aotieh* mask (a formalized design based on an animal face). During the Chou period bronzes were often inlaid with gold, silver, and such substances as malachite, and new shapes were introduced.

The manufacture of bronze objects on a large scale continued to the Han dynasty. After its introduction about 600 BC, iron gradually replaced bronze as the most important metal for the manufacture of tools and weapons, while developments in the ceramic industry overtook the manufacture of bronze vases. By the early centuries AD the art of bronze casting became concentrated in the making of mirrors, usually round and gorgeously decorated on their backs. These objects first became widely used in the Eastern Chou period, and are possibly the most characteristic products of the bronze artists of the Han and later dynasties.

A Han dynasty incense burner of gilded bronze. It shows a celestial mountain with clouds and small figures. The incense was placed inside the vessel and the fumes rose through holes in the elaborately decorated lid.

halberds, bows and arrows, axes and spears. The ko was mounted on a long wooden shaft; it was used particularly against chariots and, in later periods, against cavalry.

Casualty figures would have been lower during the Shang than at later periods, since prisoners were needed as human sacrifices. Later in Chinese history the numbers of people killed in battle or massacred in captured cities were horrifyingly large.

Religion

Shang religion involved both ancestor worship and the veneration of gods in heaven and deities on earth. Ancestors were thought of as being still a part of the family, carrying on their affairs in the after life for the family benefit. Sacrifices of animals or even of people were made to ancestors, especially those of the royal family. Ancestor worship grew from this period into an integral part of Chinese life. The most powerful of heavenly gods was Shang-ti, who ruled in Heaven and had control of agriculture. Regular

sacrifices to him and to hosts of other deities were important.

During the Shang period people believed in three universal levels: the heavenly, the human, and the earthly. Man was at the centre of these and the centre of the unity of all three. People believed that the universe could be manipulated by sacrifice either to gods or to ancestors. These sacrifices must have been accompanied by music played on instruments such as chiming stones, the ocarina (a small wind instrument), drums, bells, and probably others now lost.

The Chou

The Shang period laid the foundations of the Chinese way of life, which later dynasties developed but did not radically alter. In about 1100 BC the Shang dynasty was overthrown by the Chou people, who came from Shensi province in western China. According to the oracle bones, the Chou state was originally a feudal state of the Shang, paying tribute and supplying men and arms to the Shang king.

The first part of Chou rule is known as the Western Chou, since the capital cities of the dynasty, Hao and Feng, were in Shensi. This period lasted until 771 BC, and was followed by the Eastern Chou (771 to 481 BC) with its capital near Loyang in Honan, to the east. This is also called the Ch'un Ch'iu or Spring and Autumn period, from the title – *Spring and Autumn Annals* – of the first accurate chronology of Chinese history, written in the 6th century by Confucius. The final stage of the dynasty is called the Chankuo or Warring States period; it ended in 221 BC, when China was unified in an empire for the first time.

The Chou dynasty lasted for nearly a thousand years – the longest of any in Chinese history – and is the first historical period. Inscriptions were no longer made on blade bones, as divining in that way had gone out of fashion, but texts cast on to bronze vessels grew in size and detail. Official records and archives were kept in capital cities, but most were burned in 213 BC by the Ch'in emperor. Books were usually made from inscribed strips of bamboo, but some were made of tablets of jade, held together by metal wires. Sometimes lengths of silk were written on. A great literature began to develop during

Some of the earliest coins in China were shaped like little spades or knives, like the one above. It dates from between 680 and 260 BC, and was made of cast iron – a process used by the Chinese some 1800 years before it was developed in Europe.

A bronze yu of the Shang dynasty, used for storing and heating wine. It shows the Shang delight in heavy decoration, with birds ornamenting the body and a bull's head on the handle. Vessels like this were cast in a mould made from a number of pieces.

Animals in Chinese art: a Shang bronze elephant, found in a burial; a Han pottery figure of a dog; and a Chou chariot-mounting of gilded bronze in the form of a bull's head.

A Han dynasty pottery hu, *probably used for storing wine. It is intricately decorated in many colours, the design including applied animal masks.*

the aristocracy, the gentry, peasants, and, lowest of all, the merchants.

Supremacy during the Eastern Chou shifted from state to state, ending in the 3rd century BC with the Ch'in emperor, leader of one of these states, seizing power. Curiously, the final centuries of the Chou period, fraught with desperate strife as they were, saw great developments in art, and philosophy. And the political confusion of the times provided an opportunity in the long run for a strong imperial unity to be established that has lasted in China in some form to the present.

Technology

Chou technology mostly developed from that of the Shang. The most important advance was the introduction of iron-casting in about the 6th century BC – some 1800 years before it was developed in the West. Iron was used for everyday tools, knives, hoes, sickles, and so on. But it did not replace bronze totally until much later, especially for weapons. These can only be made from forged iron – a process which the Chinese seem to have developed later than casting.

The introduction of iron led to a decline in the use of stone tools for agriculture, but the carving of stone, jade, shell, and bone was carried on in the Shang tradition. The pottery industry moved south and the Yangtse region became established as its centre, producing great quantities. Ceramic vessels were decorated with paint, glaze, lacquer, or tin foil. Roof tiles, elaborately decorated, are characteristic of the later Chou.

Warfare

Making war was one of the chief activities of Chou times. As the centuries passed the intensity of the struggles grew. War became more scientific; the treatise on war by Sun Wu in the 6th century is a careful analysis of tactics. Enormous armies were kept by the feudal states; in the Warring States era four states were said each to have kept a million men under arms, and three others 600,000.

Chariots were still the most important strike force until the late centuries BC, but they were no good in hilly country and useless in front of a walled city. They were eventually replaced by cavalry. An important Chou invention was the crossbow.

this period. The works of the Confucian school, and the Taoist writings of Laotze and his followers (both 6th century BC) are part of this tradition. So is the *Sun Tzu* of General Sun Wu, the classic work on military tactics, which was written at the same time.

The Chou continued the old feudal style of government of the Shang, decentralizing power more and more and apparently reducing the real authority of the king. Political events of the dynasty were related entirely to the problems of authority within the feudal structure – the waning of the king's power and the growth of strength of individual tributary states, which combined against one another or against the king.

Chou feudal lords were autocratic rulers. Their power was based on their walled cities; their authority came in theory from the king, who acquired his rights from heaven. This led to the later imperial title 'Son of Heaven'. The rulers held monopolies in salt and, later, iron. Four classes of people were recognized in Chou society:

Some soldiers now wore armour, usually of leather-bound wood and sometimes with bronze attachments.

Long walls such as the Great Wall of China were built along state borders against invasions from marauders, while great waterways were built along which troops could be carried. These included the canal connecting the Yangtse and the Huai rivers, constructed in 407. (At the same time, canals for irrigation were being built.) These great feats of engineering cost the lives of many thousands of the workers concerned. Slaughter was terrible in battle and the inhabitants of captured cities were massacred. In 262 BC 400,000 soldiers were reported to have been buried alive by a victorious general; whole cities were depopulated.

The Ch'in and the Han

In 221 BC the king of the state of Ch'in to the west conquered all the other states of China and established himself as emperor. His state had become powerful partly through vast irrigation schemes which enormously increased food production and brought great prosperity. But his was a turbulent reign and only four years after his death his dynasty was driven from the throne. The king was responsible for the appalling 'Burning of the Books' in 213, in which nearly everything written in earlier centuries was destroyed, in an effort to stop people harking back to the customs of the past. In 202 BC, following a great struggle, the Han dynasty was established by the Emperor Liu Pang. It lasted for 400 years.

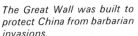

The Great Wall was built to protect China from barbarian invasions.

Right: The sage Confucius.

CONFUCIUS

Confucius was born in the year 551 BC in the town of Ch'ü-fu in the hilly part of Shantung province. In Chinese his name is properly K'ung-fu-tzŭ. At 22 he founded a school of philosophy, drawing pupils to him just as Socrates was to do a little later in Athens. His pupils commented upon and expanded the Sage's teachings as did Plato the ideas of Socrates, his master.

Confucius claimed no originality of thought, only that he was the transmitter of the wisdom of past times and that upon these ancient principles he based his philosophy. He was reacting against the degeneracy and confusion of his age, and he hoped that by teaching feudal rulers the gentler ways of the past he might bring peace. In this immediate purpose he was unsuccessful as the violent history of his age demonstrates all too clearly.

At the age of 19 Confucius married, and until he began his teaching held various public jobs. From 530 to 501 he taught and wrote, in 500 acting as magistrate in his province, minister of works, and then minister of justice in his province. He resigned when he realized that he had failed to turn the ruler of his province from his evil ways. From 496 to 483 Confucius wandered about the feudal states of north China trying in vain to reform their generally corrupt rulers. Finally, from 483 to 478 Confucius returned to his native province to complete his literary tasks including his one original work, the Ch'un-ch'iu or *Spring and Autumn Annals*. Confucius died in 479 and was buried at his birthplace. His family continues in unbroken descent to the present day.

Confucius believed that virtue would be instilled in people by example, and particularly the example of people of high rank who make efforts to emulate the ways of the ancients. The development of this virtue in an individual accompanies restraint and propriety. In family relations or in dealings with other people he taught the golden rule: 'What you do not want done to yourself, do not do to others.' Although the whole system is based on the good conduct of people towards their parents and elder brothers and sisters, ancestor worship is not a part of the teaching of Confucius. He seems to overlook it although it conveniently emphasizes his ideas of divine order and the importance of higher and lower status within this system. In other words, society is ordered in a certain way. Man must accept this order and obey those superior to him. Society is made perfect by the cultivation of the individual and the example he sets to his inferiors. The philosophy of Confucius does not allow for progress in the usual way, and it is for that reason Confucian ideas have been so roundly criticized in modern China.

The study of the works of Confucius and his followers became the centre of learning in China. Even the famous civil service examinations were based upon a knowledge of his work. Although it was not universally popular in his day, the philosophy of Confucius became widely accepted after his time. Rulers appreciated his view of their divine right to reign and ordinary people were attracted to his recognition of their rights and of their individual happiness. Confucianism became embedded in Chinese life and religion and has remained so for nearly two and a half thousand years.

From 221 BC on, great efforts were made to unify and stabilize the empire, and to reorganize it now that the feudal order had broken up. Roads were laid out connecting the capital with provincial cities. The Great Wall was completed, connecting up the stretches of wall built in earlier centuries as protection against invasion. Noble and feudal privileges were abolished, responsibilities going instead to educated people or members of the imperial family. Standard weights and measures were introduced throughout the empire.

Government of the Chinese empire was based upon a series of distinct social differences bound up with the political responsibility each carried. The emperor was at the top of the pyramid. Protected and secluded, the Son of Heaven was responsible for major policy decisions and relations between the empire and the gods. Below him were the officials who governed in practice, and below them came the mass of the people. Two levels of government existed in Han times as later, central and provincial. In the capital a small number of senior officials consulted the emperor on important matters, passing down his decisions to nine ministries among whom were divided all the major tasks of central government including the military, coinage, food transport, and price maintenance.

Han provincial government consisted

A pottery model from a Han dynasty tomb, showing a pigsty. Many such models were placed in the tombs of this period, showing people and animals as well as buildings, and they have provided us with a vast amount of information about the architecture and life of the times.

A group of painted pottery figures showing acrobats, musicians, and dancers. They date from the Western Han period. Such performances were a feature of Chinese life.

of division of the empire into a series of commanderies and small kingdoms. In the year AD 1–2 there were 83 such commanderies and 20 kingdoms. The former were governed by Grand Administrators, and the kingdoms were ruled by petty hereditary monarchies related by blood to the emperor. In practice these kingdoms were hardly any more free of central government control than the commanderies. Both these categories of province were divided into prefectures, further subdivided into districts and then into wards. At each level a government official was in charge of local affairs to the extent of his area. Provincial officials took charge of communications in the empire, providing systems of runners and riders carrying despatches. The speedy transport of officials from one place to another was helped by the provision of systems of stations with fresh horses.

Government officials were chosen, beginning in the Han dynasty, by means of a selective process based upon an examination. The character of the earliest of these examinations is unknown, but in later centuries a detailed and scholarly knowledge of the classical literature of China was a prerequisite for any high civil office. This system of civil service examinations continued in China until the early years of this century.

Trade between Han China and foreign countries was largely restricted to luxury goods not produced in China itself. The

Chinese traded silks, iron, bronze, and lacquer work for such items as horses and jade from Central Asia, pearls from the south, wild animals, and slaves. A thriving community of traders existed in China at this time.

In this period of peace and stability the arts and crafts flourished. Architecture became more elaborate, and tombs were now always built of hollow bricks, often beautifully painted, moulded, stamped, or incised with scenes of daily life. These tomb decorations are the source of much of what we know of Han life in general. Splendid clay models of buildings, in great detail, found in Han tombs tell much of the style of architecture of the times, from humble farm houses to multi-storied towers and mansions for the rich. Grave goods were elaborate indeed at this period and include the fabulous jade suits of the princess Tou Wan and her husband, in each of which more than 2000 jade tablets are held together with knotted gold wire. In this fashion the bodies of the dead were thought to be preserved.

The end of the Han

The Han dynasty came to an end in 221 AD with a series of revolts and civil disturbances. Three of the generals commanding armies engaged in putting down these uprisings broke up the weakened Han empire to form the next historical period known as the Three Kingdoms. The Han had ruled for longer than any other imperial dynasty and had made real the idea of a unified China. Old ways of life in China remained firm, especially on the rural level. But the Han were great

innovators and set up a system of government and authority that in essence remained until this century. The Chinese were able to spread their influence by force or by cultural expansion over vast areas of east Asia. The Japanese use Chinese characters as their writing, while art styles and architecture throughout continental east Asia show some Chinese influence. The unity provided by the strong Han administration was one means by which links with other parts of Asia were maintained and the interchange of ideas carried out.

The insistence of the Han dynasty on centralized government was its greatest contribution to Chinese political thinking, for this principle has inspired leaders in China ever since that time.

A stone relief from a Han dynasty tomb; it depicts a market scene, with fish for sale and pigs and cattle being led to the slaughter. The vessels in the foreground probably contained food and wine. The interiors of tombs of the period were lined with such tiles showing scenes of everyday life.

Ancient China saw almost ceaseless warfare among its states. The Han empire ended the worst of this strife. Here, Han soldiers are engaged in hand to hand fighting. All the weapons of the time are used: ko-halberds (one is held by the soldier in the right foreground); lances; composite bows; and crossbows. Casualty figures were dreadfully high.

Glossary

A

ACHAEAN The name by which the Greek heroes describe themselves in the poems of Homer. Greeks of this period (the Bronze Age) are usually called Mycenaeans by modern historians. The Achaean League (formed 280 BC) was an alliance of Greek cities defeated by Rome in 146 BC.

ACHAEMENIDS The ancient Hakhamanish dynasty of Persian kings, beginning with Cyrus I (?600–529 BC) and ending in 330 BC with the defeat of Darius III by Alexander the Great.

ACROPOLIS The highest point of an ancient Greek city. It was intended both as a citadel with strong defensive walls, and a sacred enclosure containing the chief temples of the city.

ADZE A heavy cutting tool used to trim timbers. The head, of stone or metal, curves to a flat, horizontal blade. Before the invention of an efficient saw, the adze was the most important of wood-shaping tools, especially in ship-building.

AMULET A body ornament in the form of a ring, bracelet, brooch, or pendant, believed by the ancient Egyptians and others to have the power of warding off evil. Great numbers of amulets have been discovered in a wide variety of designs: in Egypt the eye of Horus and the sacred scarab beetle were especially popular.

ANCESTOR WORSHIP The revering of deceased members of a family or tribe. In various forms ancestor worship was practised by many societies, for example those of ancient Babylon and Egypt, as well as Rome during the republic. Of all the great civilizations, it was in China that ancestor worship became most generally established at every level of society. It was strongly developed there by the 11th century BC and continued until the 20th century AD.

ARAMAEANS A group of Semitic-speaking tribes which settled large areas of northern Syria between the 11th and 8th centuries BC. During the same period some of the tribes occupied a large part of Mesopotamia, from where, despite constant pressure from the Assyrians, the Aramaeans successfully spread into Babylonia. Most importantly, the Aramaeans were the dispersers of the alphabetic writing system, and Aramaean became the international language of the Near East from the 7th century BC until the Arab conquest in the 7th century AD.

ARCHAEOLOGY The study of Man's past through the material objects and structures which have survived into the present.

ARCHIVE A systematic record of events compiled for official purposes. The term can also describe the institution or building in which such records are stored.

ARYANS A name loosely and somewhat misleadingly applied to a group of people who originally spoke the Indo-European family of languages. The supposed migrations of these peoples through Europe, the Near East, and India account for structural similarities between languages such as Greek, Latin, ancient Persian, Hittite, and Sanskrit. The term Indo-Aryan is sometimes used for aristocratic groups in the Near East whose names appear to be linguistically related to some of the divine names of the *Rig Veda*.

ASSYRIA The modern name given to the area controlled by the ancient city of Ashur in Mesopotamia.

AUTOCRAT A ruler who exercises absolute power.

B

BARD A tribal poet-singer whose function was to compose and declaim tales about the exploits of past heroes of the tribe. Before the spread of a written culture, the bard was an important figure who kept the tribe in touch with its own history.

BAST A strong fibre made from the stems of woody plants, used in the ancient world as the raw material for ropes, rigging, and so on.

BLACK-FIGURE POTTERY A type of decorated pottery made in Attica during the 7th and 6th centuries BC. Figures and details were painted on using a special glaze which turned black during the firing. The background was left a distinctive orange-red – a colour obtained by adding red ochre to the natural clay.

BODHISATTVA According to the Buddhist religion, one who is sufficiently enlightened not to have to spend further time on Earth. Instead of passing immediately to heaven *(nirvana)*, however, he chooses to remain on Earth in order to help his fellow human beings. Thus a *bodhisattva* is the Buddhist equivalent to a Christian saint, and is frequently depicted in attendance on the Buddha.

BOUDICCA (Boadicea) A queen of a British tribe, the Iceni, who led a revolt against the Romans. After initial successes, including the burning of London and the defeat of a Roman legion, the revolt was put down by the Roman governor Suetonius Paulinus in AD 61. To avoid capture, Boudicca committed suicide in AD 62.

BRONZE An alloy (mixture) of copper and tin, usually in the proportions of 9 parts copper to 1 part tin. Bronze, the oldest man-made alloy, was first discovered c 3000 BC. It had many advantages over pure copper, being much harder, with a lower melting-point. Bronze weapons, armour, tools, and utensils were the basis of the first European civilization in the Aegean c 1800 BC.

C

CENTAUR A mythical creature of Greek legend having the head and torso of a man and the body and legs of a horse. Centaurs were supposed to live in the mountains of Thessaly; the name, which means 'rounder-up of bulls' suggests that the centaur myth may have been based on nomadic mounted cowherds who at one time inhabited Thessaly. Centaurs were notorious for their generally savage and unpredictable nature.

CERAMIC A general term applied to any earthenware, brick, glass, or porcelain object produced by firing – a process in which the raw materials, such as potter's clay or sand, are heated to very high temperatures.

CHRISTIANITY Beginning in Palestine as a movement within Judaism, Christianity spread quickly through the Mediterranean world. The vehicle of its expansion was the Christian community – a group of people who gathered to discuss the life and teaching of Jesus of Galilee, whom they regarded as Christ (the Anointed One) and the Son of God. Initially, Christian ideas of brotherly love, and the promise of eternal life, appealed particularly to the poor. These early communities provided support and practical self-help for their members. On various occasions Christians were the victims of persecution by the Roman authorities – but Christianity survived and went on to attract converts from all classes of society. In 312 AD, the emperor Constantine made Christianity the official religion of the empire, with its two greatest centres at Constantinople and Rome. During the 2nd century AD, a formal organization of bishops had emerged, and the Pope or bishop of Rome, which became the spiritual centre of the western world came to have supreme authority, claiming descent from St Peter (who was martyred in Rome).

CHRONOLOGY The ordering of events in their correct historical sequence.

CLIENT The Latin word *cliens* described a man who attached himself to a rich patron in the hope of some reward. Historians use the word 'client' to mean a state economically and politically subjected to a more powerful ally.

CONSUL One of the two chief magistrates of Rome. The offices were created after the expulsion of the last Roman king in 510 BC, to take over the king's duties. Appointment was by annual election. By dividing supreme power between two elected officers, the Romans of the republic hoped to guard against the tyranny of one-man rule.

COWRIE A type of spiral shell widely used in the ancient world as a form of currency. In primitive or remote societies money-systems based on cowrie and other shells have been used right up to modern times.

CRYPTOLOGY The scientific study of inscriptions in unknown languages with a view to deciphering them.

CUIRASS A piece of body-armour protecting the area between the neck and the waist.

CULT The worship of a particular deity conducted according to certain traditional rules. Many cults of the ancient world remained purely local affairs; others, like those of Dionysus and Isis, spread far and wide. In the East (as in Egypt) the ruler of a state was often regarded as a god, with his own cult. The practice was revived by the Roman emperors as an instrument of political control; the imperial treasury often provided funds to finance the cult of the reigning emperor.

D

DIVINATION The art of discovering secret knowledge, such as the knowledge of the future, by contact with non-human, supernatural sources. All societies have practised divination at one time or another, although the techniques used have varied widely. Common methods of divination have included the inspection of the entrails or bones of sacrificed animals, the observation of the flight of birds, and the study of natural phenomena such as the weather or the stars.

DORIANS The name given to Greek-speaking migrants who settled the Peloponnese, Crete, and the south coast of Asia Minor in the period after the collapse of the Mycenaean civilization (c 1200–1000 BC). The dialect spoken by these people was Doric – the two other main Greek dialects were Aeolian and Ionian.

DYNASTY A succession of rulers from the same family. For historical convenience the term is also used to describe the period of time during which a particular family held royal power. Thus the Twelfth Dynasty of Egypt covers the period 1991 to 1786 BC.

E

EBLA The ancient name of Tell Mardik, a site south of Aleppo in northern Syria. Here recent excavation by Italian archaeologists has revealed a huge palace archive of clay tablets dating to c 2300 BC. The tablets seem to be written in a language containing a large number of West Semitic elements. If so, it is the earliest recorded instance of the branch of Semitic from which Hebrew, Phoenician and Aramaic developed.

ELECTRUM A naturally occurring alloy (mixture) of gold and silver, used particularly in the early coinage of the Lydians and the Greek cities of Asia Minor.

F

FEUDALISM A form of social organization in which the ruler is sole owner of all land, and has the right to claim unpaid labour and military service from his subjects.

FINIAL A decorative ornament crowning the upper part of a structure or object.

FRESCO A method of wall painting in which pigment is painted directly on to a layer of wet lime plaster. As the plaster dries the pigment becomes chemically incorporated into it.

G

GANGES The major river of north and north-eastern India, regarded as sacred by members of the Hindu religion.

GLADIATOR A professional fighter required to fight to the death as part of a Roman public entertainment. The practice may reach back to Etruscan rituals in which two warriors fought to the death over the grave of a newly buried king. Nevertheless, gladiatorial combats were rare until the late republic when competition for votes drove rich Romans to finance large-scale bloodsports for the populace. Gladiators were recruited from the most desperate elements of society – criminals, paupers, and slaves – and trained in special schools. In the arena (a word that originally meant the sand strewn on the ground to soak up the blood) various types of gladiator appeared: the heavily armed infantryman *(hoplomachus)*, the more lightly armed 'Thracian' *(Thrax)*, and swift, highly mobile fighters armed with nets *(reticulii)* or tridents *(tridentii)*. A defeated gladiator might be reprieved by the crowd if he had fought particularly well – otherwise, he received the 'thumbs up' (directed at the chest), a gesture which meant 'kill'. Even a gladiator who survived the death blow from his opponent had his throat cut later, at the morgue.

GRACCHI The brothers Tiberius Sempronius Gracchus (163–133 BC) and Gaius Sempronius Gracchus (153–121 BC), Roman statesmen who unsuccessfully attempted to introduce land reforms as a way of restoring the class of small independent farmers. Their reforms failed partly because of opposition from powerful land-owners, partly because of political misjudgements by the Gracchi themselves.

GREAVES Pieces of armour designed to protect the lower legs.

H

HELLENISM A general term for Greek culture and language, involving ideas of political responsibility, the pursuit of knowledge, the exercise of reason, and the cultivation of physical and moral health. The Hellenistic Age is a term used to describe the period of Greek domination in the East between the death of Alexander the Great in 322 BC to the Roman conquest of Egypt in 30 BC.

HELLESPONT A narrow strait which divides Europe from Asia at the north-eastern corner of the Aegean. It was crossed from east to west by Xerxes in the Persian invasion of Greece in 480 BC, and from west to east by Alexander the Great in 334 BC, the first step in his conquest of the Persian empire. In modern times the Hellespont has become known as the Dardanelles.

HERM A statue in the form of a square stone pillar surmounted by a bust of Hermes or some other deity. In Greek cities herms stood at street corners and were regarded as benevolent guardians of the areas they surveyed.

HINDI Originally, Hindi was the name of a group of dialects spoken in central and northern India. In the 7th century AD a written form of Hindi appeared for the first time. Modern Hindi, the official national language of India, was developed by the British in the 19th century from a dialect of Hindi spoken in the Delhi region. The sacred written language of Hindi was Sanskrit.

HURRIAN A people who by c 2000 BC had penetrated large areas of Mesopotamia, especially the region east of the Tigris river and the mountains of Zagros. After c 1700 BC there was a further Hurrian expansion, in the course of which they seem to have defeated the Assyrians, and occupied a considerable part of eastern Asia Minor. Here they came into contact with the Hittites. During the 14th century BC, renewed activity by the Hittites and Assyrians eliminated the areas of Hurrian power, although Hurrian cultural influence remained strong. Much still remains to be discovered about Hurrian society and language.

I

IMPERIUM In Roman law, *imperium* was the sacred power originally wielded by the king which passed to the consuls after the foundation of the republic. Much later, the *imperium* became an important ingredient of the legal basis of the power of the emperors.

INDO-EUROPEAN A group of languages possibly originating among nomadic peoples dwelling in central Europe before 3000 BC. From these languages are descended nearly all modern European and certain Indian languages. The fascinating connections between such diverse languages as Greek, Latin, Indian *sanskrit*, and ancient Hittite are the result of the widespread movements of Indo-European speaking peoples which occurred between 3000 and 2000 BC.

INDO-GREEK Literally, a fusion of Greek and Indian traditions which resulted from Alexander the Great's conquest of Taxila, in north-western India.

INDUS The major river of north-western India. The valley of the Indus was the home of the earliest Indian civilization, with major centres at Harappa and Mohenjo-Daro which were fully developed by 2300 BC.

IRON Centres of ironworking were highly developed in Anatolia, in the Caucasus mountains, and around the Caspian Sea by 1400 BC. The spread of iron technology c 1200 BC rapidly displaced bronze as the primary metal for weapons. The Chinese developed the technique of casting iron in the 500s BC, some 1800 years before it became widespread in Europe.

ISHTAR A goddess who played a prominent part in the mythology of the Babylonians and Assyrians. She was the personification of the planet Venus: like the Greek Aphrodite and the Roman Venus she was the goddess of love, but she also had a warlike aspect in which she was addressed as 'Lady of Battles, valiant among goddesses'.

J

JAINISM An Indian religion founded in the 5th century BC by Mahavira (born c 600 BC). Unlike Hinduism, of which it was an offshoot, Jainism does not regard any being as superior to Man himself. Above all, Jainists preach universal tolerance, love and non-violence.

JUDAISM The religion of the ancient Hebrews, characterized by a belief in one God, Yahweh or Jehovah, who revealed himself to Abraham and the prophets. The practice of Judaism involves obedience to divine laws enshrined in the ancient scriptures and interpreted by generations of religious teachers.

L

LACQUER A liquid, prepared from the sap of specially cultivated trees, which in moist surroundings dries to a very hard and brilliant finish. Lacquerwork was developed to a very high standard, first by Chinese and later by Japanese craftsmen. Normally the lacquer was built up in layers on a wafer-thin wooden base, but carved objects of solid lacquer were also made.

LAPIS LAZULI An opaque semi-precious stone of a deep blue colour, greatly valued in the ancient world. It was used for small ornaments and particularly for inlay work.

LAPITHS A semi-legendary people who, according to Homer, lived in Thessaly in the valley of the Peneus river. They were related to the mountain-dwelling Centaurs through their king, Pirithous, whose father Ixion was the ancestor of both races.

LAW CODES The Sumerians, the first inhabitants of Babylonia, left a number of inscriptions which show that their cities were ruled by local laws and customs. These inscriptions are not so much a table of laws as a record of the efforts of various kings to reform abuses of ancient customs by, for example, priests and government officials. Later inscriptions, such as the Code of Hammurabi (c 1792–1750 BC), offer a detailed and specific account of laws applying to questions of social class, the family, property, and crime.

LEVANT The name given to the area of the eastern Mediterranean, stretching from western Greece to western Egypt.

LINEAR A, LINEAR B Linear A was the palace script of the Minoan civilization in Crete, used between 2000 and 1500 BC. The language spoken by the Cretans remains a mystery. Linear B was the script used by the Mycenaeans to write their own language, which was an early form of Greek. It was deciphered in 1952 by the British scholar Michael Ventris.

M

MEGALITHIC Built of large stones.

MERCENARY A professional soldier who fights for pay rather than any patriotic or idealistic motive.

MIDDEN A layer of refuse, such as broken and discarded objects, food remains, and so on, usually found at the site of an ancient settlement. The careful excavation of middens can provide archaeologists with valuable evidence of the daily life of the former inhabitants.

MILLENIUM A period of one thousand years. Thus, the 3rd millenium BC refers to the period 3000 to 2000 BC.

MINOAN The name given to a brilliant Bronze-Age civilization which developed on the island of Crete in the 3rd millenium BC and lasted until c 1500 BC. During that time Crete developed into a major economic and political centre. With wealth amassed from trade its rulers built large and luxurious palaces at Knossos, Phaistos, and Mallia, while Minoan craftsmen produced objects of the finest quality.

The major site, Knossos, was first excavated by the British archaeologist Arthur Evans at the turn of this century. It was he who proposed the name Minoan, after the legendary King Minos of Crete.

MITANNIANS A people living to the south of Anatolia in the 15th century BC. Ruled by an Indo-Aryan aristocracy, the Mitannians established an empire based on the efficiency of its main military weapon, the two-wheeled chariot.

MITRA The Iranian god of contracts and friendship, the protector of truth and the enemy of falsehood. In Indian mythology, a god associated with the Sun, who with his brother Varuna, god of the Moon, supervises and maintains universal order.

MONEY Before the invention of coinage, trade was carried on by barter – the exchange of goods – or by specialized object-currencies such as the bronze knives of ancient China, or the iron spits of early Greece. Coinage was introduced in the Near East, possibly by the Lydians, in the late 7th century BC. Soon the Greek cities of Asia Minor were issuing oval coins of electrum or silver, stamped with the symbol of the city which issued them – a way of guaranteeing their value. These coins were too valuable for general exchange, but during the centuries which followed, coins of small denominations were universally issued. The Greek *drachma* was the equivalent of a workman's daily wage: it was further divided into six obols. The name *drachma*, meaning a handful, recalled the pre-coinage currency of iron spits – *obelos*.

MOTIF The dominant element in a design, especially one repeated several times.

MYCENAEANS Inhabitants of mainland Greece c 1600–1200 BC who spoke an early form of Greek. Perhaps influenced by the Minoan civilization of Crete, the Mycenaeans developed a culture based on fortified citadels ('palaces') at sites such as Mycenae, Pylos, and Tiryns. After the sudden collapse of Minoan power c 1500 BC, the Mycenaeans occupied Crete itself. Archaeological excavations have yielded Mycenaean gold and silver objects, jewellery, and weapons of the finest workmanship. Despite its power and wealth, the Mycenaean civilization was destroyed amid violent upheavals in the eastern Mediterranean c 1200–1100 BC.

MYTH The distinction between myth and legend is often confused. Generally speaking, however, the word myth is applied to stories of the gods, while legends are concerned with actual or supposed historical events.

N

NEAR EAST The general name given to the countries of western Asia, stretching in a broad arc from the Dardanelles (ancient Hellespont) to the Arabian peninsula. The term is sometimes used to include Egypt.

NECROPOLIS A cemetery or burial place.

NOMADS A people whose food supply depends on their migrating from place to place, usually following the seasons. Nomads are usually either hunters or herdsmen, who move on when the local resources are exhausted.

O

OILSEEDS A general term describing a number of varieties of plants cultivated primarily for the oil that their seeds yield. Examples include millet, linseed, sesame, and sunflower plants.

ONAGER The wild ass, domesticated by the ancient Sumerians and used to draw their four-wheeled chariots.

ORACLE A medium through which a deity is supposed to communicate directly to Man. There were many oracles in the ancient world; two of the most famous were at Delphi in Greece and at Thebes in Egypt. Normally the oracle was administered by priests of the cult, that of Apollo at Delphi and of Amun at Thebes. The reputation of oracles was obviously dependent upon the quality of the answers they gave, especially to important and powerful clients. To this end, the priests were keen students of international politics – the oracle at Delphi especially gave sound advice on a number of recorded occasions.

ORACLE BONES A means of divination employed by the ancient Chinese using animal bones, particularly ox shoulderbones and tortoise shells. A groove was cut in a bone and a heated metal point then applied nearby. The process caused the bones to crack in patterns which were then carefully interpreted. Oracle bones have been discovered inscribed with questions and answers in the earliest form of Chinese writing.

P

PAPYRUS The Latin name for a type of reed which grew abundantly in the Nile valley. The ancient Egyptians used papyrus to make a writing material: the stems were split in half, flattened and pasted together in layers at right angles to one another. The Egyptians also constructed light river craft, and perhaps even sea-going ships, from bundles of papyrus tied together. The flower sprays of papyrus were a common motif in Egyptian art.

PARCHMENT The skin of a sheep or goat, scraped, cured, and used as a writing material before the invention of paper.

PARTHENON The temple of Athene Parthenos (Athene the Virgin) on the Acropolis of Athens, completed in 432 BC.

PEDIMENT A triangular stone gable set over an entrance or window. In a Greek temple, the pediment was supported by columns at the main entrance, or portico.

PELOPONNESE The southern peninsula of Greece, attached to the northern mainland by the narrow Isthmus of Corinth.

PICTS The Romans referred to the Cruithi tribes of central Scotland as *pictae* – the painted people. The term first appears in 297 AD.

POPULAR ASSEMBLY The gathering of all the citizens of a particular state for the purposes of passing or approving legislation. The methods of convening the popular assembly, and the actual powers accorded to it, varied widely from state to state.

PORTICO A roofed entrance space, usually forming the centre of the facade of a building. The portico of a Greek temple, for example, was made up of a projecting triangular pediment supported by columns.

POTSHERD Any fragment of broken pottery. Because fired clay is virtually indestructible potsherds provide valuable evidence for archaeologists.

PROPYLAEUM The entrance gate to an enclosure, for example to a temple precinct. A famous example is the ceremonial gate to the Acropolis at Athens.

PUMICE A type of natural glass formed by volcanic action, full of cavities and thus very light in weight.

R

RED-FIGURE WARE A type of pottery decoration developed in Attica in the 5th century BC. The background was painted with a glaze that turned black after firing, leaving the main design in the plain red of the clay. The Athenians mixed their potters' clay with red ochre to give it a characteristic orange-red hue.

REPUBLIC Any state in which the citizens elect their leaders, who must, after a prescribed period, present themselves for re-election.

ROMULUS AND REMUS The mythical twin sons of the Roman god of war, Mars, and a mortal woman, Rhea Silvia, daughter of the king of Alba Longa. Soon after their birth, the twins were placed in a basket and set afloat on the river Tiber. The river overflowed and deposited the basket before the grotto of Lupercal. Here they were discovered by a she-wolf, who fed the infants with her own milk. Later they were brought up by a poor shepherd, Faustulus, and his wife. Subsequently Romulus was inspired by supernatural signs to found the city of Rome. In the course of marking the boundaries of the new city, Romulus quarrelled with Remus and killed him.

S

SANCTUARY An enclosure sacred to a particular deity containing temples and sacrificial altars at which the priests of the cult make the appropriate offerings. A famous sanctuary was that of Olympia, in southern Greece, sacred to Zeus. It was continually enriched by buildings and gifts dedicated to Zeus by states participating in the quadrennial Olympic Games.

SASSANIAN The ruling dynasty of a resurgent Persian empire established by Ardashir I c AD 224 and destroyed by the Arabs between 637 and 651.

SELEUCID A dynasty of kings, descended from Alexander the Great's general Seleukos I Nikator, who controlled the area of modern Syria, Iraq, and Persia from 304 BC to 64 BC. The Seleucid empire combined Macedonian, Greek, Persian, Syrian, and Babylonian elements.

SENATE In republican Rome, a council of some 300 members (senators), originally appointed by the consuls to advise them on questions of policy. At first the senate was an exclusively aristocratic (patrician) body, but in the 4th century BC non-aristocratic (plebeian) senators were admitted. After 312 BC, the senate became more and more powerful, taking on itself the authority to appoint certain magistrates and to act decisively in all matters of state. Its prestige was enormously increased by its successful conduct of the Carthaginian wars and its subsequent administration of the growing overseas empire. In the late republic its power was challenged by the tribunes and by military leaders like Marius and Julius Caesar. Caesar, particularly, trebled the numbers of senators, filling the new places with his own supporters. In the period of confusion following Caesar's assassination the senate's powers dwindled almost to nothing. Despite the nominal restoration of the senate under Augustus, it remained firmly subordinate to him and the emperors who followed.

SHARE CROPPING A type of tenant-farming in which the tenant has the right to work a piece of land in return for a proportion of his produce due to the landlord.

SORGHUM A type of grain, domesticated from wild grasses, widely grown in the ancient world.

STRATIGRAPHY The study of the layers (strata) of material left by successive periods of occupation on a particular site. Very careful records must be kept of the nature and position of objects found in each layer, since it will necessarily be destroyed in the process of investigation. Skilled interpretation of the successive layers allows the archaeologist to establish a time sequence (chronology) of occupation.

SUMER The area of Lower Mesopotamia, in the valley of the Tigris and Euphrates rivers. Here the world's first civilization developed c 3400 BC, with the establishment of independent cities at sites like Eridu, Lagash, Uruk, and Ur. Rapid advances were made in organization, administration, and the division of labour, accompanied by splendid achievements in sculpture and architecture. Above all, the invention of writing was of incalculable importance. The area was unified by the Semites under Sargon c 2370 BC, but despite this and later foreign conquests, Sumerian culture remained very influential.

T

TERRACOTTA A baked clay generally used in the ancient world for making functional, easily replaceable objects, such as domestic utensils, children's toys, roof tiles, and so on.

TEXT A term used by scholars to describe any piece of writing in its original form, as well as the actual words it contains.

TRIBUNES Representatives of the plebeian class during republican Rome. Originally, tribunes had no legal powers: the sanctity of their persons was guaranteed by the people, who swore a solemn oath to kill anyone who laid hands on a tribune. Later the tribunes secured the power to summon the popular assembly and pass laws binding on the whole Roman state.

TRIBUTE Goods or services exacted by a ruler from his subjects, who may include the populations of other states under his control.

TROY A fortified site overlooking the Dardanelles (Hellespont), occupied by various peoples from c 3000 BC to its destruction c 1100 BC. It was known to the Greeks as Ilion and Homer's *Iliad* tells the story of the siege and destruction of the city by a force of Mycenaean Greeks led by Menelaus. The site was identified by Heinrich Schliemann and excavated by him between 1871 and 1890.

TYRANT From the Greek word *tyrannos*, applied to a man who seizes power unconstitutionally and rules the states in his own interests. Greek tyrants, such as the Cypselids in Corinth and Peisistratids in Athens, did much to promote trade and agriculture by sweeping away aristocratic privileges. Only later did harsh tyrants give the word its present sense of arbitrary cruelty.

U

UJJAIN A sacred city in India, situated near Indore between the Ganges plain and the Bombay coast, founded about 500 BC.

V

VARUNA An Indian god who with his brother Mitra, maintained the order of the universe. He was associated with the Moon, and was also the judge of the dead.

W

WHITE HUNS Members of a tribe originally dwelling to the north of the Great Wall of China. During the 5th and 6th centuries AD they began to migrate westwards into Persia and India. In Persia the Sassanid kings were hard put to it to keep them at bay, while in India the White Huns successfully invaded and held parts of central India and the Punjab. They were finally defeated by the Turks some time after 540 AD.

Z

ZEALOTS A violently nationalistic Jewish sect formed c 4 BC to oppose the Roman colonial government of Palestine. For the next 70 years the Zealots continued intermittent guerrilla activity. After the destruction of Jerusalem (AD 70) the Zealots and another sect, the Sicarii, continued to resist from fortresses in the hills until the destruction of their last redoubt, Masada.

ZIGGURAT A temple mound built by the Sumerians, Babylonians, and Assyrians in a series of stages rising to a small shrine at the top. Rectangular in plan, the ziggurats were made of mudbrick with a casing of burnt brick. Stairways led to the top. The famous ziggurat at Babylon was the prototype for the biblical Tower of Babel.

Index

Bold numerals indicate a major mention.
Italic numerals indicate illustrations.

FURTHER READING

Setting the Scene
The Rise of Civilization   J. and D. Oates   Elsevier-Phaidon
The Rise of Man   D. R. Brothwell and others   Sampson Low

Archaeologists at Work
Archaeology from the Earth   Sir Mortimer Wheeler   Penguin Books
Practical Archaeology   G. Webster   A. & C. Black

Mesopotamia
Ancient Mesopotamia: Portrait of a dead civilization   A. L. Oppenheim   University of Chicago Press
The First Empires   N. Postgate   Elsevier-Phaidon
The Greatness that was Babylon   H. W. F. Saggs   Sidgwick and Jackson

Egypt
The Egyptian Kingdoms   A. R. David   Elsevier-Phaidon
The Egyptians   C. Aldred   Thames and Hudson
Tutankhamen   C. Desroches-Noblecourt   Penguin Books

Greece
A Concise History of Ancient Greece   P. Green   Thames and Hudson
The Greeks   H. D. F. Kitto   Penguin
The Greeks Overseas   J. Boardman   Penguin

Persia
The Heritage of Persia   R. Frye   Cardinal Books
History of the Persian Empire   A. Olmstead   Phoenix Books
The Medes and Persians   W. Culican   Thames and Hudson

The Phoenicians
The First Merchant Venturers   W. Culican   Thames and Hudson

On the Fringes
The Hittites and their Neighbours   J. G. McQueen   Thames and Hudson
The Royal Hordes: Nomad peoples of the steppes   E. D. Phillips   Thames and Hudson
The Celtic Realms   M. Ditton and N. Chadwick   Weidenfeld and Nicholson

Rome
Everyday Life in the Roman Empire   J. Liversedge   Batsford
Life and Leisure in Ancient Rome   J. P. V. D. Balsdon   Bodley Head
The Romans   R. H. Barrow   Penguin Books

The Barbarians
Barbarian Europe   P. Dixon   Elsevier-Phaidon
The World of Late Antiquity   P. Brown   Thames and Hudson

India
The Birth of Indian Civilization   B. and R. Allchin   Penguin Books
Early India and Pakistan   Sir Mortimer Wheeler   Thames and Hudson

China
Archaeology in China: Volume II, Shang China; Volume III, Chou China   Chêng tê-k'un   W. Heffer and Sons
China before the Han Dynasty   W. Watson   Thames and Hudson

ACKNOWLEDGEMENTS

5 Scala; 6/7 Musées Nationaux-Paris; 8 Ronald Sheridan; 10 *top left* Ekdotike Athenon S. A., Athens, *bottom left* Sonia Halliday, *right* Michael Holford; 11 *left* Sonia Halliday, *top right* William MacQuitty, *bottom right* Society for Anglo-Chinese Understanding; 12 Richard Starkey; 13 *top* Staatliche Museum Berlin, *centre* British Museum, *bottom* Musées Nationaux-Paris; 14 *top* Zefa (UK) Ltd, *bottom* Turkish Tourist Office; 15 *top* Michael Holford, *bottom* Associated Press; 16 *top and bottom* Professor N. Coldstream; 18 *bottom* Professor N. Coldstream; 19, 20, and 21 Mark Redknap; 24 Staatliche Museen zu Berlin; 25 *top* Musées Nationaux-Paris, *bottom* Peter Clayton; 26 *top* Musées Nationaux-Paris; 27 *top* British Museum, *bottom* Musées Nationaux-Paris; 28 *left* Musées Nationaux-Paris, *top right and bottom right* Scala Milan; 29 *top* Scala Milan, *bottom* British Museum; 30 and 31 Musées Nationaux-Paris; 32 Scala Milan; 35 British Museum; 36 British Museum; 38 *top and bottom* Peter Clayton; 39 *top* Zefa (UK) Ltd, *bottom* Middle East Archives; 40 *top* Michael Holford, *bottom* British Museum; 41 *top and bottom* Peter Clayton, *bottom* Peter Clayton, *bottom* Michael Holford; 44 *top* Michael Holford, *bottom* Peter Clayton; 45 Zefa (UK) Ltd; 46 Michael Holford; 47 *top* Peter Clayton, *bottdm* Michael Holford; 48 Michael Holford; 49 Peter Clayton; 50 Middle East Archives; 51 *top* Sonia Halliday, *centre and bottom* Ekdotike Athenon S.A.; 52 British Museum; 53 Michael Holford; 54, 55, and 56 British Museum; 58 *top* British Museum, *bottom* Ekdotike Athenon S.A.; 59 Michael Holford; 60 *top* Metropolitan Museum New York, *bottom* Michael Holford; 61 *top* Michael Holford, *bottom* Wodsworth Athenium; 62 *top* British Museum, *bottom* Sonia Halliday; 63 *top* British Museum, *bottom left* Musées Nationaux-Paris, *centre right and bottom* British Museum; 65 and 66 Robert Harding Associates; 67 Musées Nationaux-Paris; 68 *top* Musées Nationaux-Paris, *centre right* Peter Clayton, *bottom* British Museum; 69 *top* Zefa (UK) Ltd, *bottom* William MacQuitty; 70 and 71 Michael Holford; 72 Scala Milan; 73 *top* Peter Clayton, *bottom* Michael Holford; 74 Peter Clayton; 75 Turkish Tourist Office; 76 Novosti Press Agency; 77 *top* National Museum Copenhagen, *centre and bottom* Bulgarian Tourist Office; 78 *top* Sonia Halliday, *centre* British Museum; 79 *top* British Museum, *bottom* Ekdotike Athenon S.A. Athens; 80 William MacQuitty Collection; 81 *top* Michael Holford, *bottom* Bildarchiv Preussischer Kulturbesitz/Staatliche Museum Berlin; 82 Sonia Halliday; 83 *top* Alinari, *bottom* William MacQuitty; 84 *top* Bildarchiv Preussischer Kulturbesitz/Antikenmuseum, Berlin, *bottom* British Museum; 85 *top and bottom* Ekdotike Athenon S.A.; 86 Musées Nationaux, Paris; 87 *top* Michael Holford, *bottom* London Museum; 88 *top* Ekdotike Athenon S.A., *bottom* Robert Harding Associates; 89 *top* Mansell Collection, *bottom* Scala Milan; 90 *top* Zefa (UK) Ltd, *bottom* Ronald Sheridan; 91 *top* Ronald Sheridan, *bottom* Scala Milan; 93 *left* Scala Milan, *right* Michael Holford; 94 *top* Mansell Collection, *bottom* Scala Milan; 95 *top* William MacQuitty, *centre and bottom* Scala Milan; 96 Scala Milan; 97 *top* British Museum, *bottom* Sonia Halliday; 98 British Museum; 99 *top* British Tourist Authority, *bottom* British Museum; 100 William MacQuitty; 101 *top* Scala Milan, *bottom* British Museum; 102 Sonia Halliday; 103 *top* Scala Milan, *bottom* National Museum Copenhagen; 104 *top* Rhenisches Landesmuseum, Trier, *bottom* Museo Civico Archaeologic, Bologna; 105 William MacQuitty; 106 *top* R. Starkey, *bottom* Scala Milan; 107 *top* British Museum, *centre* Jordan Tourist, *bottom* NY Carlsberg Glyptotek, Copenhagen; 108 and 109 W. T. Jones A.R.P.S., F.S.A.; 110 *top* Schleswig-Holsteinisches Landesmuseum, *bottom* Ashmolean, Oxford; 111 *left* Universiteters Oldsaksamling, Oslo, *right* Schleswig Holsteinisches Landesmuseum; 112 *left* National Museum, Copenhagen, *right* Universitetets Oldsaksamling, Oslo; 113 Scala Milan; 114 *top* Scala Milan, *bottom* Mansell Collection; 115 *top* British Museum, *bottom* Sonia Halliday; 116 *top* Robert Harding Associates, *bottom* Ellen Smart; 117 *top* Air India; 118 *top* Ellen Smart, *bottom* Professor Hartel, Museum für Indische Kunst, Berlin; 119 *top* John Freeman/V. & A, *bottom* Ellen Smart; 120 *top* Ellen Smart, *bottom* Sri Lanka Tourist Board; 121 India Tourist Office; 122 British Museum; 124 William MacQuitty; 125 *top* Robert Harding Associates, *bottom* Michael Holford; 126 *top* Peter Clayton, *bottom* Courtesy of the Smithsonian Institution, Freer Gallery of Art, Washington D.C.; 127 *left and bottom* Society for Anglo-Chinese Understanding, *top right* Ashmolean Museum, Oxford; 128 *top right* William MacQuitty, *top left* V & A, *centre* William MacQuitty, *bottom* Peter Clayton; 129 *left* Society for Anglo-Chinese Understanding, *right* National Palace Museum, Taiwan; 130 *top* Danish National Museum, *bottom* Society for Anglo-Chinese Understanding; 131 William MacQuitty.

Picture research: Penny Warn